Capitalism and Sport: Politics, Protest, People
Edited by Michael Lavalette

Acknowledgements

For a book of 42 chapters to come together requires immense discipline from contributors. I'd like to thank all the writers in this volume for meeting deadlines and writing interesting and engaging pieces.

On behalf of the publishers I'd like to thank the estate of C L R James for permission to reprint the two pieces reproduced here (chapters 25 and 31) and Andrew Smith for help locating these works.

Sally Campbell at Bookmarks, Charlie Kimber, Martin Smith, Gareth Edwards and Pete Marsden have all offered critical comment and suggested key areas of debate we should explore. I'd like to thank each for their help and support.

While I was putting this book together my father-in-law, Alan Penketh, came to live at our family home. He is a former sheet metal worker and was a shop steward and activist within the Sheet Metal Workers and Braziers Union, now part of Unite. He is currently struggling against an industrial disease and showing great fortitude in his latest fight. He has spent much of the last few months watching sport, especially football, on the television—a passion we share, though not his ardent support for Blackburn Rovers! I would like to dedicate this book to him.

Michael Lavalette
April 2013

CAPITALISM AND SPORT
Politics, Protest, People and Play

EDITOR MICHAEL LAVALETTE

Bookmarks Publications

Capitalism and Sport: Politics, Protest, People and Play
Edited by Michael Lavalette
Published July 2013
Bookmarks Publications Ltd,
c/o 1 Bloomsbury Street, London WC1B 3QE
Copyright © Bookmarks Publications
ISBN 978 1 909026 30 8
Printed by Russell Press
Designed by Bookmarks Publications

Contents

Contributors

Simon Basketter is a journalist on *Socialist Worker*

Paul Blackledge is Professor of Politics at Leeds Metropolitan University

Adrian Budd teaches politics at London South Bank University, where he is UCU branch secretary

Sue Caldwell is a teacher and socialist activist in east London

Jo Cardwell is a socialist activist in London

Lionel Cliffe is Emeritus Professor of Politics at the University of Leeds, a founding editor of *Review of African Political Economy* and one-time league cricketer in South Yorkshire

Tony Collins is professor of history and director of the International Centre for Sports History and Culture at De Montfort University. He is the author of several books on the social history of sport, including *Rugby's Great Split* (1998), *A Social History of English Rugby Union* (2009) and *Sport in Capitalist Society* (2013)

Estelle Cooch is an assistant editor on *Socialist Review*

Jonathan Dart is a Senior Lecturer in Sports Studies at Leeds Metropolitan University

Gareth Edwards is a socialist activist in Portsmouth. He runs the sport-related blog inside-left.blogspot.co.uk

Keith Flett is a socialist historian and activist. He blogs at kmflett.wordpress.com

John Foot is Professor of Modern Italian History at University College London

Rita Gough is a social worker, a Unison member and a socialist activist in Lancashire

Peter Hain is Labour MP for Neath. A founder of the Anti Nazi League and supporter of Unite Against Fascism, he served as a Labour government minister for 12 years. He recently published his memoirs, *Outside In* (2012)

Christian Høgsbjerg is a PhD student in Leeds and editor of a new edition of C L R James's 1934 play about the Haitian Revolution, *Toussaint Louverture: The Story of the Only Successful Slave Revolt in History* (2013)

Vassilios Ioakimidis is a lecturer in social work at Durham University

C L R James (1901-1989) was a historian, journalist, socialist theorist and essayist. His 1963 book *Beyond a Boundary* is a seminal work on cricket and society.

Michael Lavalette is a socialist councillor in Preston and the national coordinator of the Social Work Action Network. He is author of several books including *Voices from the West Bank* (with Chris Jones), which was published by Bookmarks (2011)

Phil Mac Giolla Bháin is the author of *Downfall: How Rangers FC Self-destructed* (2012). He is an activist in the National Union of Journalists

Hassan Mahamdallie has a background in theatre and campaigning journalism. He writes on issues of race, religion and black people in the West. He was a founding member of Unite Against Fascism

Peter Marsden is an officer with the local government union Unison

Eamonn McCann is a journalist and activist based in Derry

Peter Millward is a lecturer in sociology at Liverpool John Moore's University

Ken Olende is a journalist on *Socialist Worker*

Sylvia Pankhurst (1882-1960) was a leading suffragette and founder member of the Communist Party of Great Britain

Hazel Potter is a freelance writer and consultant who spends much of the winter in the left wing of England's travelling cricket support. She is a long-term fans' activist, a former fanzine editor and current contributor to numerous sports fanzines, publications and websites

George Poulton is a PhD student at Durham University

Denis Pye is the author of *Fellowship is Life: The Story of the Clarion Cycling Club* (2004). He was a member of the club's national committee for over 20 years, and has written articles on the Clarion movement for the North West Labour History Journal. He is a retired teacher

Dave Renton is a lawyer, a blogger and an author. He blogs at livesrunning.wordpress.com

Brian Richardson is a lawyer and a socialist activist

Sadie Robinson is a journalist on *Socialist Worker*

Ron Senchak is a former boxer and a socialist activist in Manchester

Roddy Slorach is a disability activist and socialist in east London

Andrew Stone teaches politics and history in south London. He is a National Union of Teachers workplace rep

Dave Swanson is a PhD student at Manchester University

Phil Turner is a journalist based in Yorkshire and an NUJ activist

Dave Zirin is a blogger and political sports journalist with *The Nation* in the US. He blogs at www.edgeofsports.com

Introduction

CAPITALISM AND SPORT:
POLITICS, PROTEST, PEOPLE AND PLAY

Michael Lavalette

> The sports world is a lived world, like those of literature and the
> theatre, that is highly charged with human meaning. As a dramatic
> and symbolic world the sports world has its own plots, scenes, char-
> acters and settings. The game itself is the ritual hub of the sports
> universe; the team provides social structure; sports language gives
> the world cohesion; fans play the game vicariously through the ath-
> letes. Underneath and penetrating all the dramatic appeals is the
> powerful symbolism of play. The success of the sports world rests
> on its ability to build its symbolic structure on the memory of play,
> on the illusion of play, and, finally, on the fantasy of play.[1]

Lipsky's description captures the great allure of sport. But it poses
a very immediate question: what is sport? The answer is less obvious
than we may think. Are pigeon racing, chess playing, rambling or
hill walking all sports? Or are these leisure activities, and in some
sense different from "sport"?

There is considerable debate over what counts as sport. The UK
National Sports Council states it does not have a definition, which is
a strange position for a national sports body to adopt![2] The Council of
Europe suggests sport includes all forms of physical exercise (so rambling would be in). But this seems too broad and would include all
games, playing and partaking in unregulated physical activities as
well as highly regulated and institutionalised sporting activities. The
Oxford Dictionary states sport is "an activity involving physical exertion and skill in which an individual or team competes against
another or others for entertainment".[3] This seems a good place to
start. But we need to emphasise three things.

First, modern sport has developed within, and as part of, industrial capitalism and mirrors all its major features. It is dominated by
big businesses, is prone to all manner of crises and is racked by divisions of class, gender, race, sexuality and disability. Second, sport is
defined by national and, increasingly, international rules and regulations. Sport, as we know it today, was developed and regulated from
the mid-19th century onwards. The first modern Olympic Games

were held in Athens in 1896 and were followed by the Paris Olympics in 1900. Likewise the Football Association, the governing body of English football, was formed in 1863 and the first FA Cup final was held in 1872. The picture is repeated with many other sports—the body that governed Rugby Union was formed in 1871 and the break-away Rugby League was set up in 1885. The first Wimbledon tennis tournament was held in 1877, the British Amateur Boxing Federation was set up in 1880, US baseball developed from around 1882 and the first Tour de France cycle race was held in 1903.

These events and their regulatory bodies were responsible for unifying and implementing the rules and regulations governing the sports. The rules regularised sport, made it clear who were winners and losers, and allowed gambling to flourish. What often began as national bodies have now become powerful international organisations. Take for example the Fédération Internationale de Football Association (FIFA), the international governing body of association football. It entered 2000 stating that annual expenditure on football amounted to $250 billion and provided jobs for 450 million people. FIFA itself has assets amounting to £2.5 billion and 204 nations affiliated to it (there are only 193 nations affiliated to the UN).[4]

Finally, central to all sport is competition: competition between sports, between clubs and organisations, between teams and athletes and between spectators and fans. And here sport mirrors some aspects of the ethos of capitalism itself: individualism, competition, "survival of the fittest"—phrases and terms that can be applied to sport and are often equally applied to the world of capitalist competition.

So now another question: how do we understand the place of sport in modern society?

Let's start with the immense appeal of sport.

Every day millions of people watch, play, debate and reflect on sport. They revel in its excitement, its energy, its drama and the prowess of players and athletes. Watching sport can be exciting—and it can be dull. But part of the interest is that it is unpredictable, dramatic and often complex. It forms part of a public spectacle that generates passion among both spectators and players. It is an activity with an uncertain outcome and this holds people's interest and passions.

I was completing this introduction days after I had been to a football match to watch "my" team. It was just an ordinary league game. I watched them take an early lead (after 12 seconds) then throw this away to trail 3-1 (after 66 minutes), before they stormed back to win 4-3, scoring the winner with the last kick of the game. Afterwards I discussed the match with friends: the great start and magnificent ending—and bemoaned the lack of spirit and poor performance shown by the team in the middle hour of the game. Excitement, drama, frustration, anger, joy—just some of the emotions we went through on a dull wet Saturday afternoon. It was certainly better than working!

Neither was it a diversion from the struggle—whatever we may mean by that. One of the key topics of conversation before, during and after the match was the heavy-handed policing of supporters, and why working class fans were being criminalised for supporting their team, something that was debated widely in the Scottish press throughout the week following the match.[5]

To give another example, earlier this year I went to a Champions League game. We were playing the team that most consider to be the best in the world. No one gave us a chance, but despite this at the end of the match we had won. At the match there was a carnival atmosphere in and around the ground. This began before kick-off and ended sometime after the game was over. It involved supporters of both clubs who, throughout the day, had shared drinks and songs and had walked together to the ground. It was like a community party, with singing, dancing, and drinking with a range of shared emotions: excitement, nervousness and joy.

At the start of the game there was a magnificent "Tifo" (a banner display) that covered every seat in the ground and marked the 125th anniversary of the team. This Tifo was organised by and paid for by fans—not the club. It was a remarkable feat of organisation and design. It was created by a group of amateurs who had given up hours of their time to design the display on a computer, plot this so that each of the 55,000 seats in the home end would be colour coded and each fan, at each seat, would have a coloured piece of plastic to hold up following a cue from the ultras section of the ground. The result was a huge display and a piece of temporary public art.[6]

Playing and taking part in sport can be even better. Sporting activity contains elements of play that are rule bound. It promotes physical fitness and well-being, both of which are essential for physical and mental health. The contest presupposes (at least a formal) equality between competitors. In team games there is a combination of a group ethos, but with space for individual flair and skill to flourish.

On weekends across the country there are thousands of people at play on sports fields, out running, in the gym or the pool, or involved in organising often complex events that fill their leisure time: think of the levels of self-organisation that are required for sports leagues to function.

All of this is what marks sport out as part of modern culture.[7] But, as socialists, what do we say about such things? Some argue that they are trivial, irrelevant, a diversion from the struggle. But perhaps sport has similarities with other cultural practices—plays, dramas, dance, music—much of which will be trivial, irrelevant and perhaps even a diversion from the struggle!

This is not to argue crudely that there are no differences between various cultural activities. "Great art", embedded in such things as the plays of Shakespeare or Brecht, the literature of Balzac or Tolstoy, the poems of Shelley or Burns, the films of Eisenstein, the music of Coltrane or Beethoven, or the paintings of Picasso, speaks to us over time because it reveals interesting aspects of the nature of society, its contradictions and the forces that shape the world. It is much rarer, and much more difficult, to obtain such insights through sport—though it does happen.

When young black footballer Laurie Cunningham (at the time playing for Leyton Orient) and his black colleague Bobby Fisher were barracked by racists supporting Millwall, Cunningham's response was to play harder and better to show he would not be cowed. As Fisher recalls, "Laurie wasn't the type of guy who would accept it; he would want to give it back… I think he learned to get back at them in his own way, which was on the pitch".[8]

As the game came to its end Cunningham picked up a pass from Fisher and glided past several defenders before sending an unstoppable shot into the net. When the referee ended the game a few minutes later both Cunningham and Fisher turned to the baying Millwall fans and stared defiantly into the crowd with their hands clenched above their heads in a Black Power salute.[9] It was a moment that encapsulated a militant response to racism.

Similarly, when Muhammad Ali repeatedly pounded Ernie Terrell in their 1967 boxing bout while shouting, "What's my name, fool?" it said something very important about the nature of society, racism, rebellion and resistance. In the run up to the fight Terrell had refused to call him anything but Cassius Clay—his given name, rather than the name he chose for himself as a conscious political and spiritual act.

Of course, most sporting events do not contain such moments of critical consideration and reflection. But then most published novels do not provide the insight of a Brontë and most paintings don't match the heights of the work of Kazimir Malevich.

Yet for many on the political left sport is treated with a degree of disdain. Recently one of the editors of the Marxist journal Historical Materialism posted a comment on his Facebook feed. It expressed sarcastic surprise that a footballer gave a Nazi salute (AEK Athens player Giorgos Katidis,[10] an act which earned him an immediate lifetime ban from the Greek FA) and that two American Football players were convicted of rape.[11] His sarcasm seemed to say it all. What else would you expect from sports people?

In April 2013 Sunderland FC appointed the fascist Paulo Di Canio as their manager. The move provoked outrage in sections of the media and from anti-fascists across the country—including many anti-fascist football fans. The appointment led to the resignation of former Labour MP David Miliband from his £75,000 per year job as club director (a salary he took in addition to his MP's wage). More importantly, the Durham Miners Association demanded that the club hand back their banner which they had presented to them.[12]

In the Guardian columnist Suzanne Moore[13] used the appointment to decry the quality of sports journalism and the xenophobia, racism, sexism and homophobia within football. Much of Moore's attack was well aimed.

From the middle of the 19th century onwards there has been a very close relationship between sport and the print media. Reports of matches and games alongside fawning accounts of stars and clubs have been used to sell papers for years. This is a field where "churnalism" is prevalent (see chapter 9) and where vacuous "insider" stories are given prominence. Churnalism, superficiality and the endless analysing of sports events now also dominate television and radio programming schedules where commercial stations use sports coverage to boost their ratings—and their linked advertising revenues (see chapter 19).

Nevertheless, it is also true that there are some very good sports journalists—Dave Zirin (in the US), James Montague (in the Middle East), David Walsh (covering, among other things, cycling in Europe) and David Conn (covering the English Premier League), for example, who are prepared to dig beneath the surface and reveal the dark side of sport in the modern world. There are also some very good movies about sport, eg *When We Were Kings* (Dir: Leon Gast), which tells the story of the 1974 "rumble in the jungle" between Muhammad Ali and George Foreman or *Fire in Babylon* (Dir: Steven Riley) which tells the story of the 1976 West Indies cricket tour of England.

Moore is also right to attack those instances of racism, sexism and homophobia that blight the game—from Ched Evans's conviction for rape,[14] to the racism directed at Rio and Anton Ferdinand from England fans[15] or the fact that Robbie Rogers felt that he had to leave football in order to come out as gay.[16] As Moore argues, "While it continues to kick women, black players and gay people in the face while justifying Nazi salutes, how can it be a beautiful game? It is an ugly, ugly business".[17]

Moore goes on to contrast football with the Olympics and suggests what goes on in football does not happen there—perhaps a slightly naive assertion given the repeated link between athletics and drugs,[18] abuse of athletes by coaches[19] and the nationalism of so many athletic meets (or the fascism of long-time Olympics boss Juan Antonio Samaranch).[20]

But if we simply see football—or any sport—through the activities of some fans, players or athletes, how can we account for the counter-example? The fact that the footballers Cristiano Ronaldo and Freddie Kanute have repeatedly spoken out in support of Palestinian rights?[21] Or that Robbie Fowler supported the Liverpool dockers during their lockout from 1996 to 1998?[22] Or that in the 1970s many footballers signed up to Anti Nazi League statements against the far-right and that today fans of clubs have actively campaigned against the presence of Nazis on their terraces? Or the actions of footballer Kevin Prince-Boateng who stopped play in a friendly match for AC Milan, picked up the ball and kicked it at racists on the terracing before leading his team mates off the pitch?[23] Or that fans at St Pauli have campaigned against homophobia in the game?[24]

Moreover, listing the crimes of some sports people is a way of dismissing a whole cultural activity. Should we ignore classical music because Wagner was an anti-Semite, or Herbert Von Karajan, long-time conductor of the Berlin Philharmonic, was a member of the Nazi party (which he joined in 1933)? Would we dismiss all dance and ballet because Simone Clarke was a member of the BNP while she was Prima Ballerina of the English National Ballet? Or would we argue that structural Marxism raised no points of interest because Althusser strangled his wife?

Further, we may wonder why the same criteria are not applied equally to all sports and games. Marx and Lenin were both keen on chess—and there are not many more competitive or militaristic games than chess. The 1972 Spassky/Fischer World Championship match was played out in the midst of the Cold War and was, in many ways, a proxy for the real thing. But chess playing doesn't seem to bring the same level of disapproval that is aimed at other sports and games—perhaps it is acceptable because it's a cerebral rather than a physical sport?[25]

For others on the left it is not so much the individual sportspeople that are the problem, but the structure and nature of the sporting industry. It is the competition within modern sport, its domination by big business and, very often, its nationalism and militarism.

Of course, these are all aspects of modern sport.

While women and men have always played games and while play has been a central part of human culture in almost all periods of our history, modern sport is very much a product of capitalism. It is not the case that prior to capitalism there was no competitive game playing—as David Zirin[26] notes, Native American populations were often engaged in competitive sport (lacrosse) and the ancient Olympics were competitive show-pieces between representatives of different city-states. But of course, there are important differences between these examples and modern sport—capitalism has reshaped and transformed all areas of social life, and play is no different. In pre-capitalist societies people played during festivals, during slack times of the working day, or during quieter times in the seasonal calendar. Often the demarcation between "work time" and "leisure time" was blurred. As Tony Collins notes:

> Early games were sometimes non-competitive, occasionally non-physical and often inter-twinned with ritual activities… The methods of play and meanings ascribed to these games were very different

from today. They may have had a ceremonial, religious or ritual purpose. The idea of specialist players would almost certainly have been unknown. And winning was often not the purpose of play.[27]

But with the development of capitalism we start to see the commodification of sport (as we start to see the commodification of many other leisure and cultural activities).

For the landed gentry in 18th century Britain, gambling on the stock exchange was not treated that differently to gambling on the outcome of horse racing, boxing, cricket or other sporting activities. But to ensure a clear outcome rules were needed where often there had been none or few before (see chapter 1).

In the 17th and 18th centuries the new ideas of liberalism started to gain hold. Human beings were now portrayed as "naturally selfish", "naturally greedy" and "naturally competitive". The values of a competitive capitalist system were generalised and portrayed as eternal aspects of "human nature". Increasingly "sports competition"—the fact that regulated sport brought clear winners and losers—seemed to fit in with the cultural dynamic of capitalism.

By the middle of the 17th century Britain was entering the Industrial Revolution. Over the next 100 years industrialisation, migration and urbanisation would dramatically re-shape Britain's landscape. But the new factory dominated system required, as EP Thompson noted, the breaking of older "customs".[28] The system required a commitment to the clock (because "time is money"), to regulation, the law and the enforcement of appropriate "work discipline". This required a new set of attitudes from workers: sobriety, hard work, thrift and "morality". The concern with morality meant an attempt to control workers' leisure or free time and to attack those events and carnivals that took people away from work. It meant attempts to control "the crowd" and the criminalisation of working class "sports" like dog-fighting and badger-baiting (while fox-hunting and hunting with dogs remained legal in Britain until 2004!). And it eventually meant the promotion of regulated sports within working class communities by "Muscular Christianity".

Of course working class communities resisted, reshaped and rejected much of this attack. They fought and struck for the right to be paid while playing sport[29] and to challenge the enforced amateurism of many 19th century games (see chapter 19). Through watching they tried to influence sporting spectacles and challenge the sports capitalists in myriad ways. And it meant, as Collins has adapted Marx's famous dictum, that women and men "play sport, but not under circumstances of their own choosing".[30]

To understand modern capitalist sport Brohm[31] argues that we need to grasp its three principal elements:

1 Sport is not simply sport but a means of shaping public opinion and a mode of ideological framing of populations in all countries of the world.

2 Sport has become a sector of accumulation of wealth, money, and therefore also of capital. It attracts considerable amounts of money and is the most spectacular showcase of the globalised society of commodities.

3 Sport constitutes a political body, a space of ideological invest-ment in gestures and movements. It's an ideological valorisation of efforts via asceticism, training and self-sacrifice. Sport insti-tutes a bodily order founded on the management of sexual drives and aggressive impulses. Sport is portrayed as a device that pro-motes social appeasement, social integration, reduced violence and greater fraternity; but these are muddled illusions and mystifications.

For Brohm, sport is treated as a tool of ideological domination—it supports mindless nationalism, it reflects the inherent values of aggressive competition and the 'spirit of capitalism', it diverts people away from the "real" problems of everyday life and it divides work-ing people against each other through exacerbating regional, racial, religious and sexual divisions (see chapters 13 to 19).

He further argues that within the sports industry television, spon-sorship, ownership and advertising are all sources of profit. The principal mass spectator sports have become big business: football clubs are floated on the stock exchange; television rights to football, cricket and rugby (union and league) coverage involve huge sums of money and huge returns for clubs and television companies; sponsor-ship rewards individuals and clubs while the companies who pay for it are guaranteed regular adverts to audiences numbering millions.

The latest available accounts of England's top clubs give some indication of the size of business operations we are discussing.

These figures don't account for other aspects of the business (for

Table 1[32]

	TV & broadcasting revenue	Retail & commercial income	Gate & match day income
Arsenal	£85m	£52m	£95m
Chelsea	£113m	£70m	£78m
Man Utd	£104m	£118m	£99m
Liverpool	£63m	£64m	£42m
Tottenham	£59m	£53m	£32m
Man City	£104m	£118m	£99m

example Arsenal made an additional £8 million from property development in 2011/2012). Today Manchester United Football Club is a global brand. Alex Ferguson, the club's former manager, speaking at a meeting of the professional footballers association, told the audience, "Fifty years ago Manchester United support was mainly based in the city of Manchester, by the late 1960s our support reached across Britain and Ireland and today we have gone global." A survey commissioned by Manchester United and carried out by market research firm Kantar estimated there were 659 million Manchester United fans worldwide, with about half of them, 325 million, in Asia.[33]

Despite what fans may think about their link to "their" club these businesses rake in vast sums from fans on match days from ticket prices and pay vast rewards to players and directors. David Conn estimates that two thirds of the EPL's £2.4 billion income in 2011/2012 season went on wages. Topping the global league for payment for footballers is David Beckham. Beckham topped the list of the top 50 richest players in the world with a personal fortune of £175 million, Lionel Messi is second and is worth £115.5 million and close on his heels is Cristiano Ronaldo on £112 million.[34] For each, the majority of this fortune has been generated away from football in the advertising, sponsorship and branding deals that they have entered with a range of multinational corporations.

Conn also notes, "The financial rewards for the highest paid directors at Premier League football clubs vastly outstrip directors' earnings at non-football companies of a similar size".[35]

The top earning chief executive was David Gill at Manchester United who earned £2.6 million in 2011-12, followed closely by Daniel Levy at Spurs (£2.2 million) and Ivan Gazidis at Arsenal (£2.05 million).

Central to the football business model is television revenue. The commercial drive for profit has led clubs to get into bed with Sky TV (and increasingly ESPN and BT). These media organisations have a huge impact on football and increasingly both rugby codes and cricket. The English Premier League will pull in £5 billion as part of its latest television deal.[36] And of course sport is often mired in mindless nationalism—inherent in the Olympics or football world cups (see chapters 4, 6, 7, 13 and 14).

Finally, Brohm suggests this all debases those who work in sports. The sporting labour process enforces all sorts of depravations onto sports workers, only a tiny minority of whom will earn significant salaries in return. At the Olympics in 2013 middle-distance runner Nick Symmonds auctioned off space on his body for advertising purposes! He offered to tattoo his shoulder to obtain advertising revenue. More than 85 brands bid on the opportunity. Hanson Dodge Creative, an active lifestyle marketing firm based in Milwaukee, won with an $11,100 bid. But Symmonds had to cover the tattoo up during the Olympics because the IOC placed a ban on competitors advertising any but "Olympic sponsors" between 18 July and 15 August.[37]

In the chapters that follow aspects of each of these themes are discussed. The chapters look at the ways in which the sports industry debases and alienates sports workers and fans, the ways it regulates and controls the sporting product, the profits it generates for the few and the ways in which sporting spectacles can reinforce dominant social relations (chapter 1).

But if we only focus on these aspects of sport we end up with a one-sided reductionist account that cannot explain the contradictions, conflicts and resistance that emerge within sport.

So, to take one of Brohm's claims, it is certainly the case that the element of spectacle can be utilised to domesticate the audience (such as singing national anthems at big sporting events). Sports spectacles, therefore, can reinforce nationalism. But who among us was not ecstatic when George Osborne—the cutter of disability benefits—was booed at the Paralympics in 2012 (see chapter 20). Or which of us has never seen and been enthralled by the image of two black athletes in 1968 who gave a Black Power salute as the US national anthem played—and for a moment turned the spectacle on its head as millions watched? (See chapter 32.) Or who would not celebrate the grace and power of Jessie Owens at the 1936 Olympics—full as it was of Nazi symbolism—and his personal debunking of the Nazis racist myths? Or who among us does not see part of our tradition of resistance as encapsulated in the anti-apartheid movement's targeting of the 1970 South African rugby tour to Britain? (See chapter 38.)

While it is true that the regulation and codification of sport developed in the second half of the 19th century and this represented an attempt by the bourgeoisie to regulate and control sports (see chapters 1 and), it's not the case that this was always against the interests of the working class player of sport. Rules in boxing, for example, protected fighters (who always came from the most marginalised sections of the working class) and "professionalism" in rugby was a means of ensuring that working class players got paid for time taken off from work in the pit (see chapter 19).

While it is true that modern football clubs are floated on the stock exchange and operate, quite ruthlessly, just like any other big business (see chapter 4), it is not the case that this has been unquestionably accepted by football fans who often contest their clubs' histories (see chapters 35 and 37) or who look towards different forms of club ownership to avoid the business models that dominate at the top clubs (see chapter 35). There may be all sorts of issues with such responses—but they nevertheless open up a space for debate about the nature of sport, about the impact of globalisation on football (and society in general) and about the collective rights of supporters and fans to have a say in how their club is run.

It is true that competition in sport can be put to use by the ruling class for their own purposes, but it is not the case that competition in sport is always a negative factor. In the world of early 20th century boxing (see chapter 30) the "fight of the century" between champion Jack Johnson and Jim Jeffries (the first "great white hope") was a fight that was loaded with relevance about the nature of racism in the US. The mass popularity of early cricket games stemmed from competition between the "lowly" professionals and the local gentry who employed them. This competition drew crowds of thousands and their support for the professionals had a class character—they supported them against the toffs (see chapter 17). This aspect of cricket was also key to the growth of its popularity in British colonies since it gave the oppressed masses of those colonies the chance to humiliate the oppressors. In Franco's Spain the football matches between Real Madrid and Barcelona or Real Madrid and Athletic

Bilbao were about more than just football. The aspiration for Palestinian statehood is reflected in the support across the Palestinian diaspora for the Wihdat club in Jordan, formed in the Al Wihdat Palestinian refugee camp and once described by Yasser Arafat as Palestine's national team.[38]

In other words, sport and the factors that lend it a universal appeal are, like other areas of culture, capable of becoming a political battleground. To write off the importance of that battleground and reduce our understanding of sport under capitalism to the catch-all denunciation of "capitalist sport" is self-defeating.

The essays in this collection aim to explore the tensions that exist within sport. The aim is to look at sport in two linked ways: the politics of sport (the ways in which sport reflects the themes, big business ethos, alienation, etc of capitalism and sport) and the politics in sport (the various sites and manifestations of struggle over sport, its organisation, its divisions and its outcomes). We have divided the book into several sections, each made up of relatively short and accessible essays on a theme.

Parts one, two and three look at the structural location of sport within capitalist societies, the impact of globalisation on various professional sports activities (football, cricket, cycling, rugby and jogging) and the consequences (on clubs, protesters, supporters and athletes) when things go wrong. Part four examines some sporting divisions. We focus on issues of sexism, racism, Islamophobia, class and disability and their impact on players, spectators and competitors. Parts 5 and 6 look at resistance within sport—part 5 looking at the resistance of notable sporting rebels, while part 6 looks at the resistance of fans, campaign networks, athletes and workers' sport networks. Finally, part 7 considers some alternative futures and poses questions about other ways in which we can play and participate in sport.

The people who have been drawn together here come from a variety of positions on the left of politics. There is no single perspective, no single narrative and no common approach. Collectively, therefore, the book is about opening up debate on issues of capitalism and sport. It presents a series of different takes on sport in modern society from people who see themselves as political activists who enjoy sport, and think that those of us on the left have something important to say about the various worlds of sport and the resistance it can generate.

Part 1
Sport in a capitalist society

Chapter 1
CAPITALISM AND THE BIRTH OF MODERN SPORT

Gareth Edwards

The political and economic changes of the 17th and 18th centuries produced unprecedented prosperity for those who rode the wave of capitalist development. An explosion of innovation and invention mirrored, and was underpinned by, the thriving economy. For more than a century England would consider itself the centre of scientific enquiry, intellectual progress and industrial advance. It would also become the birthplace of codified sport.

Jack Broughton produced the first written rules for boxing in 1743. He had enjoyed a successful career as a bareknuckle fighter under the patronage of the Duke of Cumberland before opening his own amphitheatre in London, staging bouts and exhibitions for a wealthy clientele. In the world of horseracing the Jockey Club was formed sometime around 1752, although at this stage its influence did not extend much beyond the confines of Newmarket. It was, according to Mike Huggins, "a particularly select, self-elected, aristo-cratic, private club".[1] Much the same could be said of the Marylebone Cricket Club (MCC), whose members were drawn from the privileged elite, and which produced a revised set of rules for the game in 1788 (the first written rules had been produced by a select group of "Noblemen and Gentlemen" in 1744 and were updated 30 years later). As Mike Marqusee has written, "The same people who passed [the] laws in parliament drew up the Laws of Cricket, and for much the same purpose".[2]

The codification of sports echoed the development of the modern nation state. The ideas employed by the ruling class to organise their games were inspired by those deployed in their organisation of soci-ety: written "laws" replaced custom; "independent" officials passed judgement on transgressions of these rules; and a "neutral" authority would preside over disputes. This was especially important given that the immediate trigger for codification was gambling.

Betting on the outcome of sporting events had become something of a national obsession, allowing the rich an ideal opportunity to flaunt their wealth. The legendary George Osbaldeston, a one-time member of parliament, ran up a £200,000 gambling debt before his death in 1866. Often the outcomes of matches were contested and aggrieved parties would appeal to the courts in a bid to have bets honoured. Standardised rules were designed to keep disputes to a minimum. We therefore find stipulations to cover gambling in cricket's early articles of association, while in boxing, three of Broughton's rules outlined what constituted victory while another dictated how prize money was to be distributed.

It would be a mistake, therefore, to see these early examples of codification as attempts to create frameworks for national sports. The evidence suggests people wrote rules purely to formalise the game that they themselves were playing. Indeed the MCC and, to a certain extent, the Jockey Club were reluctant to accept and exercise their growing power. In part their evolution towards governing bodies was fuelled by perceptions of social class. Clubs would appeal to their "social superiors", asking them to adopt the role of adjudicator. This is apparent in horse racing where, "in the desire to avoid disputes ending up in the law courts, many courses placed themselves under the club's jurisdiction".[3] Even then their development was slow and fraught with argument. As cricket developed from a parochial pastime, practised in pockets of the country, towards a national sport, the MCC prevaricated on all sorts of issues—much as they do today. Overarm bowling was finally permitted in 1864, while the number of players allowed on each team was not standardised until 1884. They did at least fare better than the early attempt to create an organisation to oversee boxing. The Pugilism Club was formed in 1814 but would last only a decade, folding in 1824.

There was also an economic imperative driving codification. The popularity of the sport as a spectacle was clear as early as 1743 when 10,000 people watched a cricket match at the Artillery Ground in Finsbury.[4] Entrepreneurs were quick to spot this emerging market. The wider moves in society towards enclosure found their echo in the establishment of "grounds" on which matches were played. When Thomas Lord purchased the land which would become the home of the MCC he erected a fence round the ground and charged sixpence for admission. Simultaneously people were excluded from the game and transformed into paying spectators.

Grandstands were built at racecourses across the country and entrance fees applied. The stand at Epsom was built in 1830 and could hold 5,000 people; Ascot's appeared in 1837. Given the financial success of these developments it was inevitable that other areas of courses would be enclosed. At Epsom the main betting ring and the saddling enclosure were both sectioned off in the decade following the construction of the grandstand. At all sporting venues the sale of food and drink (particularly alcohol) provided another potentially lucrative revenue stream and helped to solidify the relationship between sport and business. Bureaucrats, bookies and brewers combined to commercialise sport, turning pastimes into industries. To that end changes to rules could help make games more entertaining and attractive. The MCC reduced the time between each innings to speed up games of cricket, and the monotony of long batting innings was tackled by allowing round arm bowling. Such changes were not always successful. The result of a revised code for boxing issued in 1838 was a series of dull, overly-long fights which left crowds cold.[5]

The popularity—and profitability—of sport was aided by a number of other developments. Railways allowed teams and spectators to travel further for matches, bouts and meets, and their results were reported quicker than ever before thanks to the advent of the electric telegraph. The sporting press grew in size and popularity. Papers had long carried information about sporting events—the *Weekly Journal* was advertising fights in 1715—but there was now an explosion of titles providing coverage: the *Sunday Times* and *Bell's Life in London* appeared fortnightly from the 1820s, and the *Sporting Review* once every month.

During the 19th century, as its popularity grew, sport acquired an ideological role that ran parallel to its commercial value. Public schools promoted and developed team games which they believed would instil the qualities of manliness and leadership in the children of the upper middle class. In addition middle class reformers put an end to working class blood sports, and the clergy preached the virtues of a healthy body and a healthy mind under the auspices of "Muscular Christianity". But it was the 18th century that had acted as the midwife of modern sports, imprinting it with its own distinctive markings: "The primacy of cold cash, and with it the subjugation of all to the rule of law".[6]

Capitalism and the poor at play

Most people in the 18th century lived rural lives, scratching out an existence from agricultural labour. The harshness of existence was offset by numerous fairs and festivals, which proved ideal opportunities for playing games. Taverns and public houses also played a central role in the lives of the poor in town and country alike: "The yards, greens and grounds of the drinking place provided the spaces in which sports as diverse as skittles, quoits, bowls, boxing, wrestling, tennis, foot-racing, cricket and any number of activities featuring animals could be staged".[7]

One of the more well-known games played at the time was folk or festival football, versions of which took place across the country and are often seen as the forerunners of football and rugby. In contradistinction to modern sport, folk football would invite mass participation. As Guttmann argues, "There was room for everyone and a sharply defined role for no one. The game was played by the entire village".[8] Certain areas made provision for separate children's games and it seems that matches were not purely the preserve of the village men. The poet Sir Philip Sydney wrote in the 16th century, "A tyme there is for all, / My mother often sayes, / When she, with skirt tuck't very high, / With girls at football playes".[9]

It would, of course, be a mistake to say that there were no rules in the various football games, although to the untrained eye the mass of bodies often looked like a sea of lawlessness. In 1602 Richard Carew produced a vivid description of the Cornish game of hurling detailing the rules that governed the match:

> The Hurlers are bound to the observation of many lawes, as, that they must hurle man to man, and not two set upon one man at once; that the Hurler against the ball, must not but, nor hand-fast under girdle; that he who hath the ball, must but onely in the others brest; that he must deale no Foreball, viz. he may not throw it to any of his mates, standing neere the goale, than himselfe.[10]

This account would suggest a game with a relatively sophisticated set of rules, but one in which codification is absent. The rules,

Sport in a capitalist society

though often customary, were the products of the players. There were no lawmakers outside of the game itself and no governing bodies overseeing the games' development. Similarly the matches themselves were devoid of officials, the players themselves dealing with any transgressions of accepted practice.

Unsurprisingly the ruling class has never been very keen on the lower orders having fun. "The idea that the poor should have leisure", as Bertrand Russell said, "has always been shocking to the rich".[11] Between 1300 and 1650 folk football was banned on at least 30 separate occasions.[12] For example Edward III had outlawed football as it interfered with archery practice, while in 1603 James I issued a Royal Decree which stated, "I debarre all rough and violent exercises, as the foot-ball, meeter for mameing than making able users thereof".[13] These sporadic attempts to prohibit playful recreation should come as no surprise. What is interesting is that they failed.

Capitalism's dynamic was driving changes that would leave no corner untouched and, unlike the previous attempts to curtail the leisure activities of the poor, its expansion would systematically erode the old ways of playing. Malcolmson suggests that "around 1800 the undermining of popular recreations was already well under way, and the process was to continue for at least another half century".[14]

The enclosure movement represented the most fundamental attack on the lives of the poor. Between 1700 and 1845 parliamentary acts led to the privatisation of half the ground that was formerly considered public space. Without common rights people faced the stark choice of starvation or searching out employment in the growing industrial urban economy.

Inevitably the quest for private ownership of land also eroded the space available for games and pastimes. By 1824 Robert Slaney could say that, "owing to the enclosure of open lands and commons, the poor have no place in which they may amuse themselves in summer evenings, when the labour of the day is over, or when a holiday occurs".[15]

Those driven from the land into the welcoming arms of the early industrialists were to undergo a profound change in the way they experienced time itself. The rhythms of life dictated by changing seasons were replaced by the demands of the factory. It was, as E P Thompson surmised, "the contrast between 'nature's' time and clock time".[16]

The leisure of the new working class was an impediment to productivity and profitability. The difficulty in forcing the inexperienced workforce to accept work-time discipline stemmed in no small part from their adherence to a number of holidays. Gradually the old feast days and festivals were eliminated. In 1761 there were 47 public holidays; by 1834 this figure had been reduced to four.[17] It was through "the division of labour; preachings and schoolings; the suppression of fairs and sports—[that] new labour habits were formed, and a new time-discipline was imposed".[18] Capitalism had revolutionised the world of work and in so doing had also fundamentally transformed the world of play.

Chapter 2
IN DEFENCE OF SPORT

Jon Dart

> The revolution will inevitably awaken in the British working class the deepest passions which have been so skilfully restrained and suppressed by social conventions, the church and the press, and diverted along artificial channels with the aid of boxing, football, racing and other forms of sport.
> —Leon Trotsky[1]

Some chapters in this collection will criticise aspects of sport, while others will show how sport can be used to challenge certain aspects of capitalism. However, there are elements within sport that are often underplayed or ignored and yet are worthy of celebrating; specifically its potential for fun, grace, beauty, human drama, excellence, excitement and spectacle.

While socialists readily appreciate a wide range of cultural activities, including music, art, theatre, Scandinavian and (certain) US TV drama series, sport finds it difficult to make the cut and often faces a hostile reception. In this chapter I want to argue that to dismiss sport, its participants and fans is patronising and that, as with much under capitalism, things are contradictory. Can you be a revolutionary socialist and still enjoy sport? Does sport encourage "un-socialist" ideas of competition? Why is wanting England to lose seen as politically progressive? In this piece I'll try to address these questions and, accepting that sport is contradictory, suggest that a more subtle approach is needed than that typically offered.

To dismiss sport as simply a modern-day opiate or "bread and circuses" is to adopt a one-dimensional, crude Marxist approach that fails to adequately explain its popularity, misjudges its content and underestimates its potential.

Defending sport often sees one pigeonholed as a dupe who is guilty of not exercising sufficiently critical analysis. It may be that socialists who don't enjoy sport have never done so and that not everyone appreciates the simple pleasure gained from running, jumping, kicking, throwing and catching. Without wishing to trivialise things, are the most vociferous critics of sport those who were the last to be picked in the school yard? Socialists need to engage with (but not necessarily in) sport and, maybe along the way, they might get to appreciate certain aspects. I don't like the jazz played by Miles Davies or John Coltrane, nor do I like modern dance, but, and here's the point, I accept that other people might like them.

As some in this collection will suggest, the charge sheet against sport is long and damning. One should not seek to defend sport when it brings out the worst aspects of people's behaviour and when, at its ugliest, it mirrors the nastiest characteristics of capitalism, in particular its racism, sexism and homophobia, and its militarism. Despite it being a product of English public schools, codified, commodified and exported with the military and missionaries, exploited by capitalists and used as a training mechanism to reproduce the workforce, many socialists still enjoy watching and playing sport and are acutely aware of these contradictions.

Sport is not the most political subject. However, when people discuss sport it is often limited to the elite level, with the focus on big business, multi-million pound contracts, new stadiums and mega-events; the sports industry/sport-media complex is only one element within sport. That sport is "everywhere" has led some to see the "sportification" of popular culture,[2] and despair at its infection of so much of social life. However, treating sport as an unrefined lump does not allow for distinction between the different levels at which people engage with sport, between those playing and watching, and ignores those elements which are worth celebrating.

Sport is one part of the entertainment industry, but its success has resulted in it receiving significant criticism from socialists. While socialists readily celebrate other leisure and cultural activities, sport is treated differently. In many leisure and entertainment situations, one is primarily a passive observer, often excluded from the experience; if you started to clap, cheer or boo a painting in an art gallery, an actor on the theatre's stage, or a piece of classical music (especially at the "wrong moment"), you would probably be escorted out of the building. It is difficult to become immersed in these activities in the same way as you can with sport, unique in the range of emotion and expression it allows. In the same way some people don't like the theatre, opera, art-house cinema, museums or art galleries, some people don't like sport; however, many people do like sport—and clearly they are not all morons! When dismissing sport, the implication is that people should do something more worthwhile with their time. Surely socialists are not required to enjoy only those activities approved of as "worthy"; isn't socialism about each to their own?

It might be more profitable if sport were judged on its own merits. I realise that this might be an anathema when everything is tainted by capitalism and that taking it out of its context is seen as a fundamental error. However, the same can be said for any (and all) leisure activity. I am not seeking to "rescue" sport, but rather to acknowledge its positive, empowering aspects, in particular to celebrate the strong element of play that can be found within all sport. Johan Huizinga and Roger Caillois explored how play can range from a free-spirited, creative, frivolous activity to one that is structured and serious.[3] Some might want to dismiss the sporting element within play as adopting a "sticking plaster" approach (much like charity), but it does not negate how sport can offer a platform to empower individuals and communities and challenge stereotypes.

Participation in sport (ie playing) can offer valuable physical and mental benefits to those damaged by capitalism. It can also act as a site of personal enjoyment, challenge and sense of community. I don't want to be seen as a cheerleader for "rational recreation" but being physically active in a competitive sports setting can complement one's mental activity—highlighting the long-standing attitudes (and hierarchy) between the mind and the body. Of course, physical activity is possible without engaging in sport, but the element of competition does add a frisson of excitement, potentially greater enjoyment and an opportunity to work with (and against) others in an artificial, transcendent space and time. Being physically active and playing sport, but also watching, can take you outside your immediate circumstances; when the whistle blows, time really does feel like it stands still as one becomes intensely and utterly immersed in an activity that, for most people, has no material outcome (this is not the case, of course, when you are being paid to perform or have bet on the outcome).

Debate on the left over the benefits of physical activity and sport has been minimal. Work and leisure are interconnected, but rather than leisure just being recuperation or re-creating ("recreation") the worker for work, being physically active, in both formal and informal settings, can enhance an individual's quality of life. Given how capitalism seeks to crush the spirit and value only productive work, we should seek to promote and exploit those activities that seek to resist the damaging effects of capitalism. Riordan[4] noted how Lenin shared with Marx "the notion of potential fully-developed individuals, of men and women who could not attain the full measure of their latent abilities under capitalism." Riordan then cites Lenin: "It is necessary to develop people's capabilities, to uncover their talents which are an untapped source in the people and which capitalism has repressed, crushed, stifled in their thousands and millions." Riordan, correctly in my view, concludes by suggesting that "under socialism and complete communism...everyone would have a chance to choose the physical activity they wanted to pursue and to attain complete self-realisation."

School sport was (and still is) for many people an unappealing and unpleasant experience due, in part, to the content and those who taught it. Most people have a horror story about their PE lessons or teacher, but outside school playing sport with friends can be fun. For many people, the hours spent playing, kicking, throwing and catching a ball as a youngster provide better memories and life skills than those spent playing on an X-box. This is not a rose-coloured spectacles view of the past; as an adult, whether playing a game of five-a-side or badminton after work, going swimming, playing in the back garden or down the local park with the kids after school, or going on a run by yourself, they all offer physical and mental stimulation which can contribute to a better quality of life. Similarly watching Gareth Bale skip past an opponent and blast the ball into the net, watching a diver (or gymnast) executing a series of incredibly complicated turns, or a cricketer hitting the ball out of the ground is an enjoyable experience.

Trying to describe the precise feeling(s) these events engender is akin to trying to describe how a piece of music, painting or theatre performance makes you feel. Watching, understanding and appreciating sporting excellence is exciting and engaging; it can increase one's heart rate, send shivers down the spine and make your hair stand on end. One fully accepts that these emotions are not going to solve the problems of capitalism—but it does not mean they are unworthy or any less than reading a Shakespeare sonnet or listening to Beethoven. Capitalism offers so few opportunities to feel good about, and within, ourselves, that we should take the opportunity to celebrate when we can.

Watching sport comes in for particular criticism and is often seen as passive, voyeuristic and a celebration of the lowest common denominator. Without question, sport coverage in the media has reached a point which, for many people, borders on the obscene. However, we don't have to watch it all (we physically couldn't watch it all). Admittedly, paying to watch instead of playing can be problematic in terms of an individual's health, but as part of balanced diet there is little wrong with watching someone perform who is at the top of their game. If you are lucky enough to afford tickets and attend a live event, the sense of community can be mesmerising. Of course, there is often a bunch of bigots (sexist, nationalistic, racist, etc) somewhere at the event—but it's not "their" game and they shouldn't be allowed to think it is. A sense of community can be gained from being part of a live sporting event, whether your team experiences victory or defeat. The humour and camaraderie of being part of something bigger extends beyond the immediate event, with opportunities for social interaction before and after, as well as providing common currency for workplace discussions. As others in this book have shown, sport can act as a significant site for displays of solidarity and resistance.

In appreciating athletic performance and sporting prowess one accepts that most (all?) elite athletes are "clinically ill" in their devotion to succeed in their chosen sport. However, this dedication to excellence can be found in other leisure/cultural activities as individuals hone their physical and mental skills and attempt to become a concert pianist, to be exhibited at the gallery, to write a piece of music, or to perform on stage; all are comparable to that required to perform on a sporting stage. However, sport is often dismissed as a crass display of muscle-bound dullards. Is it sacrilege to compare Lionel Messi or Jessica Ennis with a celebrated painter, opera singer, composer, author or actor? Those who display an elitist, sneering contempt towards sports performers and fans are only a short step from displaying scorn for the working class itself.

Sport is customarily viewed by the left in terms of its ideological and socio-political meaning. Without wanting to become a heretic, is it possible to suspend our historical-materialist approach and focus on the sensory, the aesthetic and emotion of sport? The orthodox Marxist position is to consider everything in terms of its material and historic context, locating activity within the infrastructure of economy and class; however, if we over-analyse we risk draining it (here sport) of all its meaning. Consequently, what is often missed by critics in statements on "what's wrong with sport" is its aesthetic, its potential for beauty and inspiration.[5]

Most of those watching elite sports performers will not be able to reproduce what they have seen (they might even be put off from trying), but nevertheless they appreciate the display of skill and beauty. Sports fans (odd how you are a sports *fan*, but you *appreciate* art and music, or are an opera *buff*) anticipate the sporting calendar, enjoy the drama of the event, delight in those situations which test the limits of human performance and the memories they offer. Many of us like sport because it takes us beyond ourselves and our immediate world. Unlike most musical performance, well-known plays and formulaic television drama (in which part of the enjoyment is often in the anticipation of the next element), sport is completely unscripted and is thus full of suspense. With the unknown outcome, drama and authenticity come to the fore with the predictable often frustrated.

There is common acceptance that sport has gone far beyond its original boundaries and now contaminates many areas of society; clearly the disproportionate amount of media coverage it garners irritates many people. We can rightly despair at the amount of time and space elite sport receives and how it depoliticises and diverts people from political activity which challenges the system. The starting position for socialists, in terms of revolution, should be identifying where the class are; they might be at home watching the football, darts or snooker, down the local park supporting their child's sporting performance, or at the sports centre gym, in the snooker rooms or playing a game of five-a-side. To dismiss those who support England as nationalist, right wing racists will not get us very far. To go round the workplace wanting England to lose (unless you are Andy Murray!) is unlikely to be constructive in building a foundation of future action.

People have always kicked, thrown, run and jumped—playing is part of what makes us human. As to whether some sports are more socialist than others, one could argue that socialists should celebrate team sports because of the group element. As Bill Shankly (manager of Liverpool FC during its successful period in the 1960s and 1970s) once said, "The socialism I believe in is everyone working for each other, everyone having a share of the rewards. It's the way I see football, the way I see life." Life under capitalism is a struggle; is there anything wrong with finding something that is exciting, enjoyable and occasionally dramatic? I wouldn't want a socialist society without the fun gained from playing and watching sport. As a parent I want my kids to know the pleasure, community and confidence that come from being physically active and being part of a team. To paraphrase Pat Stack, it is better to spend an evening supporting the local team rather than drinking yourself into oblivion or downloading pornography from the internet.[6] Sport is contradictory, neither inherently good nor bad; what we need is a more serious engagement, assessment and appreciation of those who like sport and why they like it.

Chapter 3
SPORT AND CAPITALISM

Adrian Budd

Sport is not alone in containing paradoxes and contrasts, but they are often starker than in other areas of life. Millions approach participating in or watching sport in a state of excited anticipation, and later experience exhilaration and a powerful sense of belonging to a team, yet revelations of match-fixing, doping and financial chicanery in sport appear regularly in the media. The 2012 London Olympics provided stirring images of global villagers in mutual enjoyment and celebration; yet national competition can develop into something more sinister, including the racism of the English Defence League. Grass-roots participation and reconnection to our bodies and so to a less alienated sense of self are aspects of sport, but so is the spectacle of Formula 1 motor racing that is more a high-technology trade fair than a sport. For sports with mass popularity, like football in Britain or cricket in India, the rise of corporate hospitality and of ticket and replica-kit prices threatens to derail mass participation.

This chapter presents some ideas on how to understand the contradictory nature of capitalist sport, thereby allowing us to embrace and enjoy sport while recognising its limitations and maintaining a critical distance from it. For its sternest critics the capitalist hallmark with which sport is stamped justifies either its rejection or, at best, its belittling as a trivial distraction from more serious matters. Yet sport's positive aspects can point towards a more just and equal society in which mutual respect flourishes. These are, however, only tantalising glimpses of the future, for the full development of sport's more positive aspects depends less on the internal dynamics of sport itself than on wider emancipatory processes.[1]

Capitalist social relations and sport

Emerging from and initially coexisting with earlier social practices and relations, capitalism gradually subordinated all of society to its own logic. The pastimes that the labouring classes had enjoyed during brief hours of leisure—at fetes, harvest time, etc—underwent processes of "sportisation", a transformation that reflected the dominant characteristics of the wider social system.[2] Capitalism takes various historical and national forms, but at the core of all are two key sets of social relations that express, more or less precisely, what are sometimes called capitalism's twin separations.

The first is the separation of the working class from the means of production, forcing workers to sell their labour power as a commodity to a class of owners of the means of production simply in order to live. The buyers of labour power pay wages which generally represent less value than workers produce. Capital thus exploits the working class which, producing for an alien power that dominates its working life, experiences what Marx called alienation and a sense of being a mere extension of the bosses' machinery. Aspects of capitalism may have been civilised to varying degrees over the decades, but capital continues to treat workers primarily in instrumental cost-benefit fashion and to dictate the rhythm and pace of work. Capitalism's second key separation is of individual capitals from each other: capital only functions as capital when there are relations of competitive accumulation between firms. This reinforces the relations of exploitation since firms must aim to maximise profits if they are to avoid the threat of take over by hostile rivals. Capitalism's core relations of exploitation and competition frame all other social relations and are clearly evident in sport, particularly at a professional and elite level.

Sporting labour processes cannot be radically divorced from wider capitalist labour processes, although elite-level sportspeople are not alienated as extensions of machinery in precisely the same way as other workers, since the tools of their trade are often their own bodies. Sporting workers must accept narrowly specialised roles that maximise productivity and rationalise technique in the pursuit of victory, thereby removing the bulk of individual creativity from the labour process and constraining spontaneity and the development of many-sided personalities. Where winning is the overriding goal the pleasurable aspect of sport is diminished and activity becomes merely a means to an end. Contrary to the experience of childhood play, which is a means towards personal integration and an expression of all the faculties and abilities of mind and body, for (aspiring) professional sportspeople sport is rarely "only a game". It is a job and, as with other jobs, specialisation can disfigure and distort both the personality and the body.[3] A small elite may be very well compensated for its alienation, but this represents a tiny fraction of those who set out with aspirations of sporting success.

To develop our understanding of the relationship between capitalism and sport we have to recognise the conflicts produced by capitalism's core relations of inter-class exploitation and intra-class competition. The inevitability of these conflicts means that state force has always been a central feature of capitalism. States work to contain conflict or, when capital requires it, inflict defeats on labour movements. They also attempt to provide stable supplies of raw materials and of labour power with appropriate skills, physical infrastructures and distribution networks, and legal and administrative systems that regulate the self-destructive potentials of competition.[4] As capitalism developed and the working class became increasingly concentrated in cities and large workplaces so the significance of state regulation deepened and dovetailed with moves by capital to exercise an increasingly rigid control over routinised labour, later systematised under Taylorism and time and motion studies. In relation to industry sport became:

> a way of filling leisure time with brief, but exhilarating periods of uncertainty... The spell of physically competitive activity, far from being broken, was strengthened by the need for momentary release from a colourless world dominated by the monotonous thuds and grinds of machinery.[5]

In so far as this "momentary release" soothed accumulated work-related tensions, sport also functioned as a preparation for a return to work. The factory origins of many football teams, including Arsenal and West Ham in Britain, illustrate the connection between working class sport and capitalist industry. Employers encouraged factory teams as a means to cement workers' company identification and to instil order and the discipline of team working. Other developments reinforce this picture of working class free space and leisure time shaped by industrial capitalism. The new sports codifiers and regulators were:

> not concerned with any simple repression of recognised pleasures, but with defining, regulating and locating them in their appropriate sites. Above all, perhaps, they were concerned to shift pleasures from the site of mass activity (fairs, football matches with unlimited players, carnivals verging on riot) to the site of private and individual activity.[6]

As capitalism developed then, working class leisure activities were subject to a variety of constraints, becoming codified and bound within tighter structures, rules and spaces, such as pitches and rings. They were also time-limited in ways that elite sports were not: golf, cricket, equestrianism and yachting can last for many days or weeks. These constraints were aspects of more general processes of the regulation, bureaucratisation and standardisation of social life. Attempts to remove administrative and legal irrationalities reflected the need to manage an inherent temptation of competition, namely the exclusion of firms from markets rigged by collusion between their competitors and state officials. This could produce stagnation and the self-destruction of the system as a whole. One sporting parallel of this standardisation was the establishment of national leagues under a single set of rules, which also allowed clubs to promote fixtures likely to draw sizeable attendances of fee-paying customers.[7]

States are not only concerned with domestic regulation, however. Competitive capital accumulation has never operated within narrowly national limits and the thirst for profits gave capitalism an international dimension from its birth. Later, as rivals emerged to challenge Britain's position as the world's dominant capitalist power in the second half of the 19th century, so capitalism's international aspect grew in significance and international competition intensified. In the new conditions of inter-imperialist rivalry capitals sought protection from their home states against rivals, while the states themselves sought to protect their patches of the global economy and the producers concentrated there. This in turn entailed power projection abroad in efforts to break into new markets, secure sources of raw materials, protect trade routes, etc. Very soon economic competition had become almost indistinguishable from military rivalry between the world's leading states.

Sport was quickly seized upon as a vehicle to carry nationalist ideology into the working class and prepare young people for service in the national interest. Lewis argues that the sport encouraged in English public schools sought to develop "qualities of manliness and leadership [which were] linked to the other main ideological thread running through the public schools, that of service to the empire".[8] More generally, state military interests in a fit and disciplined population encouraged the introduction of drill for British schoolboys (the girls quietly did needlework in preparation for unflappable support for their future husbands). A similar story unfolded elsewhere. In Germany, for example, Friedrich Jahn's gymnastic system, developed in 1811 to prepare youth for patriotic war against Napoleon, became widespread. One manifestation of these trends in Europe was the birth of the modern Olympic Games, launched in 1896 as the brain-child of French nobleman Pierre de Coubertin.

The Olympics, both ancient and modern, are often presented in purely idealist terms as contributing to world peace and understanding. The embrace of internationalism by spectators and viewers at the 2012 London Games (even the fact that people began speaking to each other on the underground) suggests that there is something in

Sport in a capitalist society

this. But Ellis Cashmore argues that de Coubertin was "distressed by France's poor military efforts, especially against Germany" and "felt his country in need of a reminder of the importance of physical endeavour".[9] By 1912 competitors no longer entered as individuals but as members of national teams. The 1936 Berlin Olympics were a showcase not for humanity's unity and common interests but for Hitler's ideal of racial and national supremacy.[10] Since then the Olympics, and sport more generally, have consistently been used to inflate national pride, as well as to enrich entrepreneurs.

John Hargreaves brings many of the criticisms of modern capitalist sport together: he writes that capitalist sport evinces "specialisation and standardisation, bureaucratised and hierarchical administration, long-term planning, increased reliance on science and technology, a drive for maximum productivity, a quantification of performance and, above all, the alienation of both producer and consumer".[11] Sport, then, is big business and driven by the same logic as the wider system of which it is a part. It seems clear that sport plays a conservative social role, is in part a distraction mobilised to blunt opposition and secure acquiescence to injustice and inequality, and is therefore part of a constellation of forces barring the path towards greater human freedom. Yet millions, possibly billions, of people experience sport as pleasurable, life-affirming and a source of hope. Keeping the positive aspects of sport in mind without ignoring its capitalist nature enables us, following William Morgan, to avoid "the dangers of hypercriticism and excessive romanticism".[12] Sport is a complex contradictory part of a complex contradictory social totality, such that, it has been argued, for the working class sport is "part mass therapy, part resistance, part mirror image of the dominant political economy".[13]

Optimism, hope and resistance

In his *Prison Notebooks* the Italian Marxist Antonio Gramsci wrote against merely dreaming about a better world: "It is necessary to direct one's attention violently towards the present as it is, if one wishes to transform it. Pessimism of the intelligence, optimism of the will".[14] The current social and political reality may be difficult for socialists, but by recognising the contradictory and changing nature of capitalist society we can retain a belief in the possibility of transformation. How does this relate to sport?

Understanding that capitalism's social relations are historically specific, and therefore transient, allows us to avoid the sort of abstract transhistorical essentialism that blights arguments that fall back on the idea of human nature. People are not, as many argue, naturally competitive and acquisitive, and do not carry a genetic imprint from the hunter-gatherer past, representing over 99 percent of human history, that compels us to re-enact the hunt through sport.[15] Sport therefore is not an inevitable expression of human nature to which we are permanently fated to conform.

A second important point challenges those who reject sport for its triviality. Sport is indeed trivial in the sense that it places arbitrary rules in the way of achieving an aim: why, for instance, if a woman wishes to ski down a mountain in a hurry should she have to weave around flags to do so? But, although sports are codified and organised in broad conformity to capitalist social relations, it is this very triviality that gives sport its attraction as a contrast to the daily grind of purposeful instrumental activity—ie work. Indeed, differences in the popularity of sports may be partially explained by the apparent absence of purpose or constraint: in a team sport like football players interact in apparently chaotic ways and must rapidly improvise body movements and team formation to meet unforeseen circumstances. Indeterminacy, improvisation and apparent freedom contrast markedly with the more constrained and limited, yet possibly more instrumentally "useful", activities involved in swimming, running, rowing, cycling, weightlifting, etc.

The relative unpopularity of the more instrumental sporting activities may lead critics to argue that sport shares something with religion as a means to escape from a painful reality. These critics might paraphrase Marx's famous words that as spectacular distractions from social grievances that help cement class rule sports have become a modern "opium of the people". But we should avoid concluding that we should therefore reject sport. For Marx's understanding of religion was much richer than this isolated aphorism suggests. He wrote:

> Religious suffering is at one and the same time the expression of real suffering and a protest against real suffering. Religion is the sigh of the oppressed creature, the heart of a heartless world and the soul of soulless conditions. It is the opium of the people.

Sport in a capitalist society

That members of oppressed classes sometimes require an opiate and "illusions about their condition" is because they experience a "condition that requires illusions".[16] Sport is indeed cast within prevailing social relations and we have seen that it bears their hallmarks in the form of competition, elitism, alienation, nationalism, etc. But sport is never mere illusion or soulfulness: it is constraining in the ways mentioned above but it is, albeit to a lesser extent, simultaneously enabling.

Norman Geras argues that human needs are not just physical but include needs "for love, respect and friendship...freedom and breadth of intellectual and physical self-expression".[17] Sport can contribute to meeting many of these needs. As well as bringing physical enjoyment and providing a space for physical self-expression, participation alongside one's peers encourages sociability, sharing in a common endeavour and "mutual regard for and trust in others".[18] For many young people, consigned by capitalist education (and the class system more generally) to failure, sport may provide an opportunity to excel and therefore earn both income and respect. For spectators, notwithstanding partisan division and identification, the crowd can provide a camaraderie that contrasts with the more atomised aspects of social life.

These positives are not always consciously understood, but at important moments sport can become consciously linked to wider movements of resistance with the potential to reshape prevailing social relations and structures. A popular alternative to Hitler's 1936 Berlin Olympics was organised to take place in Barcelona in 1936. Though the games were called off on their eve when Franco's military rising began, many contestants stayed in Spain to join the International Brigades. Perhaps most famously, at the 1968 Mexico Olympics two black American athletes, Tommie Smith and John Carlos, turned their backs on the American flag and raised their gloved fists in the Black Power salute at their medal ceremony. Smith explained: "When we're winning, we're Americans. Otherwise, we're just negroes".[19] But if sport provided a space for resistance, that resistance was an expression through sport of a movement that emerged and developed beyond sport.[20] It is highly unlikely that sport will generate its own gravediggers independently of wider social transformation.

Conclusion

Sport is a many-sided and paradoxical phenomenon. It can be professional or amateur, elitist or open to all. It is dominated by a cynicism which rejects as fanciful the idea that it is not the winning but the taking part that counts but it also promotes a powerful attachment to this Olympian ideal. It produces cheats but also soaring feats of endurance, grace, beauty and power. It is dominated by big business and the quest for profit but produces acts of great selflessness and generosity. It highlights individual achievement but also provides an emotionally powerful contrast to atomisation, isolation and individual powerlessness, even if collective identity is limited by the competitive identification with one group against all others. The balance between these negatives and positives is not fixed, but it is the former that have more fundamentally shaped capitalist sport. They do not have a free ride, however.

Although it is made fragile, tenuous and distorted by capitalist social relations, sport retains a connection to the exhilaration and pleasure of childhood play, which is common to infancy in all societies and fundamental to humanity.[21] Play helps us to connect with, and integrate, ourselves without fear of social disapproval, to rediscover the joys of contact with the elements and the body as we improvise its shape, run till we drop, or jump for joy. It allows us to gain a small glimpse of an unalienated socialist future and provides a harbinger of a future festival of the oppressed. It can therefore encourage us to question the nature of society and to ask why our leisure time, like the rest of our lives, is largely constrained by competition, repetition, routinisation and regimentation. For these reasons, movements of resistance to prevailing society often find a resonance in sport. But "the promise of sport as a realm of freedom can only be contested but never finally claimed within the context of capitalist social relations".[22] Only socialism will allow us to live in real freedom, and when that arrives the shape of sport, possibly even the very idea of sport, will be fundamentally different to today.

Part 2
Global sport

Chapter 4
THINK LOCAL, ACT GLOBAL: FOOTBALL AND GLOBALISATION

David Swanson

One of the many songs fans sing at matches starts, "We love you, we love you, we love you, and that is why we follow, we follow, we follow..." Now, there are not many commodities that get serenaded like that by so many, apart maybe from the iPhone. But a commodity is what football is, and an increasingly "globalised" commodity at that. Take the English Premier League (EPL). On one recent weekend 131 out of the 220 players in the starting line-ups, eight out of 20 managers and 11 out of 20 club owners were from outside of the UK.[1] And what about those watching? The most accurate figures for 2010/11 show a cumulative global total of 4.7 billion viewers for the season.[2] Meanwhile, one EPL team, Manchester United, claims 659 million supporters around the world, including 108 million in China, 55 million in Indonesia, 35 million in India and at least six in Manchester itself.[3]

This chapter traces some of the key elements in the process of football's globalisation. This includes the marketed consumer product, televised football, and aspects of production such as the players. Finally I look at some of the resistance to these trends. Along the way, some questions, such as, "How does football fit in with theories of economic globalisation?", "Are football clubs really a business if they never make money?", and, "Where is all this going?" get raised, though not necessarily answered!

The rise of commodification

The transformation of football in the direction of atomised passive consumption has a long history. Prior to the development of industrial capitalism football was a mass participation game played between villages (or parts of bigger towns), where the object was to get the ball into the opponents' village by any means necessary (see chapter 2). In reality, the object seems to have been to have a festival of "craziness" with the game, with no real physical or temporal boundaries, as the excuse. The rise of capitalism, with its tyranny of the clock and the carving-up and privatisation of public space, put paid to our fun. There is a myth that the public schools of England then invented the rules of what we call football today. This is a bit like the idea that Robin Hood must really have been a lord. We ex-peasants were more than capable of expressing the discipline of capitalism and coming up with a way to play the game ourselves.[4]

By 1850 workers had managed to win having Saturday after-noons off and it was the one bit of free time people had to do anything (since nothing was allowed to happen on a Sunday). By the 1870s going to watch football had started to take off, and the years that followed saw the formation of many of the clubs and leagues that we know today. The clubs were mainly organised by churches and workplaces, both of whom wanted to distract workers from alcohol and other "unhealthy" pursuits. Attendance at matches rose from there, with the average attendance in the English first division at 27,000 in 1922. It peaked even higher after the Second World War—the same average by then was 39,000[5] (a long decline then follows—by 1989 the average top flight attendance was down to 17,000, but this has been reversed since and is now almost back to its peak).

If the first shift is from mass playing to mass watching, the next shift is to mass communication. First, if we exclude clips in cinema newsreels, comes radio. The first game to have a live radio commen-tary (featuring Arsenal) was in 1927. From that point on you could listen in the comfort of your own home without having to have any real contact with any other human being (although at least your imagination was still involved). Soon after, television appeared. The first match to be broadcast was in 1937 (featuring Arsenal and, er, Arsenal reserves), and live FA cup finals and internationals soon fol-lowed. But not many were watching. Even by 1955 only 26 percent of working class homes had televisions. By the time the first Match of the Day was shown (featuring, surprisingly, Arsenal) in 1964, how-ever, all this had changed. By the early 1970s, despite attendances falling, Match of the Day was being watched by 12 million people and its ITV equivalent by another 8 million.

By the early 1980s the commercial potential of TV football became clear. Live league matches started to be shown regularly, at first by ITV and the BBC. But by 1988 the BBC could no longer compete (that deal was worth £11 million per year to the league compared to £2.6 million for the previous deal). Then along came Rupert Murdoch, and ITV could no longer compete either.

In the early 1990s the then new satellite broadcaster Sky/BSB needed a reason for people to subscribe. Coincidentally, at just this time the top teams in the football league realised they could make more money from TV rights and they broke away to form the Premier League. The deal they did with Sky in 1992 was worth £38 million a year. The next deals raised that to £168 million, then £400 million, then £568 million. The latest deal, jointly with Sky and BT, for 2013-16, is worth £1 billion a year.

As TV football rises, at first, attendance at games continues to fall. Things get worse after the tragedies at Heysel and Hillsborough. With English teams banned from Europe for a while their quality falls as the best players leave. Then the change to all-seater stadiums has a depressing effect on the atmosphere at games. It was around this time, having moved to Manchester from Scotland, I decided to go and see City play regularly. The first time I went was a real culture shock because it was so quiet. At one point in the game a kid near me got up on his seat and shouted "Cit-eh", but then his dad snapped at him, "Get down". One-nil down for most of the match, City scored two quick goals with five minutes to go, and the crowd started singing Blue Moon, but soon enough, all around me, people were muttering, "I bet they'll score again now." I never went back. But to be fair City weren't in the top division at the time and their fans had good reason to be miserable.

Things have changed for City, but also for attendances, since those lows. The other effect of seated stadiums was to make them feel safer. This pulled in some of the middle classes, who were partly awoken to football by satellite TV and more likely to be able to afford the rapidly rising price of the tickets. It also shifted the main audience to the more respectable and older end of the working class for similar reasons. Despite the TV money, match day income (tickets and pies) still makes up around a third of the money most clubs get and is essential to their survival.

The final step to globalisation

Football initially spread out from Britain in the latter part of the 19th century, carried by trade and the empire, by engineers and soldiers, to Europe and beyond. With a few exceptions, it only really took root in Europe and Central and South America (though the first Africa Nations Cup was held in the 1950s). But it wasn't until 1994 that the World Cup was first played outside Europe or Central/South America, and a winner from outside those regions still seems a long way off.

The international tournaments and the European club tournaments played a role in developing football locally and widening horizons. And televised football is a product that can be sold anywhere. The first real taste of this in the UK followed Italy's World Cup win in 1990, in a decade when there was always an Italian team in the Champions League final, and Channel 4 started showing games from Serie A. Similar processes to what had happened with television and the EPL took place across Europe and the big leagues started to stretch out beyond their borders. The overseas rights for the first EPL deal only made around £40 million, about a fifth of the value of the UK rights, but the latest three-year deal is worth an extra £2 billion (compared to £3 billion for the UK).

Figures like that mean that even the bottom club in the EPL will get around £60 million a year from TV money, with the winner getting £100 million. As with capitalism generally, this means the rich get richer and the poor get poorer. With this sort of money, the gap between the big leagues and the rest gets wider and the gap between the divisions in each country gets wider. And, of course, the gap between the top teams and the others in their league increases too, which is why there's only a handful of clubs in most leagues with a realistic chance of winning. The Champions League contributes to this process by piling on extra millions to those who qualify—to the ones who are already wealthier than the rest. Winners of the Champions League can pull in around £50 million extra. On top of that, the better teams do on the pitch, the more they can sell merchandise and get sponsorship deals, increasing the gap even further.

Despite this, even most of the top clubs tend not to make money. The vast sums of money they have are recycled into transfer fees and wages as they desperately try to stay at the top. Meanwhile further down, those in danger of falling out of the league spend like crazy to make sure they don't lose access to the millions of TV money, and everyone else above them then has to do the same. In the process some clubs, like Leeds, fall and struggle to recover. But most clubs just carry on with more money being poured into them by the expanding TV market. One club in Scotland did sadly die in 2011 having chased after the wealthier leagues and clubs, not realising the world had changed (see Mac Giolla Bhain, this volume). But even there a zombie Rangers has emerged, pretending that nothing really happened.

So who is making money from football? The media companies like Sky, although they overstretch themselves attempting to keep hold of the market; Nike and Adidas who produce much of the merchandise; the top players and agents definitely. But the clubs, other than those at the very top, or those such as Porto who have figured out a way to buy cheap and sell high, not really. And they don't seem to pay much tax either.[6]

Will the bubble burst at some point? Yes, but maybe not for a while. Even with competition from other packaged and commodified televisual sports like baseball, the potential markets are still huge. Take the US. Despite the growth in grassroots football and the celebrity of David Beckham, the EPL only averaged 185,000 viewers per match there for the season 2011/12. La Liga, despite a huge Spanish speaking population, only got 115,000 and Serie A 54,000. The average live global audience, outside the UK, for EPL matches, despite the headline number given at the start of the chapter, is only about 3.5 million. There's potentially a long way to go yet.

Meanwhile, the big leagues and clubs continue to draw in all the best players from around the world. If you go back to the 1970s and 1980s cross-border transfers were a rare occurrence, if you ignore the undefended border between Scotland and England. A handful left England to line their pockets in apartheid South Africa, and in America's first wave of infatuation with football. Then, following the 1978 World Cup, a handful of Argentinian players appeared over here, and other "stars" left England to play in the wealthier leagues like Italy. Of these, Luther Blisset has probably had the biggest impact, with an anarchist group naming themselves after him there due to his loveable ineptitude.[7] As the big leagues pulled in more money from television, and the deregulation of neoliberalism impacted with the Bosman ruling in 1995 securing free movement of workers, the best players were sucked towards England, Spain, Italy and Germany. The thrill of seeing players like Aguero, for those in the lucky countries, is undeniable, but it hides many negatives. Chief among them is the sheer waste of human life as big clubs monopolise as much young talent as they can from around the world. Few of them have a realistic chance of making it and they are often left to struggle alone in a foreign country when they don't make the final step up. "You're left to fend for yourself," says Jean-Claude Mbvoumin who campaigns for better support for exploited young African players. "The main danger is that of young players being treated like objects. The success of players like Samuel Eto'o or Didier Drogba leads to increasing numbers of children being developed purely for financial gain".[8]

Where next?

Globalisation is itself nothing new, in the sense of trade being international. What is meant to be new is that multinational companies transcend the national state, and can move production anywhere to avoid restrictions and find cheaper labour. In wider economics this is largely a myth; companies still rely on particular national states to represent their interests, and much production is at least difficult, and sometimes impossible, to move at all.[9] In football the situation is similar. It was a struggle to move Wimbledon to Milton Keynes, let alone trying to move, say, Chelsea to Cambodia. Football clubs, and even multinationals like Sky, are tied to the countries where they have sympathetic governments.

One recurring possibility is of a European super league of some sort. This seems like it would be in the interests of the big clubs. Companies like Sky have a base in countries such as Germany and Italy, and a sort of state structure exists in Europe. But the European Union is struggling to hold itself together in the face of the economic crisis, and competing media companies exist, each with their base in a national state, and football clubs are tied into their national structures. Here, as elsewhere, globalisation's failure to transcend the state has at least severely slowed down the process, despite televised football appearing to be the perfect commodity to achieve the dream of neoliberals.

Globalise this!

So is there an alternative to all this? Of course, some people don't mind the game the way it is. Football provides a feeling of escape from the miseries of everyday life just as much as *EastEnders* or trainspotting, and people are entitled to their escapes. And why shouldn't that include watching a European super league with all the best players in the world, or switching support depending on who is winning? You're not better than them; they're just getting their kicks how they can.

The pull of accepting how things are but wanting things just to be a bit better is powerful in the real world since changing everything seems so much harder a task. You see this in football fans too. If only our club could find an insane billionaire owner we could be at the top and we could sign some genius mercenaries too. Or, like for some fans of my own club (and me too at times), it takes the form of an obsession with making sure the business is run properly, adopting the moneyball transfer strategy, copying clubs like Porto in order to survive and succeed in this football world that's tilted against smaller leagues and smaller clubs.[10]

Another alternative is to try and escape the globalised capitalism version of football and follow a lower league team. Even non-league football has its charms. I once went to a Stalybridge Celtic game where after every goal kick the ball would bounce five or six times before anyone got near it. The atmosphere was intense with the opposing fans screaming abuse at each other through the first half to the point where it looked like things would kick off. But at half time it's not just the teams but the fans who swap ends and as they filed politely past each other they'd nod to their opposite numbers and say, "Alright", and, "How do". When the whistle blew for the second half they were back to screaming at each other.

Even better are the fan-controlled clubs. Of these, the best known include AFC Wimbledon, who made it into the football league, and FC United (see Millward and Poulton, chapter 36) still in the seventh tier but attracting good crowds and about to build their own ground. This is a minority pursuit though. Close in spirit are the ultras and fan groups across the world campaigning against the commercialisation of the game (see Zirin, Ioakimidis and Doleman, all in this volume). The desire for something better and less corporate in football reflects the desire for the same in every aspect of life. Sometimes the two can connect, like with the "Justice for the Hillsborough 96" banners that appeared on terraces across Europe or, at its most developed, with the bravery of the Egyptian ultras in Cairo's Tahrir Square and their role in the wider revolution there.

So is there a revolutionary solution to the global corporate football dream where everyone is sat alone staring at their 3D HDTV and expressing their individuality through choosing their favourite commodity: Barcelona or Real Madrid, Pepsi or Coke, iPhone or Blackberry? Not really. It's only football after all, and most of humanity has better things to worry about. Or how about this: next Tuesday we all take the day off, your workplace against mine. We'll start in the middle and the first to get the ball through the other's front door wins. Agreed?

Chapter 5
CYCLING: HISTORY AND GLOBALISATION
John Foot

For every cycling fan, every place, every journey, every hill, is also a voyage into the past. Geography, history and memory are deeply interconnected in the minds of all cycling enthusiasts: mythical victories, defeats, accidents and breakaways. All of this past cannot be understood in isolation from real, actual places. It only exists on maps, be they in people's minds or on real, paper representations of the world. So Mont Ventoux will always be associated with the tragic events of 1967, when Tommy Simpson collapsed and died during the 13th stage of the Tour de France. The same is true of the great cycling mountains and passes of Italy. The Stelvio inevitably recalls Fausto Coppi, riding in the snow in 1953, leaving all others in his wake, way below, down in the valley. Meanwhile, the Mortirolo reminds us of Marco Pantani, in the rain, in 1994. But cycling also has other ways of telling its history. The history of doping is inevitably linked to two Italian places. There is Savona, as in the end of the stage after which Eddy Merckx tested positive in the first, great, unforgettable doping case and controversy. And then there is Madonna di Campiglio, the beautiful mountain town where Pantani was thrown out of the Giro. Thirty years separate these two turning points in the history of the sport.

Other sites and places are inevitably connected to the lives of the great cyclists. Alfredo Binda was "the trumpeter of Cittiglio", a tiny village near Lago Maggiore. Fausto Coppi was born in the tiny hamlet of Castellania and is buried there with his brother, Serse. He did all he could to escape from that place, but it never really left him. Gino Bartali came from Ponte a Ema outside Florence, and today there is a huge museum in his honour and a massive statue-fountain. Inside there is the usual collection of bikes and posters, with the occasional flash of humanity, such as the cyclist's sandals. There is also a bar dedicated to Gino, L'intramontabile.

Each and every race has its key moment, its pass, its central geographical feature which makes the difference between winning and losing. On the Milano-San Remo this key place is the Passo del Turchino, and the tunnel from which Fausto Coppi emerged in 1946, on his way to an extraordinary 14-minute win. Pierre Chany wrote a whole book about that moment, including this famous piece:

> The tunnel was of a modest dimension, about 50 metres, but on the 19th March 1946 it achieved exceptional proportions to the eyes of the world. That day was long [as] six years and lost in the bleak obscurity of the war. One could hear a rumble from the depth of those six years and suddenly it appeared in the light of the day an olive green car which raised a cloud of dust. "Coppi is Arriving" announces the messenger, a revelation that only the initiated could have foreseen.[1]

For the Giro di Lombardia, the mythical climb is the Ghisallo, with its church dedicated to cyclists, its museum and its statues of Coppi, Bartali and Torriani. The race is not really won or lost on the Ghisallo, but it is that climb which captures the imagination of the fans, even today. And some hills take on mythical importance not because they are particularly difficult, but because of context. Monte Bondone is a fairly regulation climb, but it entered into cycling's history books on 8 June 1956, when freak weather caused havoc with the race, leading to dozens of cyclists dropping out. That day Charly Gaul's ride was an epic, something that encapsulated a whole career, and symbolised the end of an era of the sport. He later said of that day on the Bondone, "It made a mark on my life, in joy and regret".[2] After 1956 cycling was never the same again. Today a stage like that would never even start.

The globalisation of cycling

Cycling began to become a globalised sport with the arrival of television in the 1950s. From an event with an air of permanent mystery and a sense of hearsay, where nobody really knew what had happened in any race at any particular time, not even the cyclists themselves, television began to commodify the sport and remove these doubts. TV also had another long-term effect on the sport. Why bother to stand by the side of a road for hours in order to see a few bikes rush past, when you could see everything, and get expert commentary, from the comfort of your own home? Television also led to a massive increase in the role of sponsors. Fiorenzo Magni, the great Italian cyclist who was also known as the "third man", was the first to use a sponsor on his shirt (for Nivea cream) in the 1960s. Whereas in the pre-televisual age the sponsorship of the race was transmitted through radio adverts (the name of the team, for example), newspapers and through the crowds by the sides of the road, with television things changed forever.

In Italy and France the cyclists themselves took part in adverts, and more and more sponsors' names appeared on their shirts, their bikes and inside the "caravan" that accompanied the Tour and the Giro. On the track sponsorship was even easier. The Ignis "white goods" company, which had made a fortune from Italy's "economic miracle" of the 1960s, sponsored numerous track races, organising music concerts and posh dinners to accompany the racing. It was said that the great sprinter Antonio Maspes would stop during sprints in front of a large Ignis banner, thus guaranteeing huge exposure on live television for the company. The removal of national teams from the Tour in the 1960s was also part of this process, which led to the sponsor itself becoming all-important. The advantages for companies were obvious. Whole stages would be transmitted live, thus allowing for lengthy "adverts" for products and team sponsors, at a cost which was prohibitive if linked to proper scheduled adverts.

But this first stage of globalisation nonetheless remained within the confines of a sport which still had links with its populist, peasant and working class past. Right up until Eddy Merckx came onto the scene, most cyclists were from poor backgrounds, and most had taken up the sport either directly through their work or as a result of poverty itself. And the money they could make was relatively small, leaving aside the great champions who did indeed become rich. The very fact that Merckx was seen as "bourgeois" (he was the son of a shopkeeper) was an indication of how proletarian the sport had been up to that point.

The true leap towards globalisation of the sport only came with the arrival of a successful group of US cyclists in the 1990s. Greg Lemond was the first of these, but it was Lance Armstrong who symbolised a sea change in the sport and the way it was understood, towards the end of that decade. By concentrating on just one race a year—the Tour de France—Armstrong and his team changed the whole concept of the cycling season. In the past riders would participate right from the spring through to the winter (often beginning with the Milan-San Remo, and ending with the Giro di Lombardia). Armstrong changed all that. He was only interested in the Tour. Nothing else mattered. And the visibility his success gave that race led to a vast quantity of money coming into the sport.

Armstrong opened up the US market for European cycling, becoming a national hero who would hang around with US presidents. His double role as cancer survivor/charity worker and international sporting hero (these two images were obviously linked) led to a mixing of publicity for his charity (Livestrong) and his sponsor (most notably Trek). A whole team of people would paint the roads with Trek and Livestrong slogans before each stage. Armstrong's life story (told in countless books and documentaries, and propagated by a largely willing press corps, with a few notable exceptions) drew millions of people into a sport for which they had previously had no interest. He was a money-making machine for himself, his sponsors (Nike, Trek, Radioshack, Giro, FRS, Oakley, Shimano and so on), the Tour, international cycling as a whole and cycling companies the world over. During the Armstrong era cycling went through a worldwide boom, both as a sport and as an activity. On the back of the Armstrong boom the cycling authorities reached out to new markets. In 2007 UCI president Pat McQuaid promised China's new stage race (planned for 2009) would be "as important and popular as the Tour de France".

But the Armstrong era, and the period which preceded it (going back to the mid-1980s) was also a period of another kind of globalisation, the globalisation of blood doping. Through doctors in Italy,

Spain and France, most of the cyclists who rode professionally during the 1990s and much of the 2000s participated in various forms of blood doping practices. This doping was organised often at team level and was created through international links. Doctors were paid handsomely for their work, often via secret bank accounts in Switzerland and elsewhere. Blood from Italy was found in fridges in Spain, and drugs were taken across international frontiers where they were occasionally seized. This was an international criminal conspiracy, which involved cyclists, managers, sponsors, the media, the cycling authorities and even, at times, those who were part of the anti-doping process. Criminal globalisation mirrored a process of sporting globalisation.

In 2012 this system unravelled in retrospect, thanks to an extraordinary investigative report carried out by the US anti-doping agency. Armstrong was stripped of his seven Tour titles (which were left blank, taking account of the doping practices of most of the other cyclists over that period) and the sponsors, who had made so much money out of him, abandoned him en masse. Some even asked for compensation. An anti-history of that period of the sport emerged, made up of startling confessions (as in bestselling books by Tyler Hamilton and David Millar, but see also the prescient account by Matt Rendell of Marco Pantani's life and death) and brave investigative journalism (David Walsh and Paul Kimmage are the most important figures here).

So the era of boom was also an era of bust. The glorious years of expansion and wealth were underpinned by EPO and testosterone injections and bags of blood. They were also built on corruption and lies. Now the sport is at a crossroads. An extensive judicial investigation into Dr Michele Ferrari is coming to a close. More details will almost certainly emerge of doping practices and international networks of cheating which are ongoing, and not just linked to the so-called "Armstrong era". This is surely the last opportunity for cycling, given the shock felt by many who had been drawn into the sport during the golden years of expansion, globalisation and sponsorship.

Team Sky is in many ways the most global of the new teams (it started racing in 2010). It is a team run with almost military efficiency, which uses a vast media empire to build consensus and power. Team Sky claims to be "doping-free", and has cleared out all of its staff with any past or present links to doping practices. But is this because doping is now bad for business, just as hidden practices of doping were extremely good for business in the 2000s with Armstrong and others? Whatever the truth, we are light years away from the golden age of the 1940s and 1950s. It is difficult not to look back with some nostalgia to those pre-televisual days, where riders would fix their own punctures and sometimes push their bikes up hills that were too steep. That was a sport that was close to, and almost symbiotic with, the people. Cycling today is an integral part of the "society of the spectacle".

Chapter 6
CRICKET AND GLOBALISATION: FROM ICC TO IPL[1]

Andrew Stone

> Always denied entry by the English Gentry
> Now we're driving Bentleys playing Twenty20.[2]

On 18 April 2008 Brendon McCullum of Kolkata Knight Riders smashed the bowling of the Royal Challengers Bangalore to all parts of the packed M Chinnaswamy Stadium, Bengaluru. Scoring a blistering 158 runs in just 73 balls, the big-hitting New Zealander took his team to a massive total of 222 in their allotted 20 overs. Their demoralised opponents replied with a pitiful 82 all out. In the 59 matches played over the next six weeks the Indian Premier League (IPL) attracted an average 58,000 spectators per game and an estimated television audience of 220 million.[3] Big, bold and bloated, the IPL had arrived, and cricket's reputation as an aristocratic, backward looking relic had never looked so outdated.

But that was the baptism. The birth of the corporate behemoth came in two press statements that January. Issued by the Board of Control for Cricket in India (BCCI), they notified the world that (a) Sony Entertainment/WSG had bought the TV rights for the IPL for ten years for $1.03 billion and (b) the winning bids for the rights to the eight proffered "franchises"—ie the clubs—amounted to $723.59 million.[4] Two years later Brand Finance, a marketing consultancy, valued the IPL at $4.13 billion.[5] Leaving aside the spurious exactitude exhibited by the valuation, it reinforces how interlocked cricket now is with the embrace of big business. It also helps to explain why the chaos attendant on all market systems is becoming increasingly obvious within cricket, with fixture competition, disputed governance and widespread corruption just some of the elements threatening the world game.

Reformers and reactionaries

Twenty20 is a form of cricket launched, with an atypical lack of myopia, by the English Cricket Board (ECB) in 2003. The ECB devised this short-form version of the game (it can take as little as three hours to complete) to attract a new, more diverse audience than normally attends first class county cricket. It was, in these terms, a notable success, more than doubling spectator levels by 2005 to around half a million.[6] Combining fast-flowing cricket with tannoyed MOR music, mascots, cheerleaders and the occasional manufactured pop band, it was a bitter pill for the traditionalists who fill most county committees, but no doubt one sugared by the increased gate receipts.

The image of the typical cricket administrator as a reactionary, faintly ridiculous public school mediocrity is not without historical foundation. In an amusing article in 1962 the establishment's favourite cricket writer, E W Swanton, defended the fact that the Marylebone Cricket Club (MCC), which wielded so much power over English cricket then, should have an appointed presidency. He did so on the basis that "it eliminates politics", and that the committee was "frequently being refreshed by men distinguished in other walks of life". The roll call of post-war presidents at that time comprised a general, a lord, two earls, three knights, two viscounts, a field marshal and three dukes (including the prince consort).[7] They generally embodied the views of "golden age" luminaries such as Harrow old boy and amateur England captain Archie MacLaren, who thundered in his 1924 book, *Cricket Old and New: A Straight Talk to Young Players*, that an innovator was "the Bolshevist of the cricketing world" and it was "about time he was suppressed".[8]

The argument for cricket to be repackaged and sold off as "cricketainment"—a word so inelegantly coined by IPL founder Lalit Modi—is strongest when used in opposition to such privileged opponents of change. The first class game has been so obviously out of step with modern life—played in England to generally minuscule "crowds" over four weekdays (*increased* from three days in 1988). Discussions on holding a one-day competition began in 1873 but were scuppered by county committees, then revived and rejected again during the Second World War, before finally seeing the light of day a mere 90 years after their initial proposal. To suggest such change was glacial might be accurate if we were not living in an age of rapid climate change.

The ICC

Until recently the International Cricket Council (ICC) has typified such institutional inertia. The ICC is in many ways cricket's United Nations. This is not intended as a compliment. It mirrors that body's claim to universalism, while both, in reality, are a forum for the interests of their constituent parts. Both have a clear hierarchy in which major powers cajole and coerce their weaker counterparts. The ICC has a three-tier structure—ten full members, who are entitled to play test matches, 36 associate members where cricket is "firmly established", and 60 "affiliate members".[9] The full members dominate the executive board and control the rotation of the presidency. Their representatives are rarely worthy of the name, a mixture of bureaucrats, political appointments and cut-throat businessmen (and they are almost entirely men).

The modern ICC is an evolution of the Imperial Cricket Conference founded in 1909. It was the brainchild of South African Abe Bailey—a protégé of the brutal imperialist Cecil Rhodes. Lord Harris, the first English representative, was chairman of the London-based Consolidated Goldfield of South Africa.[10] Cricket has long facilitated the political and commercial networking for sections of the ruling class. Despite the failure of its first venture—a triangular tournament between founders England, South Africa and Australia—the body remained, meeting once a year so members could "ventilate" opinions. Long-time ICC secretary Jack Bailey opined that it fulfilled the "function of Buckingham Palace",[11] whatever that might be. Its 1926 meeting confirmed that it should comprise "governing bodies of cricket in countries within the empire", enabling West Indies, New Zealand and India to join.[12] When South Africa left the Commonwealth in 1961 it was allowed to continue to play test matches until a massive anti-apartheid movement resulted in abandoned tours and (to the great distress of much of the MCC) a sporting boycott lasting two decades until domestic resistance ensured that apartheid began to crumble. As the ICC website now admits, "Since its inception, the ICC had been run as a virtual appendix to MCC"—even their secretaries were the same until 1993. Such amateurism has, however, now gone the way of the Gentleman and Players (see chapter 17). 1993 also, as the ICC delicately puts it, "saw ICC with its own office for the first time, though this was still at Lord's, with a separate office soon established for commercial purposes in Monaco".[13] The ICC is now mainly based in Dubai, no doubt for equally benign missionary purposes, and nothing to do with tax avoidance.

Change and continuity

There are numerous examples of innovations which have faced official resistance during the long development of the game—from overarm bowling, to googlies and doosras (deliveries designed to spin in the opposite direction to that expected by the batsman), to ball-tracking technology for dismissal appeals. Not all such proposals have been beneficial—the experiment of allowing tactical substitutes, which undermined the principle that any player could, in a given situation, be an all-rounder, was mercifully dropped. But the authorities have for so long cultivated an appearance of disdain for reform, that it becomes tempting to take a default position of supporting it, whatever its source.

Yet the instigators of change in the modern game are rarely motivated by the desire to increase the participation and enjoyment of players and supporters—or at least not as ends in themselves. Like any good capitalist, their aim is to commodify human activity into a saleable product. The previous generation's Modi—media magnate Kerry Packer, who threatened to split the game irrevocably in 1977 with the launch of World Series Cricket—is often described in cricketing literature as a revolutionary. However, his grudge against the "old school tie" was that the Australian Cricket Board (ACB) had denied his Channel Nine coverage of domestic test matches. A cut-throat capitalist riding the initial wave of neoliberalism, he could not believe that they had prioritised a privately-made deal over his own higher offer—as he said in exasperation, "Come on, what's your price? We're all harlots".[14] He claimed to speak for the interests of players, but when his hostile takeover of the international game was less successful than anticipated, he made a "historic compromise" with the ACB to secure what had always been his main objective, TV coverage.

The same drive lies behind Rupert Murdoch's interest in the game. The single biggest power in baseball, he also controls live to air test and one-day international cricket in England until 2017, and in April 2012 his company Star TV paid 3.85 billion rupees (£473 million) for broadcasting rights to India's home international games for the next six years.[15] His News Corporation also has a stake in ESPN Star Sports, which is funding the Champions League Twenty20 to the tune of almost $1 billion for its first ten years. The tournament is owned and run by the boards of India, South Africa and Australia, who contribute four, two and two teams respectively "by right", with other countries required to enter a qualifying competition.[16] Murdoch has described sport as "a battering ram" to gain access to national markets.[17] The reason he is willing to invest so much in India is easy to explain—Indian cricket reaches audiences of some 400 million people, and is now the economic superpower of the world game, responsible for an estimated 70 percent of its income.[18]

The result has been the enrichment of a tiny class of administrators and business executives. Former BCCI chief Jagmohan Dalmiya was the pioneer, rising to the position of ICC President. India's ascent began in 1983, when they won the World Cup despite entering as 66-1 outsiders with a chair of selectors who considered the event "artificial" and "irrelevant".[19] Building on the resultant commercial nationalism, Dalmiya helped to mastermind India's bid to co-host the 1987 competition and, to the great fury of the English administrators, once again in 1996. TV revenue was the key, and exploiting this enabled him to add $20 million to the ICC accounts (previously bumbling along with around $30,000) via a forgettable knockout tournament in 1998.[20] However, when former friend and ally Inderjit Singh Bindra turned against him,[21] an administrative turf war began which led, in December 2006, to Dalmiya's expulsion from the BCCI. Sentimentality once again outbid in the world of cricketainment.

Scandal

One outcome of the growing emphasis on TV rights was that venues became less and less relevant. Thus Sharjah, in the UAE, hosted more than 200 international matches in the two decades from 1984. Playing often to small crowds of Asian ex-pats, they paid for themselves through a combination of legal broadcast deals and illegal international gambling. The spectre which dominated the early years of the English game, so much that a set of "laws" (ie the rules of cricket) were required to settle gambling disputes, now returned turbo-charged by instant communication and credit. The scandals around match-fixing in the 1990s led to bans for life for three international captains—Pakistan's Salim Malik, India's Mohammad Azharuddin[22] and South Africa's Hanse Cronje, and fines for two more—Waqar Younis and Wasim Akram, along with punishments for a number of other leading players.[23]

The ICC could take no credit for uncovering the Cronje case, which was revealed by chance by an Indian Central Bureau of Investigation (CBI) operation. However, they did commission a report by the head of their new Anti-Corruption Unit, Sir Paul Condon, former head of the Metropolitan Police. This was an interesting appointment given the Met's less than spotless reputation for probity. The report recognised "at least 20 years of corruption linked to betting" and bemoaned that "corrupt practices and deliberate under-performance have permeated all aspects of the game".[24] Yet despite ongoing rumours of corruption, the next major sting was achieved not by the ICC, but by Rupert Murdoch's late unlamented *News of the World*. Pakistan captain Salman Butt and his bowlers Mohammad Asif and Mohammad Amir were convicted for "spot-fixing"—the deliberate bowling of no-balls at specific times—in the Lord's test.

The Indian CBI has identified 1978 as the turning point. Though it points to the resumption of India/Pakistan fixtures as precipitating the match-fixing, it may also be relevant that this was the period of the World Series cricket conflict. If the sole aim of every cricketer is to sell their talents to the highest bidder, as Packer asserted, what happens if that bidder happens to be a bookmaker? Certainly the massive and growing inequality of rewards cannot have helped matters. In the wake of Packer the incomes of top players were boosted the most—initially English test match fees went from £200 to £1,000 per test.[25] Since the advent of central contracts a decade ago established English test players now receive a basic pay of over £400,000 per year, which is topped up by win bonuses and appearance fees. This is more than ten times what an average county cricketer can expect[26] (such as, for example, Mervyn Westfield, jailed in 2012 for spot-fixing in a one-day match for Essex)[27] And it is almost 20 times the wage of Pakistani internationals. But as the snaring of such well-remunerated players as Cronje shows, corruption is not the result of a lack of money in the sport, but a surfeit of it—and the subordination of everyone within it to the needs of profit both legal and illegal.

The IPL has itself been engulfed in governance scandals, with wide-ranging allegations of misconduct levelled at its now suspended founder, Lalit Modi. In April 2010 the *Times of India* revealed a confidential tax investigation which had been languishing in the hands of the Indian government for six months. It reported that "Mr Lalit Modi has had a trail of failed ventures and defaults till four years back but has a lifestyle now that includes a private jet, a luxury yacht and a fleet of Mercedes S class and BMW cars all acquired in the last three years".[28] It linked this newly acquired wealth to his silent stake in three of the IPL franchises. These and more serious charges of nepotism and involvement in match-fixing are denied by Mr Modi.

"Cricketainment"—the hyperbolic commentary, the interminable adverts, the celebrity bandwagon—may have found its apogee in the IPL, but there has been no shortage of attempts to emulate it elsewhere. One of them, the Indian Cricket League, was strangled with monopolistic relish through player bans by the BCCI. Others, such as the Big Bash in Australia and the Sri Lanka Premier League, have prospered thus far on a more limited scale. In combination with the Champions League they have posed a huge challenge to the ICC's Future Tours Programme, an attempt to rationalise the bilateral arrangements which make it so hard to compare the records of international teams. The historic pre-eminence of international cricket is thus seriously threatened for the first time, but the IPL city franchise model is no more benign. Far from banishing nationalism, commercialism often fuels it—after the Mumbai terrorist attack not a single Pakistani player was bought at the 2010 IPL auction, despite Pakistan being World Twenty20 champions at the time. And Lalit Modi's rationale? "They [the franchises] are spending money. And they want to get the results".[29] But did he mean sporting or financial results?

Epilogue: Stanford's century

A Texan billionaire is not the most common sight on Lord's cricket ground, and the arrival of Allen Stanford there on 11 June 2008 was even more remarkable—he flew in on a gold-plated helicopter accompanied by a black box stuffed with $20 million in crisp notes. Former cricketing greats and the English Cricket Board (ECB) fawned around him, chairman Giles Clarke gushing that "Stanford is a great legendary entrepreneur and he has the entrepreneur's ability to spot an opportunity and seize it".[30] The "legend" told the world about his plan for annual winner-takes-all games between England and the West Indies for the sum in the box. He named the contests "Twenty20 for twenty", but what no one seemed to see coming (save for *Private Eye* and anyone who had looked into Stanford's business activities) was that Stanford's Antiguan empire was built on sand. An estimated 92 percent of his bank's capital was fictitious, and he swindled some 30,000 investors in a massive $7 billion Ponzi scam.[31] He is now serving a 110-year prison sentence in the US. Only one Twenty20 for twenty was played before Stanford was caught out. Needless to say, England's players didn't win. And cricket? That didn't come close.

Chapter 7
THE MEANING OF MURDOCH: SPORT IN THE NEW WORLD ORDER

Tony Collins

In 1996 Australian media baron Rupert Murdoch addressed shareholders of his News Corporation at an annual meeting in Adelaide. His aim, he announced, was to "use sports as a battering ram and a lead offering in all our pay television operations".[1]

In 1992 he had paid the English Football Association £304 million to televise the newly created Premier League. The following year his US Fox Network paid $1.58 billion to broadcast American football. In 1995 he established his own Super League rugby league competitions in Australia and England and provided the financial underpinning for international rugby union's decision to abandon amateurism and turn professional.[2] By the start of this millennium Murdoch had become the most important player in world sport.

Other media companies struck similarly lucrative deals with American baseball and European soccer. In 2008 Indian cricket created the Indian Premier League (IPL), explicitly as a television product based on English soccer's Premier League. Almost all of sport's new riches were a consequence of the deregulation of the European television market that had begun in the late 1970s and the subsequent technological development of pay-per-view cable, satellite and digital delivery of programming.[3]

But sport's seemingly irresistible rise was also a consequence of the imposition of the "New World Order", the late 20th century counter-reformation led by Ronald Reagan and Margaret Thatcher. The defeats of trade unions, the dismantling of welfare provision, the collapse of the social democratic project and the implosion of the Soviet Union led to the almost unchallenged supremacy of capitalism and its ideology. And as went society, so too followed sport: to quote Bertolt Brecht, "The old strode in disguised as the new." Sport benefited from the deregulation of markets and provided a gushing font of rhetoric for capitalist politicians and ideologues.

Like the newly fashionable "free market", sport was nothing if not competitive, dividing winners from losers, the most important social distinction of capitalism. American football coach Vince Lombardi's infamous saying, "Winning isn't everything. It is the only thing," summed up the capitalist Zeitgeist.[4] The use of sport as a metaphor for life as ceaseless competition became increasingly prevalent. Business adopted the language of sport. Teamwork, attitude, commitment, contest: the lexicon of the locker room became the badinage of the board room. Supporters' identification with and loyalty to a club or sport, especially that of the most hardcore or "authentic" fans, became interchangeable with the "brand" and "consumer loyalty".

The break-up of the USSR and the Eastern Bloc countries in the 1990s, renewed immigration into Europe and North America from countries impoverished by "free-trade agreements", and the eagerness of the US, Britain and the West to use their military might in defence of their imperial interests, exacerbating national and racial enmities, found their reflection in sport. The "globalisation" of sport was and remains primarily a media phenomenon. Sports acquired a global audience, yet, with the exception of soccer, its geographical template had not qualitatively changed nor had its traditional hierarchy been threatened. Soccer, the one truly global sport, increasingly became an arena for the open parade of national rivalries and ethnic chauvinism. "There are no black Italians" chanted racist Juventus fans during their match against Inter-Milan in 2009.[5] Across Europe soccer stadia were the sites for the most virulent displays of public anti-Semitism since the 1930s.[6]

Although the scale and speed of sport's relentless commercial expansion since the 1980s appeared to be a new phenomenon, sport in the 21st century increasingly resembled its nakedly commercial forebears of the 18th century. Unashamedly part of the entertainment industry and played for profit, it became a fashionable bauble for super-rich patrons. Baseball, IPL and football clubs of all codes became status symbols for the wealthy in the same way that cricket clubs, race horses and pugilists were for the British aristocracy in the 18th century. Roman Abramovich at Chelsea and Daniel Snyder at the Washington Redskins in the 21st century were little different to the cricketing Earls of Tankred and Winchilsea in the 18th century, apart from the fact that today's plutocrats do not expect to play alongside their expensively acquired rosters of stars.

If the economics of sport now resembled those of the 18th century, the continuing desire of sports administrators to regulate and control their athletes was firmly based on the 19th century model of Victorian amateur sport. Amateurism was dead, but its structures of discipline lived on. In fact, there was no contradiction between the commercial exigencies of sport and the strictures of its administrators. The two went hand in hand, as Clive Woodward, the British Olympic Association's director of sport, made clear to his athletes in 2011: "It drove me nuts in Beijing [at the 2008 Olympics] because there were a couple of people who took great pride in walking around the village with a Nike T-shirt on. [Adidas] is our sponsor and this is our team kit. All I'll say is that those athletes were nowhere near the podium and I'm not surprised because they didn't have the discipline".[7] In North America the NBA and the NFL introduced dress codes and "personal conduct" policies that applied to their (predominantly black) athletes' lives outside of the playing arena.

As amateurism collapsed, the continuing desire of sports administrators to demonstrate the moral value of sport shifted their focus from policing payments to players to pursuing so-called performance-enhancing drugs. The "enemy within" for sport was no longer the "veiled professional" working class athlete or the Soviet-bloc "shama-teur" but the "drug cheat". The arbitrary rejection of certain types of pharmaceuticals—a version of the Reagan administration's "war on drugs" of the 1980s—led to increasingly draconian testing and disci-plinary measures being taken against athletes. In 2004 the World Anti-Doping Agency (WADA) introduced its "whereabouts" system that effectively turned elite athletes into prisoners on parole.[8] This forced athletes to nominate one hour per day, seven days a week, when they would be available for unannounced drug testing. Being somewhere else, failure to complete the required paperwork or pro-viding incorrect details of training schedules were punishable offences. Informers and spying were also encouraged. At the 2012 London Olympics, cleaning staff and security guards working in the athletes' village were "educated" so that "if they come across behav-iour that is untoward" they would report it to the IOC.[9] These unapologetic police state measures were of course justified as being necessary to stop "cheats".

The concerns of the 19th century amateur moralists were also echoed in 21st century sporting paranoia about gender. Although levels of formal equality had risen in the latter part of the 20th century—by 1984 even the International Olympic Committee had accepted that women were perfectly capable of running marathons—the boundaries between male and female were more strictly policed than ever. In soccer FIFA banned female Mexico striker Maribel Dominguez from playing for the Mexican men's second division side Celaya FC in 2004 because "there must be a clear separation between men's and women's football".[10] In 2009 the case of Caster Semenya, an 18 year old black South African woman middle-distance runner, once more brought the gender paranoia of sport to the fore. Suspected of "being a man", she was forced to undergo an "examination" in which "her feet were placed in stirrups, her genitals were photographed and her internal organs were examined".[11] Following an international outcry Semenya was eventually allowed to compete again.

The International Association of Athletic Federations (IAAF) even granted itself the power to determine the most intimate part of human identity: the sex of an individual. Indeed, any IAAF race-day medical official was given this right. "The Medical Delegate shall also have the authority to arrange for the determination of the gender of an athlete should he [sic] judge that to be desirable," read rule 113 of the IAAF Competition Rules. The IOC requires transgender athletes to have had sex reassignment surgery at least two years before they compete as women.[12] And despite the fact that similar medical conditions can also be found in men as well as women, male athletes are not subject to testing.[13] This is because the underlying yet predominant concern of sports organisations is policing an arbitrary boundary between male and female, just as it was in its formative era of Victorian amateurism. Then as now, modern sport is founded on the affirmation of strict gender division, in which women are subordinate to the masculine ideal, and those who do not conform are condemned.

This inbuilt historic misogyny also explains the continuing deep-seated hostility to gay athletes, both male and female, in almost all sports. Of the thousands of professional male football players of all codes around the world in 2011, there was only one soccer player, Sweden's Anton Hysen, and one rugby player, Welshman Gareth Thomas, who felt comfortable enough in their sports to be openly homosexual. In women's soccer the 2011 world cup was marked by what one commentator called "lesbian panic" as Nigeria and Guinea sought to purge players suspected of not being heterosexual.[14] Such a state of affairs marks football in all its forms as probably the most reactionary institution in the world on sexual matters, outside of organised religion.

These restrictive and repressive measures against athletes intensified because of the social conservatism of the post-Reagan/Thatcher world. But sport did not merely reflect the times, it also played an active role in changing the political climate. From the 1980s the need for "security" at sporting events increasingly became a rationale for governmental attacks on civil liberties. It was the 1984 Los Angeles Olympics, dubbed at the time "the first free enterprise games", that created the authoritarian template for subsequent "mega-sporting events".[15] Combining maximum freedom for corporate sponsors with repressive measures against potential opponents, the organisers of the LA Games ran roughshod over democratic rights, banning demonstrations, "socially cleansing" the homeless, prostitutes and others, and employing thousands of additional police and military operatives. Olympic precincts became militarised zones.[16]

By the time of the 2010 Vancouver Winter Games, the Olympics resembled nothing so much as a travelling totalitarian state that pitched up in a host city every couple of years and subjected the population, especially the poor and racially oppressed, to police-state measures and celebrations of corporate indulgence. As part of the preparations for the 2010 Games, Vancouver's city council enacted laws that banned leaflets, unauthorised placards and megaphones, outlawed demonstrations unless approved by the police, allowed the police to enter homes to take down protest signs hung outside of buildings and authorised the use of military technology, such as a 152 decibel "sonic gun", against demonstrators. The Canadian secret services identified "anti-globalisation, anti-corporate and First Nations activists" as specific threats to Olympic security.[17]

Nor was soccer any different. The introduction and extensive use of closed-circuit television systems at English soccer grounds in the 1990s presaged their almost saturation use across English towns and cities today.[18] During Euro 2008 in Switzerland private security firms vetted all supporters entering the specially designated "Fan Zones" and police undertook a programme of "preventative arrests" of those they thought might commit crimes. Ominously, elements of these measures were incorporated into Swiss immigration law.[19] In preparation for the 2014 soccer World Cup and the 2016 Olympics, it is estimated that 1.5 million Brazilians will be removed from their homes to make way for the building of new sports stadia.[20] The cost of creating these capitalist utopias—in which free enterprise controls an unfree people in celebration of the glories of competition—is of course borne entirely by the populations of the host nations, not by the IOC, FIFA or other sports bodies. As with so much sport, the "magic of the marketplace" could only conjure up profit when underpinned by public subsidy.

Thus the global mega-sports event has come to be a passion play of celebration of and deference before the world capitalist order. And sport, like its capitalist progenitor, has established itself "over the entire surface of the globe. It must nestle everywhere, settle everywhere, establish connexions everywhere".[21] In the first decade of the 21st century the bond between sport and capitalism that was established in the 18th century had never been stronger or more apparent. Like the truncheons and clubs used by police against demonstrators opposing the "New World Order" on the streets of cities around the world, Murdoch's "battering ram" was aimed squarely at the heads of the working class and the oppressed.

Chapter 8
THE JOGGING BOOM

Dave Renton

Few sports are more universal than running. Both the London Marathon and the Great North Run see around 40,000 participants each year, and around 1 million people in Britain have run at least one marathon in their lives. Socialists are critics of organised sport and, in particular, of its diminished conception of popular participation, which limits the vast majority of people to no role other than as purchasers. The participation of millions in club running and amateur athletics is a weighty piece of evidence in support of our claim that richer lives would be led by all if only people were given far broader opportunities to be physically active. Yet we also know that nothing under capitalism goes untainted by profit. Even something as simple as running shows every sign of domination by global big business.

Like both Thatcherism and punk (between which its cultural politics have repeatedly oscillated), jogging in Britain began really at the end of the 1970s. Its start was a "National Fun Run" sponsored by the *Sunday Times*, for which 12,000 people signed up. The sport's rise was fuelled by the events of the Moscow and then the Los Angeles Olympics, including Steve Ovett's 800 metres gold in 1980 and Seb Coe's 1,500 metres golds in 1980 and 1984. The ubiquitous Jimmy Savile fronted a weekend television show promoting running. The London Marathon received financial support from Ken Livingstone's Greater London Council, while such corporate sponsors as Mars also tried to muscle in on the act, promoting chocolate as the perfect mid-race snack.[1] The 1981 film *Chariots of Fire* spread the message further, its Labour-voting screenwriter Colin Welland using the story of Jewish student Harold Abrahams's struggle against inter-war anti-Semitism to get in some decent kicks against the British establishment. If *Chariots of Fire* "was" running, then both left and right could identify with it: socialists with the idea it represented a realm of freedom outside the establishment's control, the right in the spirit of Thatcher's clashes against Lords Whitelaw, Carrington, Pym and the other Tory "wets".

One company closely associated with the jogging boom was Nike, whose shoes sold in Britain from 1978, the same year as the *Sunday Times* run. The company was then in the middle of an extraordinary boom, the value of its worldwide sales increasing 70-fold from $14 million in 1976 to $1 billion ten years later. Part of Nike's appeal was that it promoted itself as a young and unspecifically counter-cultural business. In much the same way that Richard Branson's Virgin began by distributing the Sex Pistols but has ended up profiting from privatisation, Nike was originally associated with a generation of runners at the University of Oregon, headed by US Olympian Steve Prefontaine and his coach Bill Bowerman.

At his death in 1975 "Pre" was the American record holder at every distance from 2,000 to 10,000 metres. In 1972 he had finished fourth in the Olympic 5,000 metre final, an extraordinary race in which Prefontaine held but lost the lead three times in the final two laps. Pre was part of the student generation who had challenged the Vietnam War. He fought a series of battles with the administrators of US amateur athletics, at the climax of which he told the New York Times:

> "To hell with love of country", says Steve Prefontaine, America's best amateur distance runner. "I compete for myself."
>
> Prefontaine said he's so fed up with the treatment of American athletes that he would change his citizenship tomorrow if given the chance. He described himself as an "internationalist".
>
> "People say I should be running for a gold medal for the old red, white and blue and all that bull, but it's not gonna be that way", Prefontaine said in an interview. "I'm the one who has made all the sacrifices. Those are my American records, not the country's…"[2]

In many ways the perfect expression of Pre's radicalism was a 1979 TV film which came out four years after his death and which ostensibly has no links to him at all. Michael Mann's The Jericho Mile is a purely fictional account of a convict, Larry Murphy, who is discovered in prison to be running mile times within seconds of the US record. Given a chance to compete in US Olympic trials, he is opposed by a local gang leader who attempts to frustrate the race but is beaten back by a united front of politicised black and Mexican inmates. The authorities then withdraw Murphy from the race. The actor (Peter Strauss) plays the part with shoulder-length blond hair and a thick moustache, making him a virtual twin of the real-life runner Prefontaine. The film is a kind of idealised, hyper-politicised version of Pre's own radical journey.

Prefontaine's coach, Bowerman, designed the first Nike shoes, supposedly on his home waffle maker. Prefontaine was the first celebrity to endorse them, while others later to get on board included John McEnroe and the former Maoist and newly-elected Green parliamentarian in Germany Joschka Fischer, photographed in white Nike shoes while being sworn in as a member of regional government in Hesse in 1985. Nike played the game brilliantly of appearing rebellious, while carving out a niche for itself as a giant corporation with a vast turnover and a global workforce largely situated in areas of the world where workers were paid the least.

For more than 30 years conditions in Nike factories have been the subject of criticism, which the company has tried to deflect by running its own in-house labour monitoring as an alternative to external scrutiny. In 1992 it established a code of conduct for suppliers; since 2000 it has published summaries of its own monitoring. To this day Nike remains an employer of sweat-shop labour and reports on the Playfair website[3] in 2011 and 2012 described Nike workers being beaten and abused, being prevented from joining unions, and factories closing without notice leaving their workers without pay. While much of Nike's labour record is open to dispute (its critics claim that many Nike workers work 15- or 16-hour shifts for wages of less than $2 a day; for its part, the company disputes these figures, and insists that it encourages its producers to recognise trade unions and pay legal minimum wages or better), one essential feature of its labour relations cannot be disputed. Of the more than 50,000 people worldwide who are engaged in actually making Nike's shoes (as opposed to its managers, marketing staff, etc) almost none are employed by Nike. It insists on manufacturing through independent contracting companies in China, Thailand and Indonesia because it refuses to be legally liable for the conditions in which its shoes are made.

The other important criticism of Nike is that its shoes have been badly designed and have made millions of runners more vulnerable to running injuries. The starting point is the shoe designed by Bowerman at the height of Prefontaine's fame in 1972. The Nike Cortez had a thick rubber outer sole and was the most cushioned running shoe that had ever been produced. Named after the explorer who subjected America to smallpox, it was also the first shoe to feature Nike's "swoosh" logo. The Cortez had this additional padding because it was intended to extend the distance that an ordinary club runner could jog, in the direction of up to 100 miles per week. Yet the effect of the padding was to make the runner's footfall heavier. The weight of the "jogging" step was moved backwards towards the heel, meaning that our spines are misaligned and our feet hit the ground harder, increasing the chance of injury. Christopher McDougall's book Born to Run demonstrates that the mis-design of running shoes, starting with the Cortez, has been a main cause of thousands of runners' injuries in each year. "Until 1972, when the modern athletic shoe was invented by Nike, people ran in very thin-soled shoes, had strong feet, and had much lower incidence of knee injuries".[4]

Over the past 30 years the average time of a male runner completing an America marathon has increased from 3 hours 32 minutes to 4 hours 20 minutes.[5] Not quite all of this can be blamed on the mis-design of shoes: the average age of those taking part in marathons has increased by six years in the same period, which ought to account for a time reduction of around 3 percent (just seven minutes) or so. This phenomenon of slowing is also evident at an elite level. Fourteen runners in British history have completed a marathon in under 2 hours 10 minutes; only two since 2000. The fastest male UK marathon runner in 2012, Lee Merrien, comes in at 73rd in the UK all-time rankings. The fastest female Briton in 2012, Claire Hallissey, was 12 minutes behind the UK women's marathon record.

The corporations have a vision of jogging as an activity which requires the mass purchase of expensive running shoes, reducing labour conditions, and driving all our bodies into premature old age. Yet running, like any interesting cultural form, is constantly up for grabs, its meaning challenged from below as well as from above. The 2012 Olympics saw copious forms of dissent expressed through running. At the moderate end was the "Real Relay", in which around 700 runners, disappointed to learn that the official Olympic torch relay was not being run for the vast majority of its journey through Britain but driven for lengthy periods by car, responded by organising their own unofficial relay. They planned and completed an 8,000-mile route modelled on the official event, save that the Real Relay torch had to be moving at every hour of the day, and that everywhere it went it had to be taken by people on foot. At the more radical end were events such as the Counter Olympics Network's anti-Olympic relay, in which runners carried a gold foil-encrusted kitchen plunger marked "End Poverty" across east London, or the Youth Fight for Jobs' Austerity Games, with teams competing in

Property High Jumps and a Race to the Bottom.

Run *Wild*, the manifesto recently published by Boff Whalley, the Chumbawamba guitarist and a former editor of the Fellternative runners' fanzine, portrays an almost Manichean struggle between the bland world of the official marathon, in which runners follow an identical route, sponsored by large corporations, seeing nothing of the countryside around them, and the free-wheeling spirit of wild running (including, but not limited to, fell running), in which participants set off to their own route, use maps, leave the cities for nature, suffer knee-gashes and falls but avoid the debilitating injuries associated with inner-city jogging in over-padded shoes, and enjoy in other words a playful, free running of their own making.

Even the dominant figure of the 2012 Olympics, the Tory Lord Coe, has in this vision a counterpart, Steve Ovett, his red vest-wearing rival from the 1970s, a kind of British Steve Prefontaine, engaged in his own war with the athletics authorities.

Asked for their views of the government two months after the Olympics had ended, barely a quarter of sports clubs supported the coalition. Over half said the government had done "a little" to promote amateur sport; a fifth said it had not done even that.[6] The world in which the clubs survive is a world which will be familiar to most readers of this book, as it is one of cuts and austerity, with such funds as there are being siphoned off to promote vanity projects associated with private companies. But club running, at its best, is a network of local organisation done in a collective spirit with plentiful examples of basic human solidarity.

Finally, if the liberated sport of the future is to require an icon in the present, who better for it to be than Fauja Singh, the holder of the world marathon record for over-90s (at 5 hours 40 minutes), who only took up running in his eighties, after finding himself lonely in London on his son's death. With nothing to do, he began racing teenagers in his local park, only to realise that he could match or even outrun them. Another sport is possible. There are many more Fauja Singhs out there.

Part 3
The sporting gods that failed

Chapter 9
RANGERS: THE SELF-DESTRUCTION OF A FOOTBALL CLUB
Phil Mac Giolla Bháin

It was once famously observed that the three most important institutions in modern Scotland were the kirk, the Scottish legal system and Rangers Football Club.

For people outside of Scotland it is difficult to convey the extent to which Rangers were Scottish football. The term "establishment club" doesn't fully deliver the reality that for all of the 20th century Rangers really were, as First Minister Alex Salmond said when the club went into administration in 2012, "woven into the fabric of the nation".

The idea that Rangers Football Club would one day be liquidated before being reincarnated into the Scottish Third Division as a new club was unthinkable. When David Murray bought Rangers in 1988, such thoughts were not merely stupid, but risible. However, it did happen.

The downfall suffered by Rangers Football Club in 2012 is essentially about three things:

- What the club did
- What the media did not do
- What the football authorities in Scotland tried to do after the fact to assist the Ibrox club

The fans were largely onlookers at this train wreck; they were consistently misinformed by club and media alike.

There is no disputing that Rangers had some embarrassing baggage. From just before the First World War until the Berlin Wall came down, the Ibrox club operated a discriminatory employment policy against Catholics. "When I came here in 1964, we had no Catholics," said former Rangers player Sandy Jardine:

Not just the playing staff, anywhere. There was no bit of paper, it was an unwritten rule. David Murray changed that and it moved on significantly in 1989 when Maurice Johnston signed. You cannot clear up 80 years of sectarianism in eight months, but we are a huge way down the road.

In 1999 manager Walter Smith said that there was a "Protestant superiority complex" around the club and that it was palpable. The huge fan base knew this and many of them bought into it.

At no time during that period did the Scottish Football Association challenge this form of sporting apartheid. The no-Catholics policy in the early 20th century was, in the days before a globalised market in football talent, a disguise for a "No Irish" policy. Rangers managed to avoid signing a single Republic of Ireland player to play for their first team since FIFA recognised the Football Association of Ireland (FAI) as a separate footballing entity playing under the Tricolour, just after the Second World War.

In the last 20 years only one of the 191 senior professional football clubs on the island of Britain did not field a full or under-21 Republic of Ireland international in their first team—Rangers.

This is a story that the mainstream media in Scotland never investigated.

Had the excluded ethnic group been Indian, I cannot imagine that the response would be the same from Scotland's Fourth Estate.

Consequently, Scotland's "establishment club" has written permission slips for racists for generations. For over a century Rangers has been a gathering point for some the most reactionary elements within these islands. The favourite song of the Ibrox support for much of the 20th century was the "Billy Boys". To the tune of "Marching through Georgia", it lauded the life and times of Glasgow gang leader Billy Fullerton and his razor-wielding associates. A member of the British Union of Fascists and a supporter of Oswald Mosley, the hard man from Bridgeton in Glasgow's east end also established a chapter of the Ku Klux Klan. However, in Fullerton's bailiwick it would be the Irish Catholics and not African-Americans who would be the target of his hatred and xenophobia.

For longer than the Cold War there was an unstated emotional contract between the Ibrox fanbase and the people in the board-room. There was also a tacit understanding between the fans and the media. The only stories that were permitted were of the fluffy, breathless variety. Everything was going to be wonderful on Planet Ibrox for all time!

The mainstream media were telling the fans that all was well with the mighty Rangers and the people in the Ibrox boardroom were spinning them a line too. Ironically, it was bloggers from the green half of the city that were ahead of the story. What they were telling Rangers fans was very serious stuff. I wrote that their club would be liquidated if they did not act. They didn't act and the club was liquidated.

One awful aspect of this saga is that their beloved club did this to itself.

The assertion that the club self-destructed is unanswerable. Rangers created their own demise through jealousy and hubris. In trying to emulate the achievements of Jock Stein's Celtic, winners of the European Cup in 1967, Rangers tried to buy that success and fell into a debt spiral. They embarked on a risky tax efficiency scheme that led to the Big Tax Case. The media were too cowardly to report and the followers too bigoted to believe.

By the time Rangers went into administration in February 2012 it was already too late for the fans to act to save their club. The truth was out there, but unfortunately it was being made available to them by a "Fenian". Subsequently, they chose to attack the messenger and ignore the message. It was a fatal miscalculation.

When the administrators were appointed, liquidation became a certainty, yet still the mainstream media kept peddling the good news fairy stories. The club, the media and the fans became locked into a denial system that only outsiders could perceive accurately. They could have acted in time had they believed what they were being told, but they chose to cling to the old certainties.

In the 1990s Celtic fans organised themselves into an effective movement which toppled the old board, before taking part in the most successful share issue in British footballing history. The cultural difference between the two sets of fans is as marked as that between the ideologies of Republicanism and Loyalism.

Quite simply, the Rangers fans waited around for an authority figure to tell them what to do.

On their own all they could manage was to form into an angrily incoherent lynch mob outside the Ibrox stadium. The crowds that gathered outside Ibrox during the summer of 2012 sounded more like an English Defence League (EDL) gathering than a group of concerned football supporters.

As well as a history of discrimination in the boardroom and a racist song-sheet on the terraces, there was a catalogue of crowd trouble on an epic scale. The last time the world witnessed this in full flow was when the mob took to the streets of Manchester in May 2008. In scenes of civil disorder not seen on British streets since the poll tax riots of the 1980s, thousands of Rangers fans battled with police. When the judge sentenced some of the Glaswegian day trippers, he noted that what the Scottish champions had visited upon Manchester was the worse night in the city's history since the Luftwaffe.

The story of Rangers is the tale of what happens when the virus of unfettered capitalism is allowed to infect sport. The club's former owner, Sir David Murray, turned Rangers into Lehman Brothers FC.

During the writing of this piece the replacement club's CEO, Charles Green, announced a share issue. The timing of this move—just before Christmas—suggests something of a financial emergency at the new club. Already there are whispers around the Glasgow sports desks that Sevco Scotland Limited (new Rangers) is desperately short of cash. All of the financial eggs seem to have been placed in the share issue basket.

The self-destruction of Rangers (1872-2012) is not a football story, but rather a tale of our times. The club was considered indestructible, but was felled by a mixture of hubris and jealousy.

Sir David Murray was a child of Thatcherism. When he bought the club in 1988 it was the year after the "big bang" deregulation that allowed the wide boys in the City of London to become masters of the universe. The story of the self-destruction of Rangers is about politics and society in Scotland. Moreover, it is about what happens when casino economics is allowed to infect sport. Sir David Murray borrowed heavily to fund his business empire and to buy star players to thrill the Ibrox faithful. Just like the Gordon Gekko subprime sharks on Wall Street, it was the 2008 banking crash that did for Rangers.

After that the club was financially crippled and the bank moved in to run it. An austerity programme was imposed (sound familiar?) to drive down the level of indebtedness to Lloyds Banking Group.

The sporting gods that failed

From early 2009 Rangers were in peril and I wrote in detail about it. However, the "Herrenvolk" hubris of the fans prevented them from mobilising to save their club.

Despite the 150,000 Rangers fans who made it to Manchester in May 2008, in April 2012 not even 10 percent of that number managed to march in their own city to save the club from extinction.

Given the centrality of Ulster Loyalism to the Rangers identity, the following analogy is apposite. The collective consciousness of the Rangers support in my lifetime has morphed from that of smug Stormont official Unionist grandee in the 1950s to that of a paranoid UDA drug dealer in east Belfast coked out on his own supply. The support over-identifies with the glory that was Pax Britannica. Match day at Ibrox in recent years has resembled a caricature of the last night of the proms.

Oh, how the EDL would love to have something equivalent in England! What they've always wanted is a club that would work with them. In many ways the far-right had that in Glasgow with Rangers. The worldview of the club, the empire loyalism and the failure to sign a Republic of Ireland player for the first team, dovetailed perfectly with those selling a xenophobic message on the streets around the stadium on match days.

The announcement that Rangers had actually won a qualified victory in the first-tier tax tribunal in November 2012 took many people by surprise, including me. The taxman announced that they would seek leave to appeal. However, even if HMRC had accepted that FTT ruling and gone away, the victory had come too late to save the club from liquidation.

All three judges observed that the club had not cooperated fully with the probe, which began in 2004. The tribunal stated that vital documents had been "actively concealed" from HMRC investigators. Subsequently, the probe took much longer than would normally have been the case. All the while the interest clock (4 percent compound) was whirring and the potential bill in the Big Tax Case kept growing ominously.

By the time the basic arithmetic made it into the media—a story which I broke in May 2010—the assessment of £24 million plus £12 million in interest charges, coupled with penalties of £15 million, was greater than the club's much written about bank debt to Lloyds.

I know of one interested party, a potential buyer with serious money, who walked away the week after that story broke.

This contingent liability of, perhaps, over £50 million made Rangers simply unsellable to anyone other than an insolvency entrepreneur. Craig Whyte bought Rangers for £1 in May 2011. Sir David Murray got the quid but, crucially, Lloyds Banking Group received the £18 million which wiped out the last of the bank debt.

The mainstream media in Scotland hailed Whyte as a "billionaire" with "wealth off the radar". In fact, although he wasn't poor, Mr Whyte was hardly a billionaire.

I was able to write a piece on my own site a month after he had bought the club, exploring how the sale could have been financed by future season ticket sales. Given the litigious nature of Rangers' new owner, I couched the piece as a satire. I applauded Mr Whyte as a fine chap with huge personal wealth and the best interests of the club at heart. I did point out in the piece that had another type of owner, someone unscrupulous, bought Rangers instead, it could have been very messy.

I even speculated about the securitisation of future season tickets. It was very tongue in cheek, but the point was made. The mainstream media finally caught up in January 2012, seven months later. It transpired that the purchase of the club had indeed been financed by selling off futures in season ticket sales. This effectively left the club without the bulk of its future income for the next four years. By then, of course, it was too late and Rangers were a month away from being placed into administration.

I was not surprised that my journalism was disbelieved by the vast majority of Rangers fans. I had been a hate figure for them since I first called out a section of the club's support for their anti-Irish racism, most notably the singing of the racist "Famine Song", in 2008. They didn't need to know anything other than that I was a Fenian. It is a simple enough worldview, and one which does not accommodate complexity, nuance or subtlety.

A key component in the downfall of Rangers was the fact that the club's supporters were part of an evidence-resistant subculture. The fans simply did not believe that their sugar daddy would fail them. Under Sir David Murray, himself a creature of the boom, Rangers had become the soccer manifestation of the Lehman Brothers model of capitalism.

The club, in the main, did not develop home grown players;

rather it bought in established professionals in their mid-twenties. It traded at a loss and existed on a never-ending flow of easy credit.

This was true of all of Murray's companies within the Murray International Holdings (MIH) empire. I first wrote about his impending financial problems in January 2009, when I predicted that MIH would default on two huge loans to the bank. The following year a debt-for-equity swap saw the bank effectively take control of Murray's businesses, including Rangers.

The banking crash of 2008 turned off a lifeline of credit that Murray, and Rangers, needed. It also collapsed the UK property market, especially commercial real estate, an area which MIH had heavily invested in at the height of the boom, with borrowed money. It was a classic bad judgement that is made inside business bubbles. It happened in London in the early 1700s, when the "South Seas" would make everyone rich, and it infected Wall Street in the 1920s.

Rangers were part of that collateral damage. Their cultural power in Scotland made it unthinkable to only a few outsiders that this downfall was possible. The club's fan base, imbued with a complacency the size of the institution itself and a deference whereby they waited for an authority figure to take charge, meant that they were largely passive as the club was liquidated.

There is now a new Rangers in Division Three, the bottom tier of Scottish football. What takes to the field now as "The Rangers" is a franchise operation owned by Sevco Scotland Limited. By their own admission the people on the 6th floor at Hampden Park were making up "rules" on the hoof to make sure that some version of Rangers was in the top flight of Scottish football.

A rebellion organised across social media by supporters of SPL clubs made sure that the new club was not allowed into Scotland's highest level. Almost immediately a Plan B was constructed whereby the new Rangers would be put into the Scottish First Division (the second tier of Scottish football) and, therefore, would only be out of the SPL for one season.

The man at the head of Scottish football, SFA Chief Executive Stewart Regan, who had previously worked for Yorkshire County Cricket, said that if the new Rangers were not allowed into the SPL the national game would experience "Armageddon" and "a slow lingering death". The fans and the chairmen of the other clubs clearly didn't believe him. Finally the new club was voted into SFL Division

3, the bottom tier of the professional game in Scotland.

Turnbull Hutton, the straight talking Chairman of Raith Rovers, emerged as the hero of the hour.

He said that the chairmen of the SFL clubs were being "bullied" by those in leadership positions in the governing bodies. He was unequivocal that there was a high level attempt to try to engineer "Rangers" back into the top flight. Hutton stated that, in his opinion, the national game was "corrupt". When "Rangers" took to the field of play this summer to play Brechin City in the Ramsden's Challenge Cup, Rangers (1872) still existed and held a membership of the SFA. It is still unclear what legal status the Rangers that played Brechin had that day, but once more it is not a story that has exercised the chaps on the Glasgow sports desks.

The National Union of Journalists' Paul Holleran told Alex Thomson on *Channel 4 News* that since Rangers had collapsed 32 journalists had approached the union reporting that they and their families had been threatened by Rangers supporters. It should come as no surprise then that in Glasgow discretion often gets the better part of journalism when it comes to matters Ibrox.

Subsequently the mainstream media continue to peddle the fiction that this new Rangers is the same club as was established in 1872 when FIFA and UEFA are very clear that it is not.

The demise of Rangers is about the collateral damage created by unfettered capitalism and a craven media bowing down before an "institution" that pandered to a racist customer base.

Chapter 10
CYCLING AND DRUGS: IT'S NOT ABOUT THE BIKE[1]

Michael Lavalette

I'll say to you people who don't believe in cycling, the cynics and the sceptics: I'm sorry for you. I'm sorry that you can't dream big. I'm sorry you don't believe in miracles. But this is one hell of a race. This is a great sporting event and you should stand around and believe it. You should believe in these athletes, and you should believe in these people. I'll be a fan of the Tour De France for as long as I live. And there are no secrets—this is a hard sporting event and hard work wins it. Vive Le Tour.[2]

The sporting gods that failed

Towards the end of 2012 the sport of cycling was thrown into disarray by a report produced by the US Anti-Doping Agency into the "systematic" doping of athletes on the US based cycling teams US Postal and Discovery Channel. Team leader on both had been Lance Armstrong, up to that point the most successful Tour de France rider in history (though he has now been stripped of all titles) and part of a global brand, "Livestrong", that promoted both Armstrong and his anti-cancer charity.

At the start of the 21st century Armstrong took cycling onto a new plane—both as an athlete (winning the Tour a record breaking seven times in a row at average speeds faster than any before or since) and as a global sport (helping to move cycling beyond its traditional borders within Spain, France and Italy). His first victory, in 1999, came the year following the "Festina scandal"[3] on what was proclaimed the Tour of Redemption. The Festina scandal indicated a huge level of doping in professional cycling and the 1999 Tour was going to be run clean—with more anti-doping controls in place to prevent the cheats from taking part, never mind winning.

For those at the heart of cycling, within the Union Cycliste Internationale (UCI), Armstrong was the right man, in the right place, at the right time. He was a good news story at a time when cycling needed some good press.

Armstrong was a powerful "sell" because of his personal history. His struggle to overcome the cancer which threatened his life, to become the undisputed champion of one of the most demanding of endurance sports, had all the qualities of a modern fairy story. His two biographies *It's Not About The Bike: My Journey Back to Life*[4] and the follow-up *Every Second Counts*[5] became global bestsellers— breaching the confines of narrow sports book markets. There was much talk of a film, and a possible career in politics after he finished cycling (he was pictured on several occasions riding out with fellow Texan President George W Bush). And he was a friend to "the stars"—he hung out with Hollywood A-listers, had a relationship with the singer Sheryl Crow and cycled with actor Robin Williams.

And this background also meant that, for the UCI, Armstrong was a lever into the world of global sport, global sports television and the lucrative US advertising and endorsement market.[6] His personal "endorsement portfolio" ran to millions of dollars and included contracts with some of the biggest sporting companies in the world, such as Nike and Trek.

But then the doping allegations that had surrounded Armstrong for years exploded. The US Anti-Doping Agency produced a report which argued that there was:

> Overwhelming evidence that demonstrates that Mr Armstrong doped throughout the majority of his professional cycling career.[7]

Armstrong and his teams were accused of being involved in the most coordinated and systematic programme of doping ever:

> The achievements of the USPS/Discovery Channel Pro-Cycling Team, including those of Lance Armstrong as its leader, were accomplished through a massive team doping scheme, more extensive than any other previously revealed in professional sporting history.[8]

Quite an accusation when you think about the history of state-directed doping of athletes in some East European countries for much of the second half of the 20th century.

The charge sheet was substantial. He regularly used EPO (a red blood cell booster), Human Growth Hormone, testosterone, cortisone and he ran a virtual blood-bank which held his tampered blood that would be infused into his arm during races. He hired and worked with Dr Michele Ferrari, who had been under suspicion for years because of his connections with a range of banned athletes. Armstrong paid Ferrari over $1 million for his services and the doctor managed his "medical regime" and transfusions. Ferrari was found guilty of organising doping in Italy in 2004, but even after this Armstrong refused to break their professional relationship.

Armstrong had been dogged by rumours that he was a doper since the mid-1990s. Indeed the UCI have recently confirmed that on the 1999 Tour they obtained four separate positive test samples from Armstrong (for cortisone use) for which they accepted a backdated exemption form. Further, when these samples were re-tested in 2005 they were shown to have EPO present. However, by this stage there was no second sample so they did not move to take action against him.[9]

Armstrong's power and influence within cycling were such that people who raised doubts about his performances—or even asked fairly innocuous questions at press conferences—were shunned and excluded from the media tent or forced out of the professional cycling circuit.

Sunday Times journalist David Walsh was effectively cut out of the cycling media circle for daring to raise questions about Armstrong's performances. As early as 1999 he was arguing that if comebacks and performances like Armstrong's look too good to be true they probably are. He wondered aloud how it was possible for Armstrong, on his first year back after his fight against cancer, to ride the race faster than in the previous dope fuelled years. He wrote a book, *L A Confidentiel: Les secrets de Lance Armstrong*, and several articles for the *Sunday Times* that raised all sorts of questions about Armstrong's team and his individual performances. The result was that Walsh and the *Sunday Times* were sued and Walsh became persona non grata on the cycling circuit.

Cyclists Filippo Simeoni and Christophe Bassons were two within the sport who drew Armstrong's ire.

Simeoni had been a client of Dr Ferrari. But in 2004 Simeoni became a witness in an Italian case against Ferrari and became a noted critic of the doping culture. Simeoni testified in court that he began doping in 1993 and Ferrari had prescribed him doping products such as EPO and Human Growth Hormone. In 2001 Simeoni was suspended for several months for doping use.

On the eighteenth stage of the 2004 Tour, while the trial of Ferrari was continuing, Simeoni joined a breakaway of six riders. The six were no threat to Armstrong's overall position and normally (on a late stage like this) would be allowed to drift away. But remarkably Armstrong shot across the gap to the breakaway group in pursuit of Simeoni.

The presence of Armstrong in the leading group caused his main rivals in team T-mobile to chase the breakaway. This would catch Armstrong but would also eliminate the stage-winning chances of the six riders in the original breakaway. The six riders implored Armstrong to drop back to the peloton (main group of riders), but Armstrong refused unless Simeoni went with him. After some argument the two riders dropped back to the peloton. When Simeoni dropped back, he was abused by other riders. Afterwards Armstrong made a "zip the lips" gesture and later said that Simeoni "did not deserve" to win a stage.[10] Because Simeoni was a prosecution witness in legal proceedings against Ferrari at the time of Armstrong's move against him in the 2004 Tour, Italian authorities threatened to bring charges of witness intimidation against Armstrong.

Christophe Bassons was another Armstrong victim. Bassons was known as a committed non-doper. In 1999 he wrote a newspaper column questioning the ethics of the peloton and insisted that, despite the claim that that year's Tour was a "Tour of Redemption", there was still significant doping taking place. Armstrong, on his way to his first Tour victory, sought out Bassons in the peloton and asked him, "Why don't you fuck off?" As the "patron" of the peloton Armstrong's influence was substantial and Bassons found himself isolated and ignored by opponents and team mates alike. He quit the Tour and soon quit the sport.[11]

Then there was Emma O'Reilly. She had been Armstrong's masseuse, a poorly-paid job as part of the cycling back-up team. In addition to her normal duties she found that she was expected to travel to Spain to pick up his drugs, to use concealer to cover the syringe marks on his arms and to dump used syringes in discreet places away from the race circuit. In the team she felt bullied and cornered, but in 2004 she spoke on the record to the *Sunday Times*. Armstrong's response was to sue her and to publicly question her character. He suggested she had drug and alcohol problems and that she had been removed from the team because of "inappropriate relationships". She was harassed by law suits and threatened with bankruptcy all because she dared to speak out.

Betsy Andreu was the partner of one of Armstrong's early cycling team mates, Frankie Andreu. Betsy was a close friend of Armstrong's and was sitting by his bedside just after he had been diagnosed with cancer. When the consultants came to ask him some questions Armstrong told her it was alright for her to stay. The doctors then asked Armstrong if he had ever used performance enhancing drugs, to which he replied by listing EPO, testosterone, growth hormone, cortisone and steroids.

The confession was a shock to Betsy who believed in "sporting fairness" and she broke with Armstrong. As a result she was traduced, threatened and bullied.[12]

Armstrong, then, was a bully and a thug. But this is not only the story of a "failed individual".

The extent of Armstrong's doping was a dagger in the heart of modern cycling and sport more generally. One of the great claims of

The sporting gods that failed

sport is that there is a level playing field, an equality of opportunity and a set of rules which ensure that people rise to the top on merit. This was always mystification, but the drug revelations have pulled away the mask of "sporting integrity and equality" and revealed sport to be an activity that is dogged by an ethos of "winning at all and any costs", even if those costs endanger the health, well-being and lives of those who labour within the sporting industry.

In his, to date, single on-the-record response to the charges laid against him on the Oprah Winfrey show Armstrong claimed that doping was something he had to do because "it was part of the process of winning the Tour" and that taking drugs got him "onto a level playing field".[13]

Yet the notion that he doped to gain access to a "level playing field" is completely misplaced. In a world of doping athletes it is those that are on the richest teams, with the richest backers, who can pay for the chemical and biological enhancements that avoid the blood and drug controls. Armstrong paid Ferrari $1 million—way beyond the means of most professional cyclists. Doping benefits the already wealthy within sports competition.

Despite the Armstrong affair, cycling is not a uniquely "dirty sport"—though misuse of drugs has been part of the terrain of the cycling since its earliest days.

A recent report by the Australian Crime Commission[14] suggested that the market for performance and image enhancing drugs has expanded dramatically within professional sport in recent years. The commission produced evidence suggesting "widespread use" of prohibited substances and illicit drugs in sport and increased evidence that these drugs were being provided by organised criminal gangs. Such connections, the commission argued, created the climate for sports people to engage in "match fixing":

> Professional sport in Australia is highly vulnerable to organised criminal infiltration through legitimate business relationships with sports franchises and other associations... There is also increasing evidence of personal relationships of concern between professional athletes and organised criminal identities and groups... [These connections] may have resulted in match fixing and the fraudulent manipulation of betting markets.[15]

The start of 2013 also witnessed the trial of Dr Eufemiano Fuentes in Spain. Fuentes stands accused of being at the centre of a sports doping ring that includes professional cyclists, athletes, swimmers, tennis players and footballers (including players at Real Madrid).[16]

In Rugby Union the former French international Laurent Benezech has claimed that doping is rife within the sport. He points to the increase in the "effective playing time" within the game as the source of concern. He claimed:

> We went from 20 minutes of effective action [in open play] to 30 minutes at the end of the 1990s which was the normal evolution due to the players becoming professionals... But now we're explaining, even though we're already at 40 minutes, that we can hit 50 and even 60... That is what happened in cycling at the end of the 1990s when logic saw us lengthening the Tour de France's stages and increasing the difficulties without it posing any problems physically to the riders.[17]

Benezech's point is effectively the same as that made by Walsh about Armstrong: if something looks too good to be true in sport, it probably is.

Sporting competition means that "winning" and "spectacle" are everything. In cycling the spectacle of high mountain finishes, increased speeds and longer stage distances is what attracts media coverage and sponsors. Cycling teams (like all sportsmen and teams) utilise sports science to help athletes recover and improve performances, and use sports technology to make bikes lighter, more aerodynamic and provide more gears, etc. The application of science and technology is part of the normal routine of modern sport.

Historically drug use was also part of the norm of performance management. In the early days of the Tour riders would use a mix of drugs and alcohol to help them get through the long gruelling days in the saddle.[18] Most famously Jacques Antiqueil, the first five times winner of the Tour (1957, 1961-1964), made no attempt to hide his doping. In a debate on French television with a government minister he said that only a fool thought it was possible to ride cycling races "on water alone". Indeed French President Charles De Gaulle, when quizzed about Antiqueil's drug use, replied, "Doping? What doping? Did he or did he not make them play the Marseillaise abroad?"[19]

But three events were important to changing official attitudes to doping in cycling and sport more generally. One was specific to

The sporting gods that failed

cycling: the death of 29 year old British rider Tommy Simpson on Mont Ventoux on 13 July 1967. It emerged that Simpson had been drinking alcohol and taking a cocktail of drugs as he pedalled up the mountain in intense heat during the thirteenth stage of that year's Tour. His tragic death reverberated across the sport.

A second element was a consequence of the entry of the USSR (and its satellites) into world sport in the post Second World War era. The USSR first appeared at the Olympics in Helsinki in 1952—and immediately came second in the medal table. Four years later in Melbourne they came out top. In the midst of the Cold War there were all sorts of complaints raised about Soviet "shamateurism", that Soviet athletes were "not really amateurs" (ie unlike the US or British athletes who were employed by the army, by sports clubs or given places at elite universities!). But by the 1960s the focus had shifted onto Soviet "cheating" through the systematic use of performance-enhancing drugs. The claim, therefore, was that, in some way, doping undermined the "sporting ethic".

The third element was the increasing moral panic about drug taking in society generally. From a current perspective it is some-times hard to remember that Britain fought two wars to protect its interests in the opium trade,[20] that up until the 1920s opium and heroin were openly available for sale in Britain and that cocaine was widely promoted as a safe "pick me up", perhaps most famously in Coca-Cola. Even as late as the 1960s GPs in Britain could prescribe heroin to addicts.

In the late 1960s, however, drugs were associated with the counter-culture. They were portrayed as part of an "unhealthy" lifestyle (that is physically, morally and politically unhealthy). Thus moves to crimi-nalise drug taking in general had an impact on attitudes towards drug taking within sports.

Modern competitive sport pushes athletes—sports workers—to the very limits of their endurance and fitness. They over-train, distort their body shape and form,[21] and compete while carrying all manner of injuries.[22] And the demands on sports workers are growing—more games, tougher courses, faster speeds, anything which enhances the spectacle and makes for more exciting television and hence generates more income for the organisers and clubs.

In this context, doing what is "right" or "necessary" becomes a code for misuse of performance enhancers.[23] Failure to "do what is necessary" shows lack of commitment to your career and your team.

When dopers are caught they are castigated and dropped from teams. Their records are scrubbed and they are abandoned as fallen stars and disgraced individuals. But doping is not about the moral failings of individuals—however distasteful individuals like Armstrong may be. Rather doping is a result of, and embedded within, the competitive, commercial sporting system: a system worth millions to the top teams, clubs and individuals who will do what is "necessary" to ensure they win. The dopers are the rotten victims of a rotten system of sport that places winning and profit—in equal measure—at the heart of their system.

Chapter 11
HILLSBOROUGH: THE DISASTER AND THE COVER-UP

Sadie Robertson

The class contempt that the entire establishment has for ordinary people was laid bare in September 2012 in an Independent Panel report into the Hillsborough football disaster.[1]

Ninety six Liverpool football fans died as a result of the disaster on 15 April 1989, and many hundreds more injured and traumatised. The dead had been crushed in two pens at the Leppings Lane terrace at Sheffield Wednesday's football ground.

In the immediate aftermath the press, politicians and police blamed the fans. The lies and the cover-up lasted for years.

As the panel report notes:

> In the immediate aftermath there was a rush to judgement concerning the cause of the disaster and culpability. In a climate of allegation and counter-allegation, the government appointed Lord Justice Taylor to lead a judicial inquiry. What followed, over an 11-year period, were various different modes and levels of scrutiny, including Lord Justice Taylor's Interim and Final Reports, civil litigation, criminal and disciplinary investigations, the inquests into the deaths of the victims, judicial reviews, a judicial scrutiny of new evidence conducted by Lord Justice Stuart-Smith, and the private prosecution of the two most senior police officers in command on the day.[2]

But the panel report shows how police caused the disaster—and how the establishment conspired to cover that up.

The cover-up began as fans were dying. The officer in charge, chief superintendent David Duckenfield, claimed that fans had broken down a gate to enter the ground and caused the crush. In fact Duckenfield ordered the gate to be opened. But his lie was broadcast round the world—and more quickly followed.

Officers were told to write their "recollections" on plain paper. This is different to the standard procedure of writing events down immediately in notebooks. Legal counsel for the police Bill Woodward QC said that this "couldn't be better. They can put all the things in that they want and we will sort them out." Peter Metcalf, a senior partner in South Yorkshire Police (SYP) solicitors, said the advantage of this was that in inquiries "pocket notebook entries can be called for and must be produced".

Police statements went through an "unprecedented" process of alteration according to the panel report. Nearly 200 were amended. Some 116 of the 164 substantially amended had comments that criticised the police removed or altered. The police said they were altering statements to remove "opinion". But some opinions remained while others were transformed into fact. So PC Burkinshaw wrote, "The general feeling is that the fans arrived too late and a lot of them under the influence of drink." That was edited to remove the first five words—turning opinion into fact.

Some revisions covered up police contempt for fans. PC Hemsworth had said, "One could not communicate with these animals." The word "animals" was changed to "people". But the scorn for fans was obvious. Superintendent Roger Greenwood briefed officers before the match. He told them that if matches didn't go Liverpool's way, fans "had proved extremely difficult to contain and moods would easily change".

Underlying the disaster were widespread attitudes that saw football fans as animals.

Trevor Hicks lost two daughters in the disaster. He recalls shouting to police on the day and asking them to do something about the crush. He said:

> I remember feeling the despair that because I was a football fan my opinions didn't matter. I remember saying to him, "If I'd had my effing suit on you'd have took some notice of me".[3]

These attitudes explain why the police assumed that those trying to escape were hooligans attempting a pitch invasion—and pushed them back into the pens. Such was the contempt that everyone who died was tested for blood alcohol levels—including children. Those who had alcohol in their blood were then checked for criminal records. The panel called this "an attempt to impugn personal reputations" that was "possibly unlawful". Like the 1990 Taylor Report into the disaster, the panel said that alcohol was irrelevant.

Yet the media reported police lies as fact. Sheffield newspapers portrayed supporters as "predominantly ticketless, drunk, aggressive and determined to force entry". BBC Radio 4 said it was "clear" that many fans had no tickets. The *Manchester Evening News* wrote that fans "kicked and hammered" on the gates. Police claimed fans had attacked them and urinated on them. They said fans stole from the dead. And they said fans threatened an unconscious woman with rape.

The panel said there was "no evidence" for the allegations. CCTV footage refutes them. Yet they were repeated across the media—most notoriously in News International's *Sun*. David Cameron took care to try and exonerate News International in his apology to the families of the dead when the report was published. He pointed out that the lies didn't originate with the *Sun* but with a local news agency. Yet how the slurs appeared and spread speaks volumes about the relationship between the police, the media and the Tories. The lies came from White's news agency just four days after the Hillsborough disaster. They got the lies from the police. A White's representative explained how this happened in the documents released as part of the panel report. They describe a "chance" meeting between a White's reporter and a senior police officer "he has known for many years". Remarkably, "the following day there was another chance meeting with a second officer". The next day "another reporter met a third officer".

The collusion between the police, the media and the Tories went beyond simply making allegations. White's forwarded Sheffield Tory MP Irvine Patnick extracts from six sworn statements to the Taylor inquiry—a month before Taylor's interim report was published. They included allegations against Liverpool fans. White's didn't explain how it came to possess the statements, which had originally been taken by West Midlands Police.

The sporting gods that failed

Members of the South Yorkshire Police Federation met four days after the disaster. Chief constable Peter Wright said they had to "prepare a rock solid story". Another Tory, Michael Shersby, was at the meeting. He represented the Police Federation's interests in parliament and said he wanted to "bring out that the police did behave magnificently". Editor of the Police Federation magazine Tony Judge declared, "We should plan with Michael Shersby a counter-attack." A version of this counter-attack then appeared in the magazine.

Shersby told home secretary Douglas Hurd that police statements had been altered to take out negative descriptions of fans' behaviour. The panel said there is no evidence of this. Shersby later invited then South Yorkshire cop Norman Bettison to meet a group of MPs in London. Bettison said that one Tory MP "confided that in his view Taylor had got it all wrong and, as far as he was concerned, he intended to put the record straight".

Patnick intervened too. He contacted Lord Justice Taylor within five days of the disaster to repeat the lies police had told him. Patnick told Taylor they would "have to be considered". Later he sent an officer involved with the West Midlands investigation into South Yorkshire Police a transcript of the Police Federation meeting with Shersby and his correspondence with White's news agency. Patnick wrote that police evidence "was not fully taken into account" at the Taylor inquiry and that he hoped that "something can be done to rectify this".

The idea that fans were little more than animals came from the top. In 1985, just after the Heysel disaster, Tory leader Margaret Thatcher claimed, "There are three sources of violence in our society: Ulster, football hooliganism and picket line violence"—a theme she returned to in her Tory conference speech in 1988.[4]

Thatcher's government was in the process of bringing in regulations to deal with football violence when the disaster happened. The panel found that "the principal concern in Whitehall following the Hillsborough disaster was its potential impact on the Football Spectators Bill". The Health and Safety Executive had found that Sheffield Wednesday's football ground was "structurally unsafe". Yet the government cared so little for the safety of fans that regulations relating to ground safety were only voluntary. The fact that fans were packed into pens at matches speaks volumes. Thatcher challenged the criticism of the police in the Taylor Interim Report published in

August 1989. She described the report as "flawed in a number of respects". When Douglas Hurd sent Thatcher a planned speech for his response, she toned it down. She wrote a note to him saying:

> What do we mean by "welcoming the broad thrust of the report"?
> The broad thrust is devastating criticism of the police... Is that for us
> to welcome? Surely we welcome the thoroughness of the report and
> its recommendations—M.T.

Hurd changed his speech accordingly.

Labour played its role in covering up the truth too. Labour leader Tony Blair's response to the idea of a partial inquiry into the disaster in 1997 was, "Why? What is the point?" The panel makes clear that then home secretary Jack Straw only ordered the Stuart-Smith scrutiny because of public pressure. Straw told the judge before it began that he didn't think there was significant new evidence or any need for fresh inquests.

It is determined campaigning that forced details about the day and the cover-up to come out. Today everyone from David Cameron to the disgraced former Sun editor Kelvin MacKenzie has lined up to apologise to the families of the dead. All claim to see that the disaster showed terrible things about a past society. In truth they show terrible things about a society that remains to this day. There was and is an establishment view of working class people as untrustworthy scum—especially when they are in crowds. That's why the police were confident that their denigration of fans would find a hearing.

Hillsborough victims and relatives of the dead are still fighting for justice. The panel ruled that 41 people could have been saved had they been put evacuated faster, put in the correct recovery position and had the medical attention they needed. It also found evidence of cerebral oedema (an excess of fluid in the brain) among some victims. This can lead to coning, where pressure on the brain pushes parts of it towards the spinal cord. Cerebral oedema was "clearly described in 31 of the post mortem records" and coning found in 16 of these. The time this condition takes to develop shows that some victims survived for longer than a few minutes. But the coroner, Stefan Popper, refused to hear any evidence after 3.15pm on the day of the disaster. He declared that all who died would have been beyond saving by that point. He had initially said

The sporting gods that failed

he wasn't sure there was even any need for inquests at all. He decided that the cause of death in all cases would probably be traumatic asphyxia.

We still live in a world of police cover-ups and collusion with the media and the government. The police slurred Jean Charles de Menezes after they shot him dead on a London tube train in 2005. They claimed that he had jumped over a ticket barrier and was an illegal immigrant. None of this justifies shooting someone seven times in the head and once in the shoulder. But it was a pack of lies nonetheless. During the inquest into his death it emerged that some police officers had altered their evidence. Some had to retract or change parts of evidence after it was shown to be false. No one has been held responsible for Jean Charles's death. Those at the top don't care about the victims of their society. They care about defending the system.

As *Socialist Worker* said the week after the disaster:

> The appalling tragedy at Hillsborough was a disaster waiting to happen. Years of politicians and police branding football fans as mindless hooligans ensured near a hundred died when they were herded into cages from which there was no escape. Those Liverpool fans died because government and police refused to treat them as human beings.[5]

That was the truth—not the lies put out by the Murdoch press, the police or the Tories.

And the fact that the whole truth has still not come out, and the families have still not got justice, shows what a rotten system we still live in today.

Chapter 12
MEXICO 1968: MASSACRE AT THE OLYMPIC GAMES[1]

Eamonn McCann

The Mexico Olympics opened on Saturday 12 October 1968. I know the date because it was exactly a week after the 5 October civil rights march in Derry, generally accepted as the day the Troubles in Northern Ireland started. The association of the Derry march with the Mexico Olympics has been firmly fixed in my mind ever since due to the intervention of hunger striker Mickey Devine.

The 1968 Olympics were politically charged from the outset. A mass student demonstration on 2 October in Mexico City had set the stage for Tommie Smith's and John Carlos's gloved-fist salute. The student protest was against the military occupation of the National Polytechnic Institute (NPI)—and the military's response was murderous. The BBC described the atmosphere at the opening ceremony as "unbearably tense". There was a huge sigh of relief when the moment passed without disruption. The fear had been that the student deaths would prompt attempts to cancel the games.

More than 40 years later it is still not known how many were murdered on 2 October. It was certainly scores, some say hundreds.

Dawn broke on the Plaza de las Tres Culturas carpeted with corpses. Dustbin lorries carried them away. It is remarkable that many otherwise estimable accounts of the global student movement of 1968 entirely leave out the Mexico massacre. But it was well enough marked at the time for Mickey Devine to interrupt my speech in Derry with a shout of, "What about the Mexican students, McCann?"

The students' demonstration of 2 October followed weeks of protests demanding free speech, fair elections and social justice. The games offered an opportunity to expose the rottenness of the government of Gustavo Díaz Ordaz. The regime was well prepared. In September Díaz Ordaz had ordered the army to occupy the NPI, regarded as one of the prime centres of student militancy.

All lectures and meetings on the campus were cancelled. Students who refused to leave quietly were battered out of the buildings. Demonstrations demanded the removal of the military and the reopening of the institute. They drew thousands of trade unionists and community activists onto the streets alongside the students. An estimated 15,000 students and others gathered on the afternoon of 2 October. They intended to march through a working class suburb and onwards to the institute. But as the crowd milled around, soldiers and paramilitary police in armoured vehicles took up positions surrounding the square.

Defence minister General Marcelino Garcia Barragan later insisted that the troops had been deployed merely to "maintain public safety". He claimed they had come under fire from within the crowd and from snipers in buildings, and were forced to fire back in self-defence. Many of the casualties, he insisted, had been struck in crossfire during a 90-minute "gunfight". But eyewitnesses were adamant that within seconds of arriving in the square soldiers had disembarked and begun firing without warning. Some accounts are unnervingly similar to descriptions of the British Paras erupting into a civil rights demonstration in Derry's Bogside on Bloody Sunday three and a half years later.

It wasn't until the release of Mexican state papers in 2000 that it was confirmed that the government had deployed snipers. In 2003 documents published by George Washington University revealed the CIA's involvement in the killings. Its "station" in Mexico City had been directly involved in planning and supplying weapons for the attack on students.

Coverage of the massacre in the Western media focused more or less exclusively on the ramifications for the games. The reaction given most prominence was that of the International Olympic Committee. Its boss, Avery Brundage, maintained that the killings had nothing to do with the "non-political" Olympics. In fact one of the chants of the crowd had been, "No queremos olimpiadas, queremos revolución!" or, "We don't want Olympics, we want revolution!"

These were the events Mickey Devine had in mind in Derry three days later. He was eventually to become the last of the hunger strikers to die, in August 1981. In 1968 he was only 15. Still, as he was to recall, "my whole way of thinking was tossed upside down at that time."

Mickey was born in Springtown Camp on the outskirts of Derry, a former US base where homeless Catholics squatted when GIs were withdrawn after the Second World War. He had a hard upbringing. Tin huts for accommodating soldiers made unsuitable family homes. Services were effectively non-existent.

Mickey's father died when he was six. He was ten when he found his mother dead. He was raised by his only sibling, a sister seven years older. It was very unusual in the Catholic working class not to come from a large extended family. This may be one of the reasons Mickey took to hanging out at an early age with fellows a few years older. One of these was Red Mickey Doherty from the Bogside, a stalwart of the Derry Labour Party and one of the key instigators of the civil rights movement.

The first time I remember being aware of Mickey

was as I clambered onto a chair to make a speech at the 5 October demonstration. About 500 of us had surged a couple of hundred yards from the rallying point at the station up to the mouth of Duke Street. We were heading for the city centre but found the way blocked by a phalanx of riot police. Behind us more police moved in. Unable to go backwards or forwards, we milled around until someone produced a loudhailer and debate began on what to do next. The first few speeches were made by "moderates". They hit out at the Unionist government and condemned the police before congratulating everyone on having "made our point" and telling us we should go home. The problem with this was the difficulty of going anywhere when we were hemmed in on all sides. Nowadays we might call it "kettling".

As the crowd became restive, I was urged to take the loudhailer by those who wanted a different direction. The front ranks were shoving harder against the police line. The cops were snarling louder. I had no clear idea what to say for the best. That's when I heard him. A small figure with a chubby face and rounded glasses. "What about the Mexican students, McCann?" he shouted.

Taken aback, I hesitated. He shouted again. "What about the Mexican students?"

His point was simple. If students in Mexico could stand up for civil rights in the face of murder then surely we were not going to slink away from confrontation in Derry. I am not sure what I would have said had Mickey not intervened. But, anyway, I made a speech which the courts later characterised as incitement to riot.

What happened on 5 October 1968 in Derry sent the narrative of Northern Irish history spinning in a different direction. By August the following year the Bogside had effectively seceded from the state. British soldiers had replaced the Royal Ulster Constabulary patrolling the edges of the area. By the end of 1970, under pressure of events, the IRA had split. Both groups that emerged, Officials and Provisionals, were recruiting steadily. Bloody Sunday in January 1972 sent recruitment figures soaring.

Mickey had joined the Young Socialists after 5 October but now, along with Red Mickey, he switched to the Officials. The following year he broke away to form the Irish Republican Socialist Party and its armed wing, the Irish National Liberation Army (INLA). This wasn't an uncommon political journey in the period. Most of the ex

Young Socialist contingent did the same.

Mickey was arrested in 1977 and sentenced to 12 years for possession of guns with intent. He refused to wear a prison uniform and went "on the blanket". In 1979 he joined the "dirty protest". When the INLA leader in the prison, Patsy O'Hara, died on hunger strike on 22 June 1981, Mickey volunteered to take his place. He died 60 days later, on 20 August, aged 27. The hunger strike was called off the following day.

Red Mickey and others among us from the class of '68 spoke at his wake. We spoke at length on occasions afterwards about the terrible sadness of Mickey's death and whether it had been worth it.

We never reached a consensus.

But I inadvertently chanced on an indication that it hadn't all been for nothing a week or two later, reading a column in a socialist newspaper. It featured news snippets from around the world: "Sydney: Bus strikers vote to stay out", "Pretoria: Cops open fire on township protest", that sort of thing. And there it was: "Mexico City: Students gather for tribute to Irish hunger striker Michael Devine."

The London Olympics "will bring the world together" was Lord Coe's mantra in the run up to the 2012 event. And maybe so, in an ersatz way. But what unites us in the depths of our being is the things we fight for together, even when we are but dimly aware of the common cause transfiguring our struggles.

Chapter 13
ANYONE BUT ENGLAND:
NOT FLYING THE FLAG IN THE WORLD CUP[1]

Socialist Worker

Many ordinary people have bedecked their houses, cars and bodies in the flag of St George to show their support for England in the World Cup.

And millions of people will enjoy the World Cup as a chance to escape from the usual routine of life.

But the media's image of a united nation is a long way from reality.

Many people simply don't care about the event. For others, the sudden explosion of the England flag on cars, houses and in pubs is intimidating—because of the history of violence and racism associated with it.

But the patriotism that sporting events encourage is useful for some people.

Our rulers encourage nationalism in sport to foster a sense of national unity. They created international sporting competitions in the late 19th and early 20th centuries to do just this.

They want us to compete with people from other countries and feel superior to them because of where we were born. They want us to ignore the main division in society—which is class.

Nationalism creates a fake "community" which can have a particularly strong appeal when the world is in crisis.

For ordinary people, this "community" feeling can be comforting and this partly explains why some accept nationalist ideas.

But just because David Cameron is flying the England flag over his home, it doesn't mean that he has anything in common with the worker who is doing the same.

Cameron, and his Tory and Lib Dem chums claim that "we're all in it together" while destroying jobs and handing more money to the rich.

Their actions show that, for them, class comes before nation. When their power and profits are threatened they demand that workers make sacrifices in the interests of the nation—which really means the interests of the rich.

These sacrifices can be accepting cuts or fighting and dying for queen and country in a war.

The right wing press has even tried to link the World Cup to the war in Afghanistan to bolster the unpopular occupation. The *Sun* newspaper's front page headline last Friday read "Fabio Capello's Khaki Army", referring to British troops in Afghanistan.

And nationalism can encourage foul forces such as the English Defence League (EDL) and the British National Party (BNP), which will try and use it to win support for their racist offensive against Muslims.

The idea that there is an "English" identity means that there are also "un-English" ones. It gives confidence to racists who want to exclude black people, Muslims and immigrants and argue that they don't "belong" in England.

The sporting gods that failed

Despite all this, some believe that there is something progressive about the way that the symbols of English nationalism are no longer the exclusive preserve of racists and the right wing.

The Umbro World Cup advert plays on this by showing people of different races and religions singing the English national anthem.

There are those on the left who think we can reclaim the idea of Englishness.

They believe that our real English tradition is one of ordinary people struggling for their rights.

But these workers' fightbacks are part of a rich global heritage, not specifically English.

We cannot defeat the jingoism of the Tories and the bigots by counterposing a more multicultural nationalism to it.

Ordinary people may live in the same country as the rich, but we do not have the same interests.

A white English born worker has more in common with a Pole or Nigerian who works in London or Sheffield as a bus driver than with a rich businessman who happens to have been born in the same country.

The struggles of the ruled against their rulers take place across the world.

Much of the flag waving of the next few weeks will not have a fundamental impact.

Many people who support England will reject the racism of the EDL and the BNP and join protests against them.

But nationalism has an insidious effect. Most workers would laugh at the idea that it is unpatriotic to strike when we should all be uniting behind the national team.

However, the Unite union said it would not call any strikes at British Airways during the World Cup so as not to disrupt fans' flights.

Nationalism, however it is dressed up, draws us closer to our rulers and divides us from other workers.

It also feeds into the drive to blame migrants—rather than the rich—for the lack of housing, jobs and services.

Socialists reject the false divisions created by those at the top of society.

It will take a fight by workers of all backgrounds to defeat our rulers, who pretend that they are on our team while they kick us.

Chapter 14
THE OLYMPICS: A NATION UNITED?

Brian Richardson

> It just cannot get better than this! This is us, our time, our country, our Mo Farah: Crowd of our time; tears of our time: Hope for all time.

Those were the words with which the usually level headed newscaster Jon Snow greeted Mohammad Farah's victory in the men's Olympic 5,000 metres final. Elsewhere there was a similar sense of hysteria as commentators rushed to celebrate the successes of "Team GB". London 2012 was, we were told, a triumph for the whole nation. We, the public, had paid billions to build the stadia and support the athletes and they had paid us back with glittering performances.

I am a sports fanatic. I also live in Stratford, the main host borough, and was one of the lucky few who managed to secure tickets to the Olympic Games. I was therefore able to observe the festival at close quarters.

Much of the sport was exhilarating and there was a real camaraderie among competitors, volunteers and spectators from all over the world in and around the Olympic venues. The flag waving aside, there is something to be said about the affection with which spectators cheered the likes of Farah, a refugee from war-torn Somalia, and the mixed race Jessica Ennis to victory. It should also be remembered that there was almost universal admiration for the feats of Jamaican sprinter Usain Bolt and Kenyan runner David Rudisha. That spirit of international friendship and respect was in stark contrast to the snarling and sexist machismo we habitually see at professional football matches.

Inevitably, the mood of euphoria around London 2012 has been compared to the events of a year ago when riots erupted just miles from the Olympic Park and spread across England. We were repeatedly told that August 2012 represented the real character of Britain, "our" togetherness, unity and commitment to fair play in stark contrast to the apparently ugly acquisitive individualism we witnessed in August 2011.

Such assertions are dangerously complacent. The Olympic Games will not be returning to Britain any time soon, but it is a fair bet that there will be further explosions on the streets. At the heart of the riots was a rage against racism and a revolt against the social exclusion and decimation of the life chances of a generation of youth. None of the issues that brought people out onto the streets have been seriously addressed. The cover ups over deaths in custody continue and young people are still harassed and bullied by the police. Meanwhile official figures announced the day after the Olympics finished suggest that the prospects for the UK economy have worsened. If a fraction of the £11 billion that was lavished on the Olympics had been spent on providing training, jobs and services for young people we might not have seen such an eruption of anger last summer.

The £264 million spent this year alone on funding elite athletes through UK Sport works out at over £4 million for each of the 65 medals that Team GB secured. Moreover, the percentage of this funding that is given to pursuits that are largely the preserve of the privileged few such as rowing, sailing and canoeing is quite staggering. Many people cycle but unlike Team GB's most successful Olympians they are not provided with millions of pounds to ride repeatedly round an indoor track chasing after a man on a moped. Elsewhere, frankly, who cares about or participates in dressage or clay pigeon shooting?

It is no coincidence that one third of Team GB's medal winners were educated privately. As a schoolboy I used to compete against Eton College and can testify to the vast array of resources they are able to offer their pupils. Dorney Lake, the £17 million site of the 2012 rowing and canoe events, is owned by the college. Similarly, former test cricketer Geoffrey Boycott recently remarked that Eton had some of the finest pitches he had ever practised on. Compare this with the state school that I live opposite, which, incidentally, was commandeered as a base for the US Olympic Team during London 2012. Instead of acres of immaculately manicured fields and state of the art equipment, the girls at that school have to make do with one modest sized gymnasium and a concrete playground, half of which was fenced off to create a car park two summers ago.

In their desperation to bask in the glory, those two Old Etonians David Cameron and Boris Johnson were engaged in their own contest to fetch up alongside their younger college alumni William and Harry and Saint David of Leytonstone at as many Olympic events as possible. In the immediate aftermath they then raced each other to the TV cameras to explain how they will deliver the headline promise to "inspire a generation".

Their hypocrisy is quite breathtaking. Days before the Olympics began, Cameron's government slipped through a new set of rules reducing the amount of outdoor space that must be available at schools for PE and recreation. Having witnessed the success of the games, he is clearly now determined to pitch his Big Society tent onto the Team GB bandwagon. At the conclusion of the 5,000 metres race he declared, "Mo Farah is a true British hero. We can all be proud." Compare that to the spiteful attack on multiculturalism in general and Islam in particular he made at a security conference in Munch in 2011. This is a government that habitually scapegoats refugees and asylum seekers. It would appear that we are "all in it together" only when it suits the prime minister.

On that very same final Saturday of the Olympics I spent the day with friends in Victoria Park, Tower Hamlets. On the way there we shared a canal path with people cycling, jogging or simply taking a leisurely stroll. The park itself was a hive of activity with diverse groups of friends and families running, jumping, skating, cycling and playing ball. Everywhere people were having fun, enjoying each other's company on a beautiful sunny day. They didn't need to be lectured about inclusivity or recreation by patronising politicians and corralled into participating in competitive sports in order to stay fit and healthy.

Cameron sneers at activities such as Indian dancing, arguing instead that children should play games where there are winners and losers. Yet this obsession with competitive sports could easily act as a disincentive to young people. The self-esteem of generations of schoolchildren in times past was crushed as they found themselves ignored and humiliated whenever teams were being picked in PE lessons. Even now, more than 30 years later, I can still recall the name and face of the boy with spina bifida who was always the last to be chosen. By contrast, I was among the favoured few; one of the first picks every time. Ultimately however, my own love of football and rugby was destroyed by coaches who castigated us for "only" winning 7-0, by an opponent who was applauded for deliberately dislocating my shoulder and by public schoolboys who screamed "Kill the nigger" whenever I received the ball.

The sporting gods that failed

Instead of centrally prescribed, top down PE curricula or government diktats, what we all need is the leisure time away from the stresses of life, nutritious and affordable food and a range of accessible recreational facilities. Those are, of course, precisely the things that are under threat as the government seeks to slash and burn public services and we are forced to work harder and for longer.

Returning to that day in the park and in the minutes before Mo Farah's race, my attention was drawn to a baby boy struggling to take his first steps while his proud father stood over him. As I watched the infant, considered the challenges that confront us now that the party is over and contemplated a truly worthwhile legacy, I was reminded of Leon Trotsky's poignant observation:

> Life is beautiful. Let future generations cleanse it of all evil, oppression and violence and enjoy it to the full.

Part 4

Sporting divisions

Chapter 15

SEXISM IN SPORT

Jo Cardwell

Nicole Cooke was one of the greatest cyclists of her generation, but the chances are, unless you are a keen cyclist, you won't have heard of her. She has won the Italian equivalent of the Tour de France twice, the world championship and Olympic Gold. She was the first woman to dominate both long-distance tour and day races. Her recent retirement was accompanied by an incredible speech that marked out her principled stand on doping and how she has challenged the gross inequality that women face in her sport.

Her retirement speech raised the issue of women's wages in cycling. As journalist Rupert Guinness notes:

> Spanish triple Tour de France champion Alberto Contador commands an estimated €5 million a year, and Australian Tour champion Cadel Evans is valued at close to €4 million. The average salary for women [professional cyclists] is understood to be €20,000, and about 20 percent race for free.[1]

Remarkably, in October 2012 the UCI (Union Cycliste International) Road Commission, headed by British Cycling's Brian Cookson, stated that while a minimum wage is required for all male professionals, there was "no case" for a minimum wage for female riders.

This is just one example of the discrimination that women face in sport. A new report from the Commission on the Future of Women's Sport shows that sponsorship of women's sport in the UK amounted to just 0.5 percent of the total market. This compares to 61.1 percent for men's sport over the same period, with the remainder going to mixed sport.[2]

The London 2012 Olympics were a showcase for women's sport

and for women presenters. However, there was a significant inequality in the numbers of women taking part and in the number of events they were allowed to compete in. Nicole Adams was the first woman to win the women's boxing title at the 2012 Games because women had not been allowed to compete in the sport before.

Baron Pierre de Coubertin, the founder of the modern Olympics, stated, "I do not approve of the participation of women in public competitions. In the Olympic games their role should be to crown the victors." When London first hosted the Olympics in 1908, only 37 women competed, compared to 1,971 men.

Early restrictions on women's sport—and women's participation in track and field events in particular—were such that a French woman, Alice Milliat, founded La Fédération Sportive Féminine Internationale (FSFI) and started the Women's Olympic Games in 1922. The growth in participation and spectator interest brought prestige to women's track and field events and meant that the IOC wanted to gain control.

They met with Milliat. In exchange for her changing the name of her event from the Women's Olympic Games to the Women's World Games they said they would place ten track and field events on the IOC's 1924 Olympic programme. When it came to the games, however, only five events were scheduled. The British Women's Athletics Association boycotted the games in response.

Even today we do not have equal participation at Olympic events. Women are not allowed to compete in the 50 kilometre walk. It was only in the 1980s that women were allowed to run the marathon. The incredible achievements they have made in this event and many others have meant that women's struggle to be treated seriously as athletes has not escaped the public's attention.

A survey shows that 61 percent of sports fans want to see more women's sport on TV, and 63 percent believe that individual sportswomen and women's teams are as skilful and exciting to watch as their male counterparts. Sports fans also believe women's team sports are more aspirational than men's and that women's sport has a brighter future than men's.[3]

In social media we can see the trend continuing. In the run up to and during London 2012 of all social media conversations about the top ten athletes, of whom five were women, 60 percent were about women athletes.

figures from Wildfire...found that star athletes—Usain Bolt from Jamaica, Roger Federer from Switzerland and Russia's Maria Sharapova—powered their home nations to the top three spots for countries with the most global reach. US gymnast Gabby Douglas picked up a record number of Facebook followers...[followed by]... Marcel Nguyen and Camille Muffat.[4]

It can't therefore be claimed that sports fans do not want to watch women's sport. The battles of Nicole Cook, Nicola Adams and their predecessors have paid off, to a certain extent.

However, in sport, like every other area of capitalism, women's experience is tarred by oppression. Not only are they still barred from certain events but they are underrepresented in the boardrooms and their sport is seen as secondary to men's, as can be seen from sponsorship and media coverage.

These themes have been present for over 100 years of organised sport.

The story of Alice Milliat is emblematic. She was born in a Victorian era when women were thought too inadequate to be able to do sport. Female exertion was limited for fear that too much activity might "dislodge" the uterus, "robbing future generations". One text from 1874 even warned that "a single ride on horseback, a single wetting of the feet...may entail lifelong misery".[5]

In cycling the crouched racing position over dropped handlebars was thought too aggressive (both for women and "refined men"!). But sitting on a bike was thought "dangerous", something that might "ignite passions" and damage the woman's body.[6]

The development of sports and its governing bodies towards the end of the 19th century is documented elsewhere in this book, but this took place at the time when women were ruled out of sport. For upper class women, they were able to engage in some sport and leisure, but at a more restricted level. For working class women, sport was out of their reach.

The story of Dick, Kerr Ladies, discussed elsewhere in this book, is a great example of how things changed for working class women when they were brought into the factories during the First World War. The number of factory women's football teams blossomed. But the fact that the FA banned women from using any of its grounds shows the extent of discrimination.

The response of some involved in women's sport was to develop different rules for women—rules that were seen to fit more with a woman's supposed lesser physical abilities. However, even in these times there were some women who broke the mould.

When American Gertrude Ederle swam the English Channel in 1926, she did it in 14 hours and 31 minutes, beating the records of the five men who had made the swim before her.[7] In 1924 Sybil Bauer sought to compete with men in the Olympics. At the time no man had come within five seconds of her time.

In many sports separate rules inherited from these times apply even now. In badminton women's singles only play to 11 points while men play to 15. It would be absolutely ludicrous to suggest that women couldn't endure four more points. In tennis where the women's final at Wimbledon regularly draws higher TV ratings than men's, women only play to two sets (best of three) while men play to three (best of five).

In the 1996 Atlanta Olympics when mountain biking was introduced, the men's course was 40 to 50 kilometres, and the women's 30 to 40 kilometres. Again it is unbelievable to suggest that women couldn't compete over an extra 10 kilometres.

It wasn't until 1981 that the IOC allowed women to run the marathon. As Ellis Cashmore points out in his book *Making Sense of Sports*, between Briton Dale Grieg's first official run in 1964 and today the world record for the women's marathon has improved by 1 hour, 5 minutes and 21 seconds. In the same period the men's record has improved by just 5 minutes, 2 seconds.[8]

When women are allowed to legally compete in an event, they can perform on at least comparable terms to men. When television companies intervened in marathon events to insist that women start their races prior to men they stopped one of the very few mixed events from happening. On many occasions women have beaten men in marathons. It is highly probable that they would reduce their times further in mixed competition.

The notion of physical limitation of women in sport is totally ignorant of the huge difference athletic training can make to the body. Women's bodies have proved to be as responsive to training as men's. Further, the vast majority of sports are not dependent on physical strength alone. Even when you look at women power lifters, the difference resistance training makes is remarkable. An untrained woman can be as much as 50 percent percent less efficient than men, but at peak training level a woman's lifting strength can be within 5 percent of trained men.[9]

It is instructive to look at sports where one can argue that physical strength is not the determining factor, such as rifle shooting. This has been part of the Olympics since 1896. Margaret Murdoch competed with Lanny Basham in the 50 metre three position shooting event at the 1976 Olympics in Montreal. They tied in first place, but the judges broke the tie and awarded Basham the gold and Murdoch the silver.[10]

Murdoch claims that "there was more than one squabble" among officials after her performance and she contends it spurred them to seek separate and different women's shooting events. By 1996 in Atlanta men's and women's shooting events were completely segregated, with seven events for women and ten for men. In nearly all comparable events men have more shots, more targets, or as in the pistol event, shoot from 50 metres while women shoot from 25 metres away from the target.[11]

The physical differences between men's and women's bodies not only become significantly reduced when athletic and resistance training is involved; there are clearly times when women outperform men. For example, long distance swimming.

The social pressure on women to maintain femininity can be a very real barrier to their development. This can be an issue for every woman—from those who go to the gym but don't want to "bulk up" right through to trained athletes.

The terrain on which women athletes compete for recognition of their capabilities is therefore not just physical. Jessica Ennis's body has been subject to big debate. Many women are relieved to see the representation of women's bodies move away from the distorted world of models and celebrities. To have a woman's body celebrated for being strong and athletic is most definitely a step forward, but no male athlete is examined in the same way.

In women's tennis, despite the fact that Serena and Venus Williams were consistently at the top of the game, it was Anna Kournikova who was chosen by many advertising firms to be the face of women's sport. Is it any wonder that elite junior female tennis players aspire to be like Kournikova and not the Williams sisters, despite the latters' achievements?

In tennis we have an example of an incredible sportswoman, Martina Navratilova. Consider though how she and many other sportswomen are viewed and critiqued when they don't fit the feminine norms expected.

Many women who perform outstandingly are questioned as to whether they have taken drugs or whether they are really men. The South African middle-distance runner Caster Semenya was gender tested after her victory at the 2009 World Championships. She is not alone. The gender testing regime that women have had to undergo exposes the sexism at the heart of sport.

Assumptions of what is masculine and what is feminine also raise the question of sexuality. Alongside attempts to attribute strength and a competitive spirit to masculinity goes the unwillingness to accept that masculinity and homosexuality can coexist. The fact that so many gay sportsmen struggle to come out is evidence of the hostile environment created by discriminatory and unfounded constructs of sexuality and gender.

The world of sport therefore needs to change. Of course, sport doesn't take place in a vacuum, and we couldn't seriously argue that sport alone could resist the material basis of women's oppression. However, there are a number of things we can expect of sport and the institutions that correspond to it.

We can expect an equal amount of male and female sports coverage in the media. We can expect as much investment to be put into women's sports as men's. We can expect that sporting events such as the Olympics will have an equal number of events for men and women and an equal number of competitors.

We should also raise very serious objections to the segregation of sport. Why can't we have men and women competing with each other? As long as we segregate and separate we will never see the true potential of women. There is an argument that says women need their own space in sport because historically they have been sidelined by men's sport. I am not advocating that we force women and men to compete together, but enforced segregation at every level is wrong. Of course we will have to look into ways of de-segregating so that we don't disadvantage women.

In boxing for example, when it comes to measuring weight, we could develop a system where we take into account the fact that women will have proportionately more body fat than men and therefore find a way to measure muscle mass instead. This could allow men and women to compete on an equal basis.

It seems certain that if women were allowed to compete with men in the marathon, for example, we would see a real improvement in women's performance in this event.

This summer, if I was so inclined, I could go and watch Sarah Taylor make history when she plays cricket for Sussex, but such examples are too few and far between. How many other sports could develop ways of integrating women? How long will it be before we see women coaching and managing a professional football team? Would it be inconceivable to see a woman playing for a professional team alongside men?

Would mixed competing and equal representation start to challenge the notions of strength, masculinity and femininity enough to enable gay men to come out in sport?

The achievements of women in sport over the last century allow us to raise these questions in a serious way. We should celebrate their achievements, but like them, we should not accept the outdated and sexist boundaries, perimeters and rules of sport. We should expect more and we should fight for it.

Chapter 16
WRESTLING WITH THE PROPHET: THE POLITICS OF MUSLIMS AND SPORT

Hassan Mahamdallie

Muslims play sports along with everyone else. There is no Koranic prohibition on men or women taking part in sporting activities, despite some Saudi religious leaders declaring women in sports as "steps of the devil". According to the hadith (accounts of his life) the prophet Mohammed enjoyed competitive sports, including running with his wife Aisha (clerics please note), swimming and wrestling, and organising the occasional sports tournament between his companions while in Medina.

Indonesia has the world's largest Muslim population. It has a national sports day every September, specialises in badminton at an international and Olympic level and has its own football premier league. One of the top teams is Semen Padang FC, named after a cement company. Its stadium, the Haji Agus Salim Stadium, is named after one of Indonesia's founding figures, and has a women's supporters' club called Uni Spartacks.

So far, so good. Unfortunately, as with every other aspect of Muslim's lives post 9/11 via notions of a clash of civilisations and the conduct of the seemingly never ending war on terror, we are encouraged to view Muslim participation in sports through a distorted lens.

For example, sport has in some instances become a tool in the strategy of "soft power"—a way of co-opting populations to accept Western "values" and domination, the underbelly of "hard power" or military might. The British sense of "fair play" after all has its roots in empire propaganda that sought to project colonial rule as just and impartial. The opposite to British "fair play", the suspicion that foreigners don't play by the rules and are liable to cheat, is the essence of the sporting idiom, "You can't do that—it's just not cricket!"

Football is an ideal vehicle for soft power. The British Forces News website carries numerous reports of football employed as a "hearts and minds strategy". Two examples:

A team of Afghan soldiers have taken on their British mentors at football.

At the start of the match the Afghan Army players were given kits donated by Championship club Watford.

The teams played on a completely grass free pitch at the Afghan Regional Military Training Centre next to Camp Bastion.

Hundreds of Afghan soldiers were on the sidelines to cheer their team along.

They left disappointed though as the British side won 3-0.[1]

And:

Female football is a growing game in Afghanistan, but in a country where many object to women participating in any form of sport, the Afghan Ladies Football team has many obstacles to overcome.

The players practise at the dilapidated Ghazi Stadium in Kabul which—under Taliban control—was used to stage public executions. Today the shots being fired are very different.

There are real risks for the players in a deeply conservative nation where many in Afghanistan believe women playing sport is anti-religious. But that has not stopped players like team captain Zahra Mahmodi. She says she will not walk out on a sport she loves—even if that means going against the wishes of her family. Incredibly—and in defiance of opposition and the lack of playing facilities—women's football is on the up. Support from ISAF nations continues to bolster the team's aspirations that the female game will one day be universally accepted in Afghanistan. It's a goal these young women are determined to achieve.[2]

Note in the first example that the outcome was victorious for the British (naturally), and in the second example the contrast is stressed between the "barbaric" use of the stadium under Taliban rule and associations of "liberation" under British rule.

The war on terror has divided Muslims into two categories, that of Good Muslim and Bad Muslim. As US academic Mahmood Mamdani has written, "The political leadership of the anti-terrorism alliance...speak of the need to distinguish 'good Muslims' from 'bad Muslims'. The implication is undisguised: whether in Afghanistan, Palestine or Pakistan [or Algeria, Mali and so on] Islam must be quarantined and the devil must be exorcised from it by civil war between good Muslims and bad Muslims".[3]

In this context good Muslims play sports and bad Muslims don't. The problem with this categorisation is that sometimes those with power get confused as to which Muslim to put in which box. Such a confusion arose over Christmas 2012 when double Olympic gold medallist Mo Farah was detained by US border guards who suspected him of being a terrorist. "I couldn't believe it. Because of my Somali origin I get detained every time I come through US customs. This time I even got my medals out to show who I am, but they wouldn't have it".[4]

Farah must have thought, "What more do I have to do?" His astounding sporting achievement in the London Olympics was a joy to behold. The right wing attack on multiculturalism was temporarily halted as the fruits of our diverse society, including Farah, became triumphantly apparent. As a bonus all Muslims watching will have got a little frisson of religious pride when Mo knelt down post-victory to "sujood"—place his forehead on the ground as at prayer.

Farah is certainly not alone (although he must feel that way each time he spots Homeland Security). The English Premier League has its share of Muslim footballers from abroad, around 30 in the 2012 season, most of the clubs having at least one Muslim player, with big names including Samir Nasri, Soloman Kalou, Ali Al-Habsi, Moussa Dembele. Demba Ba and Modibo Maiga.

For the big football clubs the main calculation is financial, with talented players originating from north and sub-Saharan Africa particularly in demand. However, it is interesting to see the efforts that some clubs have gone to accommodating their Muslim players' and fans' religious needs. Newcastle manager Alan Pardew announced in 2012 that he was planning a prayer room for his Muslim players:

> It's something we're looking at. Religion plays an important role for some of our players.
>
> You have to respect that some players have a different religion to most of the footballers in this country. We need different facilities for them. It's important that whatever the religion, we take care of it and understand it.[5]

Newcastle was following the example of Bolton Wanderers and Blackburn Rovers, both Lancashire teams representing towns with large Muslim populations who had already installed prayer rooms for staff and supporters in their stadiums. The Scottish Premier League stole a march on their English counterpart in 2007 by announcing the intention to make prayer facilities available for fans at all their teams' stadiums. All this can play a positive role in changing attitudes towards Muslims and their religion in the minds of football supporters and wider society.

However, this progress can easily be undermined if Muslim football fans are reluctant to attend matches through fear of experiencing racism and hostility. The fascist English Defence League and its alliance with football hooligan outfits such as the Casuals United threaten the advances that have been made.

The presence of Islamophobia in English and European football is best understood by locating it in extreme racism that has dogged the game to a greater or lesser extent for decades. In Britain and Western Europe it is easy to see how racism, rooted historically in hostility to immigrants of a different skin colour, merges with a hostility to Muslims, the majority of whom are of South Asian or African descent. It's quite possible to be called simultaneously a "Paki" and "Bin Laden" while being told to "go home".

And where is the new generation of Muslim football players to come from? The popularity of Muslim football players drawn from the international scene serves to highlight the lack of "home grown" Muslim athletic talent coming through.

Shahed Ahmed, from the Bangladeshi community of Whitechapel, east London, is one of the few British-born Muslims to have played professional football. His circular journey is instructive.

Shahed began as a youth player for Wimbledon, south London, before being signed in 2004 to Wycombe Wanderers as a striker. He played five games that season and scored one goal. He was then hired by non-league Wingate and Finchley, headhunted for the Bangladeshi national team and then returned to the East End to play for Sporting Bengal United, a local club set up to encourage young Asian Londoners to play football at a high level. In a 2004 interview, while at Wycombe Wanderers, Shahed told a journalist:

> I had an offer from Bangladesh to play for the national side, but I would like to play for England since I was born and brought up here. Either way, if you are Muslim, then people expect you to perform, especially if you are in the limelight. I try not to feel the pressure.[6]

So why are there so few Muslim sportspeople coming through? It is likely to be a combination of factors, including racism and Islamophobia, ideas among the first generation that sport is not a career option or is unsuitable for young women, and low expectations of Muslims' sporting potential. However, the biggest single reason is likely to be socio-economics. Muslims represent some of Britain's poorest communities, living in deprived working class neighbourhoods with little access to the full range of sports facilities and opportunities. Pakistanis and Bangladeshis make up seven tenths of Britain's Muslim population, with young men, for example, still being much, much more likely to end up in the curry house trade or driving cabs than stretching their legs on the running track or football pitch.

English cricket is one of the exceptions, with Muslim players of south Asian origin present at county and national level. Basically, the game's gatekeepers couldn't keep them out. Even that bastion of Englishness the Yorkshire County Cricket Club (YCCC) was forced through the emergence of star players such as Adil Rashid and Ajmal Shahzad to stretch the boundaries of who was allowed to stake claim to being a Yorkshireman.[7] Another exception is boxing, historically a route out of poverty for immigrant communities, with past and future champions over the years including Prince Nasim Hamid, Adil Anwar, Amir Khan, his emerging younger brother Haroon Khan and Nadim Siddique.

While focusing on the real issues surrounding Muslim participation on the domestic front, it is useful to lift the gaze to take in the prejudices on display at a global level. Radical sports journalist Dave Zirin reported on a football qualifier during the run up to the 2012 Olympics:

> Moments before Iran's women's team was due to take to the pitch and play in an Olympic qualifier against Jordan, the team was disqualified for wearing their traditional full-body tracksuits and hijabs. Jordan was granted a 3-0 forfeit victory, crushing the lauded Iranian team's chances to go to the 2012 London games.
>
> As the Iranian players and officials tearfully objected, they were told that they had violated FIFA rules... The team were also informed that since 2007 FIFA had held the view that wearing the hijab while playing "could cause choking injuries".[8]

The culprit, loathed FIFA president Sepp Blatter, again did his bit for East/West relations when in the wake of Qatar's successful bid to host the 2022 World Cup he warned gay fans that they "should refrain from any sexual activities" that are illegal in that country.[9]

Support for the plight of the Iranian women's team should not, however, be extended to support for the Iranian authorities' ban on women attending matches alongside male spectators—the subject of the powerful film Offside, which depicted the attempt by a group of women football fans to get to see an international match by dressing up as men.

Journalist James M Dorsey, in his highly regarded blog The Turbulent World of Middle East Soccer, describes how:

> In late 1997 in Tehran, some 5,000 women stormed the [Azadi] stadium in protest at the ban on women to celebrate revolutionary Iran's first ever qualification for the World Cup finals... Men and women danced in the streets together to blacklisted music and sang nationalist songs as they did six months later when Iran defeated the United States.[10]

In the same vein while it may be tempting to applaud FIFA vice chairman Prince Ali Bin Al Hussein's efforts to boost Muslim women's participation in sport and come up with a velcroed hijab to satisfy FIFA demands, it should not be glossed over that the prince is a member of the monarchical dictatorship summed up by Human Rights Watch thus: "The kingdom has barely advanced rights protections over the past decade. Expression and association remain tightly circumscribed in law and practice, and security services enjoy a large degree of impunity for arbitrary arrests and torture, as do employers for widespread abuses against migrant domestic workers".[11]

The baleful combination of politics and sport leans heavily upon those Muslims who enjoy or excel at sports. The burden of being a "good Muslim", even in a sporting context, is a label that no one should have to carry. Oona King, the former New Labour MP for Bethnal Green, east London, got it right, albeit for the wrong reasons, when she wrote a newspaper article in 2006, headlined "What we need is a Muslim Rooney".[12]

King's plea, part of an over the top article that gifted sport in general and football in particular with miraculous world-healing properties, held a grain of truth. Wayne Rooney is a complicated and contradictory individual, who doesn't easily fit into the category of role model—which seems to me to be a good thing. For surely one definition of equality is the right to be as flawed as everyone else, and for those human weaknesses not to be linked to race or religion or gender, sexual orientation, disability, and so on.

If there ever was a Muslim equivalent of Rooney, one might hope that he (or she) would be as bad tempered and foul-mouthed a bundle of dubious behaviour as the great man himself.

Chapter 17
CRICKET: GENTLEMEN AND PLAYERS

Keith Flett

Lord Home of the Hirsel died aged 92 in 1995.

He was a Tory prime minister in the period before Harold Wilson's Labour government took office in late 1964, and was known as Sir Alec Douglas-Home.

Douglas-Home (Eton and Oxford) was also a first class cricketer for Middlesex.

An equivalent might have been if Arthur Scargill, aside from leading the miners' union, had also turned out for Yorkshire County Cricket Club. History records that he did not.

Douglas-Home's first class career ran from 1924 to 1927 and Wisden—the cricketers' book of records—records that he was a "better batsman on wet pitches". Comments from Geoffrey Boycott on the BBC's *Test Match Special* notwithstanding, the modern game has done away with uncovered cricket pitches and, as far as can be seen, the Tory party with leaders who can adeptly play on them.

In the Eton v Harrow game of 1922 Douglas-Home scored 66 on just such a pitch.

Wisden notes that Douglas-Home was at his best in cricket and in politics on a "sticky wicket"—a wet cricket pitch where the bounce and turn of the ball are unpredictable.

Douglas-Home was also president of the MCC, cricket's ruling authority, in 1966.

Even this brief summary of his career might be enough to suggest to the casual reader that cricket is stuffed full of upper class Tories.

While they are certainly not an unknown feature of the game, it is unlikely that the sport would have become as popular and widespread as it is if this was the limit of its audience.

For a start, while batting may be seen as a glamorous and stylish pursuit, someone has to bowl the ball for the batsman to hit. Bowling is a rather more arduous and generally less romantic aspect of the game, although it might be added that Douglas-Home was also an adequate medium-paced swing bowler.

This said, cricket probably above any other sport is one where a division between professionals and amateurs has been keenly felt.

The distinction between the paid professional player and the supposedly unpaid amateur was officially abolished in 1963, although divisions continue in various ways. It is certainly no accident that in the wake of the abolition the cricketers' trade union, the Professional Cricketers Association (PCA), began for the first time to exert some genuine influence from the later 1960s.

The distinction seen by spectators prior to 1963, and more particularly before 1939, was that the professional cricketer, dressed in sober cricket clothes and the amateur, usually idiosyncratically dressed, entered the field of play via separate gates.

The divisions, however, went much wider than that. The professional and the amateur used separate dressing rooms, and took their meals separately as well. Quite often the only time the professional and amateur cricketer, batting together on the field, would meet would be actually on that field.

In fact at Lord's and the Oval divisions went further. There were two dressing rooms for professionals: one for the more senior—and better paid—players and one for the rest.

David Kynaston has noted that when a new pavilion was opened at Lancashire's ground at Old Trafford in 1895 it had three bathrooms for amateurs and none at all for professionals. He describes the system as a form of "class based apartheid".[1]

It was expected that an amateur player would always be England captain even if there was a more capable professional in the side. The same was true for many although not all of the county sides.

The division was institutionalised perhaps initially in North (professional) v South (amateur) games but over time with Gentlemen v Players matches. Former Tory prime minister John Major's history of the game refers to "unpleasantness" between the north and south.[2]

The Gentlemen v Players game was a regular fixture—mostly at the HQ of cricket, Lord's at London's St John's Wood—from 1819. The professional cricketers, "players", were for decades far superior to the "gentlemen", amateur cricketers. This all changed when a certain hirsute player and medical doctor W G Grace started to appear for the Gentlemen in 1865. Grace was almost a force of nature on the cricket field and in the decades that followed the balance in the annual game shifted heavily in favour of the Gentlemen.

W G Grace was still captaining the Gentleman in 1899 when he scored 78 and they won by an innings. He last played in the 1905 match when he was aged 58 but still managed to hit 74 runs.

The situation is a little more complex than simply a toffs v plebs tussle, although there is a considerable element of that.

For example, H M Hyndman, one of the founders of the first British Marxist organisation the Social Democratic Federation, was a first class cricketer for Cambridge University, MCC and Sussex for some years in the first half of the 1860s.

W G Grace might be said to have founded something that still has an echo in the modern game—"shamateurism". Grace was not a professional cricketer but an amateur; strictly speaking he made no money from the game at all. However, with expenses and other fees related to cricket, although not directly related to his performance on the field, he made a rather good living.

In 1895 when Grace was 46 years old he celebrated both scoring 100 first class hundreds and scoring 1,000 runs in a month. Both were very considerable achievements. Several testimonials netted Grace £9,073 8s 3d, which is worth around a quarter of a million pounds in today's money.

But if then, as now, a handful of cricketers, whether professional or notionally amateur, could command significant fees for their appearance at a match the reality for most was much less romantic.

The origins of cricket can be traced broadly back to medieval times when the game was played by peasants. Histories of the game that touch on the period—for example John Major's—unsurprisingly underline the point.

Major notes that the playing of cricket was thought to be undesirable, particularly by the church, and efforts were made to stamp it out. Certainly in the early period "gentlemen" were not involved.

The move towards a more professional game with an agreed common framework of rules came with the development of industrial capitalism, the industrial working day and the ability for teams to travel round the country. Only slowly did cricket start to become a sport out of which it was possible to make a professional living.

Ric Sissons notes that the first paid cricket professionals were groundsmen, cricket coaches at private schools and bowlers.[3] Straight away we can see the gentlemen/amateurs v players/professionals distinction appearing. It was the better off gentlemen who batted on pitches prepared by a person of a lower class who might very well also be the person who bowled the balls which allowed them to bat.

Touring clubs of professional players—England XIs—were a feature by the 1850s and the fact that they were financed and organised indicates a rather more complex relationship between gentlemen and players. There was a fund to help pay the cricketers, but the money came largely from amateur patronage.

Major notes that "commercially inspired professional elevens... could be anarchic".[4] While we may wonder exactly how the Tory defines the term, the general point is probably correct and continues to be so today. Where money was the guiding factor in the formation of a cricket team or fixture the game itself might become secondary with spectators a poor third.

By the 1860s professionals and amateurs were battling for the upper hand in the game, something which no doubt underwrote the appearance of the MCC's County Rules in 1873, an early attempt to regulate the game. At this point professionals were limited to playing for one county in each summer season, thereby considerably impacting on their earning power.

As Sissons notes, the reality for most professional cricketers was not great: "Annual income was only marginally better than that of a well-paid labourer".[5] In general cricketers could be seen as akin to skilled workers. The issue was that most had employment as cricketers for only around half the year during the summer months. Surrey was the first county club to introduce winter pay, but that wasn't until 1894.

Tensions continued and some England players took strike action before the Third Test in 1896. Major wonders why it took the players so long and refers to the "timidity of the cricketer in the face of great injustice".[6] He goes on to argue that the divisions between amateurs and professionals were "absurd and insulting", and that with a salary of £80 for professional cricketers and £85 for labourers the cricketers had "cause to be aggrieved".[7]

The situation in the 20th century up to 1945 continued in much the same way. The great England cricketer found that in order to become England captain he had to switch from professional to amateur status. However, social and economic trends were playing their part and the supply of amateur players was in decline by 1939. Kynaston notes that conditions in the dressing rooms of professionals remained poor, with a notable rebel being the Surrey captain Percy Fender, who insisted on leading his team onto the field together, amateurs and professionals alike.

After the end of the Second World War the game reluctantly dragged itself into the new century, although in the first post-war season of 1946 all but one of the 17 county captains was an amateur. The great Yorkshire batsman Len Hutton, a professional, was appointed England captain in 1952.

As late as 1957-58 an MCC sub-committee concluded that amateurs had a valuable role in the game.

However, the last Gentlemen v Players game was held at Lord's in 1962. The Gentlemen were captained by Ted Dexter, who stood as a

Tory parliamentary candidate in Cardiff. The Players were led by Fred Trueman, a former Yorkshire miner, also a Tory.

In November 1962 the Advisory County Cricket Committee accepted £6,500 from Gillette to sponsor one-day cricket and abolished amateur status. The *Times* recorded, "Cricket breaks with the past."

By October 1967 Somerset bowler Fred Rumsey had organised a professional cricketers' association—in effect a players' trade union that continues today. However, as Sissons concludes, "until the 1980s professionals were not accorded the same rights as employees in any other job".[8]

While the division between gentlemen and players has been abolished for 50 years it would be wrong to think that many of the attitudes that it underwrote do not continue in some form.

Some might argue that there tends to be a preference for appointing an England captain with a public school background and more concern shown if someone who doesn't have such a schooling—Andrew "Freddie" Flintoff of Lancashire for example—is picked. These are matters of perception.

The gap between the star professionals who earn top money and others who earn their living at the game continues. The recent disputes about batsman Kevin Pietersen's place in the England team have contained an element of his desire to use his cricketing celebrity to maximise his earnings potential, where loyalty to a team comes second.

The huge sums of money available in limited overs cricket in the Indian Premier League and the central contracts offered by the England and Wales Cricket Board to leading players again emphasise a division between a small elite of very wealthy players and the rest.

In short, while the rigid class distinctions in cricket are a thing of the past, divisions based on celebrity, hence earning power and money, continue to be a major feature of the game. After all, as Kynaston notes, one of the attractions of cricket is its focus on "digging in", as former England batsman Geoffrey Boycott, once dropped for slow scoring in a test match, would have it. Another way of understanding that point is that cricket is a "game whose essence [is] steady accumulation".[9] Its structures mirror more closely than many games the class divisions in society and dynamic that drives market capitalism.

Chapter 18

CRICKET, RACISM AND THE YORKSHIRE LEAGUES: PROSPECTS FOR A MORE INCLUSIVE CRICKET IN YORKSHIRE

Lionel Cliffe

2013 marks 150 years from the founding of Yorkshire County Cricket Club (YCCC hereafter). That founding moment was right in the midst of what C L R James in his magisterial book on cricket[1] calls the "rush to organise sports associations of every kind". The first professional football clubs and the Football Association date back to that period. In cricket 1862 had seen the first team of England cricketers sail for Australia, and the following year the MCC defined the rules that authorised overarm bowling, and thereby defined how the playing of the game would evolve.

These organised sports associations had to find mechanisms that linked three categories of people: players (already by that time including a sub-category of professionals marked off from the masses who played "for fun"—although such a phrase would be frowned on in Yorkshire circles); managers, coaches and administrators; and spectators. Rules governing the playing of the game, the organisation of fixtures, and the setting out of who was qualified to play were formulated and signed up to. The social composition of the groups was shaped by the pathways that evolved to recruit them. Especially important were the avenues through which full-time players and those who ran the game emerged. From the 1860s the full-timers were drawn from two classes: "gentlemen" drawn from the ranks of the aristocracy, and working men, artisans in a new field. In fact there were already numbers of professional "players" in the county before the founding. The administrators tended to be drawn from the aristocrats and "gentlemen" ex-players, though responsible to industrial and commercial bourgeois for keeping the sweaty players strictly in line. However, cricket has still not yet followed football into the fully capitalist realm where the former clubs are incorporated businesses, with increasingly ultimate control and access to profits being managed at arm's length through holding companies.

But the "social relations" of the sport between the three groups, the conflicts of interest and the making of common cause, came to be shaped by more than just formalised institutions and rule books, but also by long-established and sometimes slowly evolving sets of practices and ultimately a "culture". Nowhere was the playing of cricket more steeped into a particular cultural tradition than in Yorkshire, and one that was so close to the broader social context and identity. In Hamilton's words:

> nowhere else was so absorbed in cricket or regarded it so earnestly; nowhere else studied it so thoughtfully or followed it with such obsessive passion…and certainly nowhere else were the vagaries of the game so cherished, so understood or so utterly and deeply felt… Those who played or merely observed cricket in Yorkshire were sure of, and never lost, an appreciation of where they came from and the proud sense of self it gave them.[2]

That proud sense of self involved what another cricket writer (Gibson, quoted by Hamilton) described as believing that they have to behave "like their fixed belief in what a Yorkshireman should be: tough, ruthless, brave, mean". The pride and the toughness certainly feed into the culture that pervades Yorkshire cricket. The belief in not needing any outside help was at the heart of the parochialism that fed the born in Yorkshire "rule" in operation (though not always applied strictly to "gentlemen" cricketers) until 1992.

On the field these attributes foster traditions of play marked by fierce determination, especially to avoid defeat, and the cautious application of technically sound skills and tactics: "Never play the cut stroke before mid-summer." The ideal bowler—in both county and leagues—was an accurate medium-pacer who could be relied on to only go for 2.5 runs per over, throughout a season or career.

The institutions set up to run the game matched these attitudes: a long and strong structure of fiercely competitive league matches, and a county machine run in an autocratic tradition. Two key figures, captains without being worth a place in the team, embody a continuity in authoritarian privileged class domination on and off the field. Lord Hawke was captain from the Golden Period in the late 1800s and up to and beyond the First World War, and then ruled as president until after the Second World War, to be succeeded by the inter-war captain, Brian Sellers, backed by a long-serving and equally ruthless secretary. The resulting "employment policies were Dickensian…[and] the recruitment policies were hopelessly anachronistic" by the 1970s when "overseas players" became an issue in English cricket, in the view of Birley's *Social History of English Cricket*. Since then the confrontational, dictatorial bosses at Headingley have managed to give the boot to more than a handful of internationals, including two England captains and two Yorkshire captains (Wardle, Close, Illingworth, Boycott, Hoggard, and in 2012 Shahzad).

This brief sketch of the emergence of the traditions and institutions of cricket in Yorkshire over a century might provide a key to issues that arose in the last 50 years as those bodies dealt with (or not) the immigration from cricket-playing countries.

Exclusion and racism

The home-born players rule was such an entrenched belief that it was even defended by over 100 MPs proposing that "Yorkshire-born" should be written as an exemption when the Race Relations Act was brought to parliament in 1976. But the rule survived until poor results and economic realities of what made for success in the game led to recruitment of English players born elsewhere, the first of which was a future England captain, Michael Vaughan, who was anyway brought up in Sheffield and had come through the county's new coaching system. This was followed by the long-delayed contracting of "overseas players" already employed for 20 years by all other counties. Among the first of these were a teenage genius, Sachin Tendulkar from India, and Richie Richardson, captain of West Indies at the time.

The rule was matched by exclusivity in the minds of the YCCC authorities. Many instances of racist statements and actions by those in authority can be assembled. A Bradford MP even levelled the charge of a "deep-rooted, embedded racism" in YCCC in parliament in 2004. Examples might include the long-serving secretary, Joe Lester, explicitly accepting in the 1970s a segregated structure of cricket, reminiscent of apartheid South Africa with its separate white and coloured crickets, when he dismissively confined immigrant players to "their own leagues". Senior former players complained in 2000 when some wrought iron decorative gates to commemorate Sir Leonard Hutton were unveiled to show some Asian people among the Yorkshire people depicted. One of the great talents to emerge in Sheffield, Devon Malcolm, an awesome fast bowler of Caribbean origin who went on to get most wickets in an innings in 50 years for

England, had to move home to be accepted as a Derbyshire player. Even then he was dismissed as mere brawn by former England and Yorkshire captain Ray Illingworth, as "not having a cricket brain".[3] The persistence of these precise racist assumptions about black cricketers I heard repeated in a radio commentary by current YCCC President Geoff Boycott in 2012 when he used the same words in justifying the prospects of one new star, Adil Rashid (see below).

But the rule and the racist attitudes of some official alone do not explain the fact that only one Caribbean player of local background has ever played for the county, and then only for a couple of games, or that none from an Asian background played before 2004. By the time the selection rule was put aside there was already at least one whole generation of black and Asian would-be players who had been born in Yorkshire, and a further 12 years were to transpire before a few were recognised at county level. By then the exclusion operated through "institutional racism", in the form of non-entry into the lower level clubs and leagues. First and second generation immigrants who came to the UK with cricket traditions and skills described how they were not welcome in trying to get games, which in some leagues required "registration", at local clubs, and how they formed their own teams in frustration. But then they had to arrange fixtures with local clubs reluctant to lay on extra games outside their regular Saturday league fixtures; and if they played with teams from their own communities that involved travel and the hiring or begging of a ground to use. Being cut off from this access also severely restricted the prospects of school-age players, as school games were curtailed by national policies, as clubs became an even more essential avenue into the youth talent-spotting and coaching structures being set up by YCCC by the late 1980s.

Responses to exclusion

Mike Marqusee[4] pointed in 1994 to the most tangible response to exclusion—the emergence of a "parallel world" of black cricket, including leagues and clubs. This was occurring on a scale still hardly realised today by many mainstream players, officials and spectators. He also looked forward in hope that these initiatives pursued by "refugees from racism" would lead to a future of inclusion: "a celebration of a common heritage and experience...[and] a potential resource for English cricket", adding the proviso, only if "English cricket is prepared to redefine its notions about what constitutes 'Englishness'."[5]

Yorkshire has a rich experience of this parallel game, a glimpse of which is offered below. A preliminary assessment is offered here of how far this alternative vision of a more inclusive culture of cricket has emerged and of what might be its prospects beyond some encouraging initial steps in the last decade.

One path in the major cities of Yorkshire in the 1970s was the formation of Caribbean Cricket Clubs, but they still had to break the cold shoulder of existing clubs in order to get fixtures. For Sheffield Caribbean CC they were able to get access to a mid-week and a Saturday league and were provided a ground by Sheffield City Council. Both it and its Leeds counterpart remain lively clubs—the latter having won their league in 2009. But they have not spawned many other clubs, perhaps as Afro-Caribbean young men seem to opt for football and athletics. Devon Malcolm, despite his exclusion by YCCC, returned after his playing career to found a cricket school in his native Sheffield.

Similar steps were taken in many parts of the UK when Asian players formed clubs and arranged matches and even mini-festivals between their teams. But a further step was taken in 1980 in West Yorkshire among the large Asian communities in Bradford and surrounding towns like Dewsbury and Huddersfield. The Quaid-e-azam League (named after the premier championship in Pakistan and in honour of Pakistan's founding leader, Mohammad Jinnah) was formed. It continues to this day and will have 27 teams in two divisions signed up for 2013—with one or two beyond the original spawning ground, in places like Sheffield and Rotherham. This league gained backing and resources from local communities and businesses, but has also developed on the field. In terms of ability it has come full circle as witnessed by an application to join for 2013 from Kashmir (Bradford) CC, who had been playing for some years in a mainstream local league, but now wanted to switch "to improve the quality of their cricket".

It is now some years since Asian clubs followed Caribbeans in joining and being accepted into existing leagues. Some clubs now run teams on different days and in different competitions which are not just multiracial but enter teams in Quaid-e-azam, say, and in long-established leagues. The cross-over even extends to many Asians being welcome to play in one of Sheffield Carribean CC's sides, which plays Sunday fixtures. It has also become common for proficient Asian cricketers to be employed as semi-professionals on a seasonal contract or per match in a whole variety of clubs. In the next village to where I live, Hoylandswaine has won the Huddersfield League (a serious enough competition to be listed in the annual Wisden) with the help of Haroon Rashid, brother of England cricketer Adil Rashid. These local "stars" are also sought to act as coaches in club and youth sides and in schools—these gigs proving handy wage supplements.

At county level these trends made possible the emergence, finally, of Asian cricketers in the YCCC sides, and even as internationals. Adil Rashid, with the rare skills (in Yorkshire especially) of being a slow leg-break spin bowler and useful batsman, has become the best known of the core of those who played for the county after 2005. Among his many feats he is the only Yorkshire player to score 100 and take five wickets in an innings in one of the annual War of the Roses matches against Lancashire. He became an England prospect and has played a few matches for the national one-day side. Another Bradford lad, Ajmal Shahzad, played for YCCC slightly before Rashid, and has played for England. Only a few years younger, Azeem Rafiq, another slow spin bowling all-rounder from Barnsley, and Moin Ashraf, a very athletic fast bowler, have established themselves as regulars in the Yorkshire side.

One set of events that may well become iconic as marking a new era was the sight of a 20 year old Rafiq being made replacement captain in the short-form 20-20 games of June 2012 (a format in which Yorkshire has never excelled, no doubt still seeing it as too trivial for them) and leading out a team including Rashid and Ashraf, which won five of the six games, one rained off, in order to take them to the national finals. This recent sea-change has three crucial dimensions. It is first a sign that at local levels the blurring of the demarcation between separate and parallel structures has gone so far that much of Yorkshire cricket has become multicultural.

This process has also involved a significant change of attitude on the part of the county as well as local authorities. The small core of stars have played through the levels: spotted to play for YCCC under-15 sides (Ashraf even in an under-13 team) and the hierarchy leading to the junior professional level of the Academy, which in turn fields a team that competes in the senior pan-Yorkshire Premier League. This in turn offers an avenue for young black and Asian players to enter the ranks of professional cricketers. And they then act as role models and provide coaching for younger would-be players, from within but also beyond their own communities.

This opening up of recruitment has been followed within a more conscious "business plan" or development strategy by YCCC which reaches out to the sizeable immigrant and particularly Asian communities. Where else can be found boys who are cricket mad playing in back streets all year round? Providing role models was arguably behind contracts as "overseas players" for Yousuf Khan, vice-captain and Imzimam ul Haq, former captain, and fast bowler Hassan, all of Pakistan, in the late 2000s. Headingley also won a bid to host a "neutral" international test match between Australia and Pakistan in 2010—although this was an expensive failure in bringing hordes of Asian spectators, probably because the cost of four or five days attendance was so high compared with a one-day international. But at least there was intent.

What these recent trends signify is not just a top-down strategy, at last, from YCCC but at least as much community led initiatives—the leagues and the diffusion out from them, the commitment of resources and even a still parallel but no longer segregated training system. The latter includes the formal institutionalisation in December 2012 of the Adil Rashid Cricket Academy (following in the footsteps of the cricket school that Devon Malcolm set up in his native Sheffield once he retired) but also the multiplicity of informal coaching arrangements at all levels of the game. An attendance list at a boys' Pathway to Progress Centre, set up under national auspices, not YCCC, in Heckmondwyke (what place could more embody Yorkshire?) had a third of the 40 with obviously Asian names.

The struggle continues

In Yorkshire the parallel structures are no longer segregated. At local level crude racist exclusion is ended and there is much intermingling and interaction. At county level a path towards professional status has been opened up for cricketers from minority communities. But the broader vision of an integrated cricketing culture built on a new idea of Yorkshireness and Englishness still faces struggles ahead.

One measure of the task is offered by the current position of the Asian players who emerged through the YCCC structures. Adil Rashid, who was seen as a future international player, has seen his career falter. Seemingly no longer in England's future plans, his form deteriorated in 2011 and 2012, so that he no longer commands an automatic place in the Yorkshire side. It was in this context of his loss of confidence, so vital to a bowler of his type, that his county president, his employer, explained to the listening public that he has no cricketing brain—though he still retains iconic status among the Pakistani community of West Yorkshire! Shahzad, the other player with appearances for England, was involved in a row with the managerial and coaching staff at Headingley. He claims it was about his role in the team and the type of cricket he was expected to play: to curb his attacking instincts and be more of a defensive bowler, a reversion if true to a long tradition in Yorkshire cricket. He was told he was not wanted at YCCC, played a season on loan to Lancashire and has now been signed up by Nottinghamshire (interestingly he says of his 2013 move aged 27 that it is the first time he has lived away from the family home). Azeem Rafiq already went through a period of suspension from playing after making public his disputes, again about his playing role, with the coach of the England Under-19 side in 2011. It is hard to get to the bottom of these disputes but the fact that there have already been more than one does raise the possibility that players and managers are not yet on a mutually supportive wavelength.

Chapter 19
RUGBY LEAGUE: SPORT, CLASS AND POLITICS
Paul Blackledge

Modern football can trace its roots back to late medieval England where it was generally played by large groups of young men in a myriad of local forms. Our knowledge of the sport is largely confined to odd reports of the death or injury of participants. All we can say with certainty is that by the time of the industrial revolution football was suppressed from above because of the perception that it was a source of social turmoil.

If this action, alongside the dramatic reduction in leisure time in industrial Britain, meant that by the turn of the 19th century football seemed to be on its last legs,[1] its revival famously came through the English public schools. It was from these institutions that it returned, in a changed form, to the English working class from the mid-19th century onwards through the medium of "muscular Christianity". Ex public schoolboy clergymen set up football clubs in the towns and cities with a view to instilling team spirit and godliness into the hearts of young workers.[2]

But things didn't work out quite as the middle class reformers had hoped. Almost from the first football developed a dynamic of its own. On the one hand, games between local teams created the need for rules. And it was from the subsequent process of formalisation that the codes of rugby and association football (and Australian Rules, Gaelic Football and American Football) initially diverged and then split.

On the other hand, class tensions grew within both codes. From the mid-19th century onwards "sport", as Eric Hobsbawm wrote, "provided much of the formal cement" which gave cohesion to the English middle and upper classes.[3] Indeed what C L R James wrote in *Beyond a Boundary* about the role of cricket in summer was equally true of football in winter: the British ruling class "took over the game of cricket and in the public schools established the rigorous code as a means of uniting and disciplining their class".[4]

However, whereas the muscular Christians aimed to spread their middle class ethos downwards, they soon found that once they had let the working class genie out of the bottle it became increasingly difficult to control it. In particular, mass working class participation in association football (soccer) from the 1870s onwards went hand in hand with the growth of a heightened competiveness. By contrast with the earlier ethos of fairness, cup competitions fostered a utilitarian spirit of winning at any cost: and workers who were used to operating through a division of labour to get the job done in factories tended to excel in this more disciplined culture. This, alongside the fact that the newly-free Saturday afternoon was initially confined to the industrial section of the working class, helps explain how northern working class clubs came to dominate soccer by the 1880s. If the teams made up of working class players tended to beat teams made up of middle class participants on the field of play, the boisterous behaviour of working class supporters tended to alienate middle class supporters off it.

In this situation, soccer was no longer able to provide the social cement to hold the middle classes together. Mindful of these developments, those who ran the Rugby Football Union (RFU) set out to keep their sport a preserve of the middle classes. In the 1880s this meant wilfully losing previously rugby-playing northern and especially Lancashire clubs to soccer through a refusal to countenance (popular) cup competitions. The RFU were clear about their intensions: they'd rather rugby was less popular than have more working class participants, and where this meant wrecking their own sport, as it did in Lancashire and Yorkshire, they did just this. This process culminated in the 1895 split between the old establishment and the increasingly powerful big clubs of Yorkshire and Lancashire through which the Rugby League (initially the Northern Union) was formed.[5]

Rugby League immediately distinguished itself from Rugby Union by its comparative vibrancy. For instance, in the decades leading up to the split, rugby had been in a process of development into a faster and more spectator-friendly sport, a tendency which included a reduction in the size of teams from 20 to 15 a side. However, after the split, and in an attempt to claim for itself the mantle of tradition, the Rugby Union essentially ossified around the rules of 1895, while the Rugby League instituted, among other reforms, reductions in the size of the team, first to 13 then to 11 and back to 13 again, in an attempt to extend the pre-split tendency to foster a faster and more open game. If the main aim of these reforms was to create weekly spectacles which would make money for the owners by attracting large crowds of hard-working, fee paying fans, they also fostered the creation of a game through which generations of northern working men could find some outlet for their creativity.

In his excellent study of the class dynamics at the heart of the division between rugby's two codes, *Rugby's Great Split*, Tony Collins shows that it is impossible to understand the events of 1895 outside the social, cultural and political context of the 1890s in general, and the class struggle of the period in particular.[6] In fact, rugby's split occurred in the wake of the upsurge of working class struggle known as the New Unionism (1889), and a decade after a team made up of northern workingmen (Blackburn Olympic) nailed the myth of the effortless superiority of the English middle classes when they beat the last team of amateur ex public schoolboys (Old Etonians) to make it to the FA cup final in 1883.[7]

Fearing that developments in soccer pointed to the future of rugby, the Rugby Football Union focused all its attention on ensuring that rugby did not follow football down a route that would lead to mass working class participation. This had in fact already occurred in parts of Lancashire and Yorkshire, where the demand for "broken time" payments—to pay players for wages lost when playing for a team—had been taken up by the businessmen who owned the big clubs to ensure that they got the best possible team on the pitch, and therefore the highest possible take at the gate. For the authorities who ran the game this was anathema, and they insisted that only those who could afford to play without pay should be able to do so. It was, for the most part, a game for the middle classes and they wanted to keep it that way. Moreover, as they saw it, the alternative was to foster working class idleness by providing an easy way out of industry. London Tory politician and president of the RFU Arthur Budd expressed the general feeling of rugby's authorities at the time: "The answer then to those who urge that the working man ought to be compensated for the loss of time incurred by his recreations is that, if he cannot afford the leisure to play the game, he must do without it".[8]

At a gerrymandered vote in 1893 that set the scene for the split of 1895 (though the establishment would have probably won anyway), the RFU defeated a motion that would have allowed workers to be compensated for loss of earnings while playing. In the wake of the eventual split and for the next century (with slight relaxations during the two world wars) this form of social exclusion was policed by rules that made just about any contact on the part of members of the Rugby Football Union with anyone associated with Rugby League grounds for an automatic ban from Rugby Union.

It was this pariah status that helped give Rugby League, as Tony Collins points out, its sense of identity—not just northern and manly, but also resolutely working class.[9] Interestingly, Collins compares the consciousness of Rugby League's sense of otherness with social democracy. Both were ideologies rooted in working class life that were critical of existing social hierarchies, but which essentially naturalised the status quo. So while Rugby League proved its patriotism in both world wars, its sense of democratic egalitarianism meant that on many issues it was much more progressive than other British institutions. For instance, the first black man to play for the national side, Wigan's George Bennett, won caps in the 1930s after leaving Wales because the racism of the Welsh Rugby Union acted as a bar to his selection to their national team—indeed no black person played for that team before the 1980s. In 1972 Clive Sullivan became the first black man to captain a national British sporting team. And

Wakefield Trinity attempted to sign John Carlos, America's 200 metre bronze medal winner at the 1968 Olympics, after he'd been sent home in "disgrace" for giving the iconic Black Power salute during the medal ceremony. Nevertheless, if racism was kicked out of the front door, Collins shows how it returned through the back. Coaches thought in stereotypes, and black players almost universally played centre or wing. Moreover, the parochialism of those who ran the sport meant that, while there was always a smattering of Jewish players—particularly in Leeds—they never reached out to the Asian communities which grew up across the north in the post-war period.

This reflected broader contradictions. Rugby League was egalitarian, but it was also manly and hard; it was democratic, but it was also parochial and inward-looking. Just like social democracy, therefore, it reflected the fact that working class life exists both in and against capitalism. This is nowhere truer than in the dialectic at the core of the game between those who ran the sport—the members of the middle classes, largely small businessmen in general and publicans in particular, who, at the time of the split in 1895,[10] saw rugby as a means of making money rather than primarily a means of social cohesion—and those who played and watched the game, largely members of the manual working class. It was this tension that fuelled the popular upsurge of supporters against Murdoch's Super League in 1995, but which undermined this movement as Rugby League's authorities couldn't imagine an alternative to his plan (or, more importantly, to his money).

Collins is right to point out that Rugby League reflected a sense of northern working class identity, but he mistakenly suggests that this was a working class culture. This point is easily countered with evidence deployed by Collins himself. The strength of Rugby League teams when compared to their Rugby Union alternatives is best understood, he argues, as a reflection of their work situation. Writing of the dominant team of the inter-war years, Collins points out that "for spectators whose day to day lives were based on synchronised, collective labour of the town's textile mills, the Huddersfield side was the embodiment of working class industrial collectivity at play".[11] One has only to think about this statement for a moment to realise how misleading is the concept of working class culture. The fact that the discipline of the team reflected the capitalist discipline of the workplace suggests that we are talking about bourgeois culture, understood not in a crude sense as the mores of the bourgeoisie, but rather as the contradictory culture of a capitalist society.

As Edward Thompson insisted in a criticism he made of Raymond Williams's early work, culture is best understood not so much as a static "way of life" as it is as a dynamic "way of struggle".[12] Among the lessons of the history of Rugby League is that working class involvement in sport generally is best understood neither, as those who tend to romanticise such things suggest,[13] as a simple expression of the values of ordinary people nor, as one-sided critics such as Marc Perelman argue, as mere alienation.[14] Rather there is a tension between creativity and alienation: working class participation in sport reflects the constant struggle to maintain a sense of dignity in a world that reduces workers to the status of cogs in a wheel: while it is important that we do not romanticise this aspect of sport, it would be equally foolish to lose sight of it.

Chapter 20
WHAT'S DIFFERENT ABOUT THE PARALYMPICS?

Roddy Slorach

Channel 4's big gamble paid off. As London 2012 presenter Arthur Williams put it:

> Our worst fear was that people would shrug their shoulders. Instead we have left our audience captivated. Everybody who has watched the Paralympics has been changed by what they have witnessed. If there is anyone out there who disagrees, they're lying.[1]

A record 2.7 million tickets were sold for "the second half" of London 2012, packing out every venue. Twelve million UK viewers watched the Paralympics opening ceremony. Spectators and contestants alike embraced the atmosphere as well as the events themselves. As one disabled visitor at the Paralympics said, "It feels like some kind of weird and wonderful bubble. Instead of being stared at or patronised, everyone treats you like an equal."

The GB Wheelchair Basketball Association reported almost 7,000 visits on its "find a club" web page in the weeks after the Paralympics. In 2008 the Blackhawk Mallards club in Woking had just seven registered players. It now has 28 and fields four teams, two in the men's national league. The enthusiasm extended to other sports in which GB teams did poorly, such as sitting volleyball. A month after London 2012 Volleyball England was planning to launch at least three new clubs.[2]

But London 2012's success was not without precedent. Participation in disability sports saw a similar boom four years previously. Attendances rose steadily at each of the Paralympics after the poor turn-out for the Atlanta (US) Games in 1996. At Beijing 2008 some spectators were bussed in or bribed to attend to ensure venues were full, but huge crowds also gathered in shopping malls to watch the TV coverage. The success of the Beijing Paralympics led to TV rights for London 2012 being put out to tender for the first time, in turn attracting significant corporate sponsorship. The total world TV audience for both was 3.8 billion.[3]

China's recent dominance at the Paralympics reflects its economic success. Coming a mere 28th when it first took part in the Paralympics in 1984, China topped the medals table for the first time in Athens 20 years later—increasing its medals share to double that of its closest rivals at both Beijing and London. Before and after their winning bid to stage the 2008 Games China's rulers invested massively in sport. More modest investment in the UK saw its Paralympics team drop to third place after coming second in each of the three previous Paralympic Games.

According to the World Health Organisation, 80 percent of the globe's 1 billion disabled people live in developing countries. This isn't reflected in the medals tables. African countries won a total of 27 gold medals at the 2012 Paralympics—five less than Australia, which has less than a fortieth of their population. Nineteen of the largest 25 squads at the 2012 Paralympics belonged to the OECD industrialised nations' club, and the biggest nine teams comprised almost 40 percent of the 4,200 contestants. Others come from emerging economic powers like Brazil, Russia and South Africa. Ukraine and Iran have also developed strong Paralympic traditions.

The disparity is particularly evident in the more high-tech sports. None of the world's poorer countries took part in the cycling events, where the GB team's machines were universally acknowledged to have the edge. During the opening ceremony commentator and former Paralympian Ade Adepitan pointed out that athletes from developing countries were competing in wheelchairs hugely inferior to those used by teams such as GB or France. Specialised wheelchairs used in athletics, basketball or tennis cost up to £5,000 each, while the running blades pioneered by Oscar Pistorius cost around £15,000. Virtually all of Kenya's 13-strong squad were blind or partially-sighted runners, and only one uses a wheelchair. Poorer countries are therefore restricted to competing in only a few events.

As Peter Walker has noted:

> some less developed nations' success in Paralympic events has come directly from war. Sitting volleyball is enormously popular in Iran—the country won five out of six gold medals since 1988—and has long been popular with injured veterans from the brutal war with Iraq. Iran's main rivals, Bosnia and Herzegovina, who won the 2004 title, are captained by Sabahudin Delalic, who lost a leg in 1992 in the Balkan conflict.

He adds that Cambodia, one of the world's poorest countries, also has one of the "highest ratios of amputees due to landmine blasts, but managed to send only one of them to compete at London 2012".[4]

According to a study by Sheffield Hallam University, "population and Gross Domestic Product explain about 53 percent of a nation's success in the Olympic Games, and more than 60 percent in the Paralympic Games. A big population means a big pool of talent to fish from, and wealth means good healthcare and the money to spend on sports training and facilities".[5] In contrast to its main Paralympic rivals, the US still lacks universal healthcare and has only a limited welfare system.

This partly explains why the US, the world's leading economic power, won five of the last six Olympic Games but only managed sixth place at the 2012 Paralympics—lower than Britain, Australia and Ukraine, despite its population and GDP being over twice the size of these three combined. Paralympian athletes successfully sued the US Olympic Committee in 2003 for chronic underfunding. Broadcasting giant NBC was widely criticised for its sparse coverage of the 2012 Games, which were almost universally ignored by the rest of the US media.

Kazakhstan and North Korea also performed markedly worse in the Paralympics, winning no medals there but several at the Olympics. In contrast, Austria, Nigeria and Algeria won many more Paralympic medals than Olympic medals. Several war-torn countries—Rwanda, Bosnia Herzegovina, Iran and Iraq—entered more athletes for the Paralympics than the Olympics, with Iran finishing joint tenth in the final medals table.

The Paralympics, like the Olympics, involves a tiny elite of athletes who come in the main from privileged backgrounds, and whose lives and achievements have at best questionable relevance to the rest of us. Unlike its bigger relative, the Paralympics remains a "niche product", its £20 million in sponsorship deals a fraction of the £750 million for the Olympics.

Oscar Pistorius arrived in London as the poster boy for the Paralympics. A rich white South African and a serial gold medal winner, his true-life tale of triumph over adversity made him an ideal brand image for corporate sponsors. To compete in both the Olympics and Paralympics, Pistorius first had to overturn legal claims that his prosthetic carbon fibre blades gave him an unfair advantage. This victory against a conservative sporting establishment made him a hero and an inspiration to others—including his conquerors at London 2012.

No longer "the fastest man on no legs" or the sole "blade runner", it was not so much defeat as his reaction to it which first tarnished Pistorius's clean-cut image. After the T43 200 metres final he complained that the winner, Brazilian Alan Oliveira, had cheated by switching to longer running blades three weeks before the games. Oliveira and others who had idolised him as a role model were shocked. The irony in Pistorius of all people making such a complaint was missed by much of the media. But with an income estimated at £2 million a year, his privileged background also gave him a huge advantage over most disabled athletes.

As the Paralympics have become more prestigious and competitive, so the pressure on individual athletes to win—often by illegal means—has also increased. One established technique involves "boosting", where competitors with spinal injuries deliberately injure themselves in order to raise blood pressure and improve performances. Two Russian powerlifters were suspended at London 2012 for taking human growth hormone, and a Georgian tested positive for steroids. Monique van der Vorst won two silver medals in paraplegic handcycling for Holland in Beijing, but later admitted she could always stand and walk when she won a contract as a professional road racer.

Paralympians are categorised into one of six main impairment groups, then "graded" into classes according to the severity of their impairments. This is why there were 25 different finals for the 100 metres sprint alone (13 for men and 12 for women), and 14 classes in swimming. An athlete classified as a 9 in freestyle, for example, could be a 10 in butterfly, as different strokes may be harder depending on impairment. Inevitably, some classification decisions have been disputed.[6] Some athletes try to cheat their class in order to compete against others who are more severely impaired and increase their chances of winning. As the prizes, sponsorship and recognition increase, so more scandals, rows over technology and classification irregularities will surely follow.

The Paralympics draw on a relatively small pool of athletes, particularly once widespread discrimination is taken into account, so participation across the events is uneven. Only swimming and athletics were represented across all ten impairment groups at London 2012, and there were no qualifying rounds for a whole series of events due to a shortage of eligible participants.

Boccia and goalball are sports unique to the Paralympics. Wheelchair rugby—"murderball"—differs sharply from its outdoor namesake. Fast, furious and complex, it won many new fans in London. Like other Paralympic events, it has become widely recognised as a sport in its own right. The way in which different grades of players are deployed is a key part of a team's success, making it more akin to a particularly violent game of chess.

The complexity of the classification system; the distinct rules; the debates about how to ensure a level playing field for competitors; athletes with contrasting impairments competing in the same events; the additional obstacles disabled athletes face—all this is part of the Paralympics' unique appeal.

The rise of the Paralympics is above all a consequence of long-term and wider social change—the arrival of disabled people into the workplace and wider society. The long economic boom after the Second World War also brought medical and scientific advances which led to more severely disabled people living longer and living independently. Where heating water or lighting a fire was previously a major problem, turning on a tap or electric radiator is usually not. Full employment, a welfare state and the expansion of social services helped prompt the emergence of a disabled people's movement, which helped win further benefits and rights, including social support to achieve a level of independence. These reforms are now under threat from neoliberal policies and austerity cuts.

As actress Liz Carr predicted, we saw "more disability on TV in 12 days than we have in the previous 12 years", and the narrative was indeed primarily "about exceptional and inspiring individuals".[7] The message to disabled people—that they too could achieve if only they tried hard enough—was made explicit with disability deniers Atos being made one of the Paralympics' main sponsors.

London 2012 did offer some positive images of disability. But in a society facing huge austerity cuts, where over half of all disabled people are unemployed, and where constant media scapegoating has led to increased discrimination, views on disability have become more polarised. So an ITN/ComRes poll found that, while 85 percent of those polled thought Paralympians are great role models, only 56 percent believed discrimination against disabled people would decrease because of the games.[8]

The prospect of any once-trumpeted wider legacy in Britain seems as equally remote for disability sports as it does for wider society. Past Paralympians Tanni Grey-Thompson and Ade Adepitan have warned that benefit cuts will undermine wider access to sport. Contrary to promises made before the games, the Tories are selling off school playing fields. Even where there are locally accessible transport and sports facilities, the costs of coaching, equipment and training are beyond the means of most would-be disabled athletes.

Physical recreation and play are about the enjoyment of one's body, human company and the environment. Under capitalism sport incorporates elements of these into timed systems of competition, incorporating both a division of skills and an obedience to arbitrary rules—an ideal preparation for the modern productive process.

The main needs of disabled people include access to health, social services and education. Making these accessible to everyone, regardless of wealth or need, represents a far more worthwhile goal than the pursuit of ever more Paralympic medals.

The extra needs and costs of disability have won some recognition in elite sport. Elsewhere the trend is in the opposite direction. The Paralympics "bubble" did provide a glimpse of society's ability to truly provide for, and utilise the skills of, disabled people. But for that to happen will require getting rid of the competition for profit that drives capitalism and which shapes all of modern sports.

Chapter 21
FROM THE FACTORY TO THE FIELD:
THE STORY OF DICK, KERR LADIES FC (1917-1965)[1]

Pete Marsden

Bend it like Beckham and *Gregory's Girl* are both cinematic depictions of the
hurdles facing young women wanting to play football on equal
grounds with their male counterparts. Both films depict the obstacles
which lie in women's path both within sport and in wider society. Yet
flash back around half a century and we can find a Pathé news film
which reveals the story of a women's football team, made up of shop
floor workers from a Preston munitions factory: Dick, Kerr Ladies FC.

The players of Dick, Kerr Ladies FC were the true pioneers of
women's football, trailing a path for women's sporting equality. Yet
they were also the victims of an appalling abuse of power by the
Football Association (FA), which hated the idea of women participating in sport—so much so that on 5 December 1921 it took a decision
to effectively prevent women's teams from playing on any FA ground.
This decision set back the development of women's football in
Britain for almost a half century until the "ban" was lifted in 1969.

The Preston-based team was set up in 1917 at the Dick, Kerr munitions factory to raise money for charitable causes, such as disabled
servicemen wounded in the war. David Lloyd George had taken the
parallel decision to recruit women to the workforce, following the
introduction of conscription into the armed forces in 1916, and over
700,000 women would soon be working in the munitions industry.[2]

In Preston there was a long history of women engaged in paid
employment. Nationally in 1918 over 423,000 women were members of the various textile unions when the national female
membership of trade unions was just over a million. Such members
were concentrated in the Lancashire mills and associated trades.
Women made up the bulk of the membership in the various unions;
52 percent in textiles, 75 percent in cotton and 82 percent in textile
dyeing and bleaching. This history of women identifying with trade
unionism carried over to the munitions factories. Female membership of the general labour unions grew from 24,000 to 216,000
during the war years and women made up 80 percent of members.[3]

The subsequent move to support women's football teams was

intended to improve the morale and status of women workers in key wartime industries. This gave a fillip to women on the shop floor at Dick, Kerr who were keen on setting up a team. This was also instrumental in subsequent support from management to allow players unpaid time off from work and the use of factory playing fields on which to train. This was a time of changing women's attitudes and attitudes to women, with a challenge to Victorian conservatism and the growth of agitation for women's suffrage, both through the Suffragettes and Suffragists. As Gail J Newsham said, "Women wanted to work, they wanted to vote and they wanted to play and they were no longer prepared to accept their so called 'place' as being the only one that the society of the day would allow".[4]

Dick, Kerr FC's popularity grew dramatically. On Boxing Day 1920 at Goodison Park they drew a crowd of 53,000 with between 10,000 and 14,000 spectators being locked out—a record crowd for women's football—35,000 spectators watched them take on Bath at Old Trafford; 25,000 people turned out to witness them destroy a Rest of Britain team 9-1 at Anfield; and 22,000 watched the return fixture in Paris before a pitch invasion ended the game 1-1 five minutes from time.[5] Playing 67 games for charity in 1921 they attracted crowds of over 900,000 spectators.[6]

These figures illustrate that the team were drawing larger crowds than their male contemporaries. Barbara Jacobs said:

> They were massive stars by then… Not only were they brilliant footballers, but were doing a week's work and then turning out to play football in their spare time—and they were giving all the money they earned to wounded and invalid soldiers. The funds of various cities like Liverpool depended totally on it.[7]

Resentment from the male-dominated soccer establishment soon grew. A further factor in the growing animosity directed at the team was their decision to play matches to raise money for trade union causes. The immediate aftermath of the First World War witnessed a period of intensified class struggle in Britain—with 1919, in particular, bringing strikes across engineering, mines and railways. Even the police in London and Liverpool went on strike.

In March 1921 the mine owners announced a 50 percent reduction in miners' wages and when the miners refused to accept this they were locked out. The team members, such as Lily Parr, one of the stars of the team who hailed from "the poorest part of Saint Helens", played games to raise money for the families of locked out miners. Similar matches were organised in mining areas in Wales and Scotland.

As Barbara Jacobs said:

> Women's football had come to be associated with charity, and had its own credibility. Now it was used as a tool to help the labour movement and the trade unions. It had, it could be said, become a politically dangerous sport, to those who felt the trade unions to be their enemies... Women going out to support their men folk, a Lancashire tradition, was causing ripples in a society which wanted women to revert to their pre-war roles as set down by their masters, of keeping their place, that place being the home and the kitchen. Lancashire lasses were upsetting the social order. It wasn't acceptable.[8]

The FA's mean-spirited and sexist attitudes led to all-women's teams being effectively barred from using FA pitches. However, it would be far from accurate to see this organisation's enmity as representative of all layers of British society. Undoubtedly there were many men who found it difficult to accept that women could play football. Attitudes within the crowd were mixed, with some contemporary accounts focusing on the players' appearances and retaining their "feminine characteristics" while playing a "male sport". Yet there are plenty of progressive male voices, such as William Crook who saw Dick, Kerr play on several occasions just before the 1926 General Strike. He went to matches because he enjoyed watching a good game of football and, he noted, "Dick, Kerr Ladies has some brilliant players".[9]

Preston North End allowed the use of their ground and training pitch (at a cost), ex-footballers (including Bob Holmes one of PNE's "Invincibles") coached the team, and they were even supported by John Kerr, the firm's managing director and Conservative MP for Preston.

The decision to effectively hamstring the charitable work of the team and deal a death blow to the women's game was justified in a smear campaign. On 5 December 1921 the FA unanimously passed the following resolution:

> Complaints having been made as to football being played by women, the council feel impelled to express their strong opinion that the

game of football is quite unsuitable for females and ought not to be encouraged.

Complaints have also been made as to the conditions under which some of the matches have been arranged and played, and the appropriation of receipts to other than charitable objects.

The council are further of the opinion that an excessive proportion of the receipts are absorbed in expenses and an inadequate percentage devoted to charitable objects.

For these reasons the council request clubs belonging to the association to refuse the use of their grounds for such matches.[10]

The accusation of misappropriating charity monies was felt particularly keenly by the Dick, Kerr players. The team had raised an estimated £70,000 for charities, £14 million at current prices. As working class women the only way they could afford to play during working hours was to be reimbursed for their travel costs, accommodation and loss of earnings. Alice Kell, the captain, spoke for the other women when she said:

We play for the love of the game and we are determined to carry on. It is impossible for us the working girls to afford to leave work to play matches all over the country and be the losers. I see no reason why we should not be compensated for loss of time at work. No one ever receives more than 10 shillings per day.[11]

The medical establishment was also drawn in to provide spurious advice about the danger of football to women's health. Dr Mary Scharlieb, a Harley Street physician, said:

There are physical reasons why the game is harmful to women. It is a rough game at any time, but it is much more harmful to women than men. They may receive injuries from which they may never recover.[12]

The captain of Plymouth Ladies argued:

The controlling body of the FA are a hundred years behind the times and their action is purely sex prejudice. Not one of our girls has felt any ill effects from participating in the game.[13]

In response to the FA's dictates the first meeting of the English Ladies Football Association (ELFA) took place in Blackburn on 10

December 1921. At the time there were about 150 women's teams in England and 25 clubs were represented, rising to 60 at the next meeting in Grimsby. The ELFA introduced its own set of rules and regulations, including reducing the size of the pitch and using a lighter football. It also decreed that no woman was to play for a team that was more than 20 miles from her home; a rule which handicapped Dick, Kerr who had a policy of recruiting the best available players from the country.[14]

The FA's decision dealt a fatal blow to women's football and to equality generally and confined women's football to "muddy fields and obscurity".[15] The team were further handicapped over the years as men returned from the trenches and women were released from the factory. Team manager Alfred Frankland tried to alleviate this trend by finding work in a nearby mental health hospital for a number of the women, so allowing them to continue to work and play.

After the team had played Bolton Ladies in aid of the War Memorial Fund in 1947 the Mayor of Stalybridge said:

> I hope you will go ahead and fight the FA which is a narrow bigoted authority. From one who has been involved in the game for 30 years, I personally resent it.[16]

Although such words were indicative of much support, the FA's hostility to women's football continued unabated through the years. In 1947 the Kent FA suspended a referee because he refused to end his association as manager and trainer with Kent Ladies FC. The Kent County Football Association said, "Women's football brings the game into disrepute". Then in 1962 the local football association even stepped in to stop a match being played by Dick, Kerr in aid of the Wigan Society for the Blind.[17]

As Gail J Newsham argued:

> So, that was that, the axe had fallen, and despite all the ladies' denials and assurances regarding finances, and their willingness to play under any conditions that the FA laid down, the decision was irreversible. The chauvinists, the medical "experts" and the anti-women's football lobby had won—their threatened male bastion was now safe.[18]

Dick, Kerr continued their slow demise, a decline mirrored by the women's game in general, and finally stopped playing in 1965. Their period of extra time was not without its highlights, with innovations such as the first women's international game, wartime floodlit games illuminated by searchlights, and a tour of the United States in which the team played and beat a number of men's teams. In September 1937 they won the unofficial "championship of Great Britain and the World" when they beat Edinburgh Ladies 5-1 at Preston.[19] At their demise Dick, Kerr Ladies FC's impressive playing record over 48 years read: played 828, won 758, drew 46, lost 24.[20]

Women's football owes an enormous debt to these Lancashire working women; without their efforts we would not be able to witness something in the region of 4,500 women's teams playing nationwide. This is not to suggest that the struggle for women's equality in sport has been achieved or is anywhere close to achieving a level playing field. Indeed, to date only 0.5 percent of sponsorship goes to women's sport while men's sport gets the lion's share at 62 percent. Simply browsing through any sports website can reveal many sexist attitudes.

Yet Dick, Kerr's is an inspiring story. As Gail J Newsham said:

> It's easy to say now that they were hugely important. But put it in the context of Emily Davidson throwing herself under the king's horse at the Derby and Emily Pankhurst being arrested at Buckingham Palace—then there was Dick, Kerr Ladies travelling the country with people paying to see them play football. Everybody looked up to them. As one of the players said to me before she died, "We were famous you see, and everybody wanted to see us".[21]

Dick, Kerr Ladies FC remain working class pioneers of women's football and equality in sport and represent a high water mark in efforts to achieve emancipation in the factory and on the playing field.

Chapter 22
CYCLING TO SOCIALISM: THE CLARION CYCLING CLUB

Denis Pye

In 1891 Robert Blatchford left his well-paid job at the *Sunday Chronicle* in Manchester after refusing to stop advocating socialism in his popular weekly column. He was joined by his brother Montague and two sympathetic fellow-journalists, Alex Thompson and Edward Fay.

Renting a tiny office, they brought out the first issue of a penny socialist paper, the Clarion. By 1908, devoured every weekend in working class homes throughout the land, its circulation topped 90,000. Though its avowed aim was to "make socialists", the Clarion from the beginning was no po-faced, hard-edged paper for politicos. As well as the politics, each issue in the 1890s featured reviews of music, theatre and books, a women's section, reports of cricket and football, children's stories, notes for ramblers, and a column for cyclists.

Two years after the establishment of the Clarion a Socialist Cycling Club was launched by readers in Birmingham. Six members of the Labour Church in the city met under the chairmanship of Tom Groom to discuss how they might "combine the pleasures of cycling with the propaganda of socialism". They soon changed the name to the Clarion Cycling Club, after their favourite paper, and over the Easter holiday weekend Tom and his comrades undertook their first cycling tour. He wrote a report about it for the next issue of the Clarion, stirring other cycle-crazy socialists into action. By January 1895 five more Clarion Cycling Clubs were in existence: in the Potteries, Liverpool, Bradford, Barnsley and Manchester. Over the next 20 years the growth of the movement was remarkable. At the end of 1913 there were more than 200 such clubs, and a total membership in excess of 6,000. They were not all convinced or committed socialists, but there were enough activists to have a significant influence in the formation of Independent Labour Party and Social Democratic Federation branches in many parts of the country.

The Cycling Clubs were only the first of many Clarion-based organisations catering for the cultural and leisure interests of readers, but the cyclists were always at the centre of the movement. Easter 1895 saw their first Annual Meet at Ashbourne in Derbyshire. On Easter Sunday morning over a hundred Clarionettes (men and women) gathered in the open air outside the Izaak Walton Hotel in Dovedale to set up the National Clarion Cycling Club. It was here that the famous trumpet badge, designed by a Birmingham member, was adopted.

In the years up to 1914 the Easter Meet became a gathering not only of the cyclists but of other groups organised through the paper: the Vocal Unions (choirs), the Field Clubs (ramblers), the Handicraft Guilds and the Dramatic Societies. So, although the aim of the Clarion, in Blatchford's words, was to "teach the principles of socialism in the simplest and best words at our command", the non-political parts of the paper were of equal importance to most readers. All the various cultural, social, leisure and sporting activities promoted by contributors offered a whole new way of life outside the toil and drabness of the world of work and crowded urban living.

In some ways the Clarion movement was an attempt to pre-figure life under socialism as William Morris described it in his utopian novel *News from Nowhere*. Indeed, those who started the Manchester Clarion Cyclists' Clubhouse at Bucklow Hill in Cheshire called it the "first socialist guest-house". Between Easter Meets this and the other residential clubhouses which followed up and down the country provided centres, easily reached by bicycle, for all the activities and interests promoted in the paper.

In 1896 Julia Dawson, writer of the women's column in the *Clarion*, suggested that a horse-drawn caravan be used as a kind of missionary van to preach the socialist gospel in small towns and villages where it had seldom before been taken. That summer a small group of women volunteers set out from Chester in a newly-decorated and equipped vehicle. They toured Shropshire and Cheshire, then went through Lancashire, Yorkshire, Durham and Northumberland. Every day they addressed meetings ranging from half a dozen people to several hundreds. And the efforts of the women vanners were aided by Clarion cyclists who rode out from the big towns into the countryside at weekends carrying copies of the paper, socialist leaflets, and Blatchford's million-selling penny pamphlet *Merrie England*. After appeals for funds more vans were put on the road. Their tours went on into the 1920s—always relying on the cyclists to make the open-air meetings more effective.

In many ways the Clarion, as a movement, was a casualty of the First World War, even though some of the choirs, dramatic societies and clubhouses lingered on to the Second World War and beyond. After 1914 there was a steep drop in the circulation of the paper, from around 60,000 to under 10,000 copies a week, largely as a result of what Robert Blatchford saw as his "patriotic stand" in support of the war. (He had already dismayed many readers by his support for the war against the Boers in South Africa.) After staggering through the 1920s the *Clarion* became a monthly in 1927, and ceased publication in 1934.

Paradoxically, however, the death of the paper and the decline of other Clarion organisations coincided with a dramatic increase in the membership of the National Clarion Cycling Club, which reached an all-time high of over 8,000 in more than 240 local sections by 1936. This was the heyday of cycling, with ten million bikes on the road compared with only 1 million cars. And many Clarion cyclists, having dropped the "propagation of the principles of socialism" (even though it was still part of the national club's aims and objects) were not just interested in weekend runs and touring. An increasing number (mainly young men, but some young women) were involved in competitive cycling, on road and track.

Interest in racing had started in a small way in the 1890s, though it was at first frowned upon by many socialist activists. Manchester led the way, organising an annual sports meeting at Belle Vue, which continued until it was moved to the Fallowfield track in 1930. Between the wars racing on the road meant individual time-trials; mass-start road races were illegal in Britain, though not on the Continent. Twenty five and 50-mile time-trials took place in semi-secrecy, with the riders dressed in black alpaca from the neck down to wrists and ankles.

At the 1930 conference during the Buxton Easter Meet the National Clarion CC elected its first racing secretary, who announced his dedication to what he described as the "clean amateur competition" of time-trialling, with no tactics, crowds or nationalistic rivalry as on the Continent. The socialist foundations of the Clarion CC interested only a small minority of the "racing lads"—though with some notable exceptions. The brothers Alex and Jack Taylor from Glasgow (the former a Scottish national champion) both declared their socialist commitment in 1939.

As Alex wrote:

> Our biggest asset lies in our being a working class organisation. When a rider competes in the Clarion name, the success of that rider reflects credit on the Clarion, and this indirectly helps the Clarion cause of socialism... The knowledge that he is riding for a principle...gives new energy to tired legs.

And his brother wrote that he was "proud to ride for the Clarion because I believe that the propagation of socialism should still be the main object of the club, especially in these days of crisis following crisis, when the weaknesses of our present capitalistic system are becoming so glaringly apparent".

It was in international competition, however, as part of the Workers' Sports movement that some Clarion cyclists gave expression to their club's socialist foundations. The most spectacular workers' sports events in the inter-war years were the Olympiads held in various European cities. A preliminary event took place in Prague in 1921, where the Clarion team won a trophy which is still in the club's possession. The first Workers' Olympiad proper was staged in Frankfurt in the summer of 1925 under the slogan "No more war". Britain's sole representatives were six Clarion cyclists who between them in various events took four second places and three third places. Two years later in Prague Clarion cyclists took the first four places in a mass-start road-race.

Divisions between the Labour Party and TUC on the one side, and the Communist Party on the other prevented the formation of a single Workers' Sports organisation in Britain. Two Clarion members were expelled from the club for competing in a Red Workers' Spartakiade in Moscow in 1928. Two years later the National Workers' Sports Association was set up, and a team including Clarion cyclists was sent to the 1931 second Workers' Olympiad in Vienna. Here Colin Copeland of Oldham Clarion won a gold medal in the 20 kilometre track event.

The Communist-dominated British Workers' Sports Federation organised an international sports festival at Dorchester in 1934 to mark the centenary of the Tolpuddle labourers' sentencing to transportation for their part in organising a farm workers' union. Cyclists and athletes came from Czechoslovakia, Belgium, Switzerland and Palestine, and the Clarion cyclists won two events.

The Workers' Olympiads were organised in opposition to the official international Olympic movement. As one Clarion member wrote about the Red Workers' Spartakiade, "Instead of competitors taking part as Englishmen or Frenchmen, Germans or Russians, they assemble as workers, and instead of the blatant challenges of various national anthems, the song which stirs the pulses of the socialist sportsmen and women is the Internationale."

At the Clarion CC's 1936 Easter Meet in Chester a 200-strong National Conference condemned the staging of the Olympic Games in Berlin that summer. The resolution declared that:

Fascist Germany, by racial discrimination and religious and political persecution, has aroused the horror and contempt of the sportsmen of the whole world. This conference calls for the transfer of the games to another capital, and refuses to participate in any games in Hitler's Germany.

In opposition to the Berlin Games a People's Olympiad was organised in Barcelona, with the aim of giving a "lead to youth to suppress fascism and war", but the start of the Civil War in Spain put a stop to the event. A number of Clarion cyclists who had travelled to Spain to take part joined the International Brigade, and two were killed in action.

The Third Workers' Olympiad took place in Antwerp in 1937. Once again Clarion cyclists joined the British Workers' Sports Association team, even though cycling's ruling body, the National Cyclists' Union, like the Amateur Athletics Association, threatened to expel anyone who took part in this "political event". Despite the threat, a three-man Clarion team came third in the 50 kilometre time-trial. In 1938, however, the NCU got their way when the Clarion cycling team, ready to travel to Rotterdam for what proved to be the last Workers' Olympiad, were forced to withdraw, or be banned from competition at home.

The British Workers' Sports Association resumed activities after the Second World War, but the international body to which they were affiliated became a victim of post-war politics when it refused demands from the Western sports organisations to exclude Communists. When the BWSA renewed its international affiliation the Labour Party and TUC withdrew their financial support and the association was wound up in 1960.

By this time the National Clarion Cycling Club was in decline, although it had benefited for a time after the war years from a renewed burst of interest in cycle touring and racing. Membership had reached over 6,000 again in 1949, but like other cycling organisations it suffered as a result of the dramatic increase in car ownership in the 1960s. It was only when a cycling revival began in the late 1970s that the steady fall in national membership was arrested. Today the membership is reckoned in the hundreds, but is rising again, as is the number of local sections.

From the late 1930s there had been attempts by some members

and sections to move the Clarion Cycling Club away from its commitment to socialism. These were renewed more strongly in the 1950s amid Cold War fears of "red" influence, and have continued to the present day. At the Easter Meets in 2004 and 2007 motions to remove the words "support for the principles of socialism" from the constitution were only narrowly defeated. Just as disturbing for members on the political left was the treatment of the national secretary elected in 2003, who succeeded in increasing membership by emphasising socialism in an effective publicity campaign. He was forced to resign from his position in 2006, and was subsequently expelled from the club. His successor said that the National Committee "does not want to spread the view that we are a socialist organisation". Meanwhile, a breakaway group has set up the National Clarion Cycling Club (1895), with the aim of maintaining the century-old dedication to socialist principles. They would echo the words of founding father Tom Groom, who wrote not long before his death in 1945:

> Of all the Clarion organisations...the Clarion Cycling Club alone remains fully alive. And so long as it keeps true to its objects: Mutual Aid, Good Fellowship, and the Propagation of the Principles of Socialism, it will have good cause and reason for keeping alive.

Chapter 23
PEDALLING DAYS[1]

Sylvia Pankhurst

I was 14 years of age and my sister, Christabel, two years older (1896), when we first joined the Manchester Clarion Cycling Club. For the next two years we rode with the club almost every Sunday. We knew, of course, all the Clarion people: Robert Blatchford "Nunquam," Montague Blatchford "Mont Blanc," "Dangle" A M Thompson and Edward Fay (the "Bounder") and the rest.

We read them weekly and saw them sometimes. Edward Fay's funny articles in the Clarion were too funny for me, for I was never amused by the jokes which make most people laugh, only by the funniest things which happened, as it were, by accident. But when the "Bounder" (Edward Fay) came to stay with us we all liked him tremendously. He had that lovable quality which makes one feel a man is an old friend when first one meets him. We were all very sad when he died.

Mrs Bennett, an active member of the Clarion Club, taught us to ride. The first time she led us into the main road I was surprised to find myself in collision with a pony and trap which met me from behind a furniture van. The pony's head struck me hard on the right arm and shoulder, and down I went with a bang. I saw stars. Mrs Bennett took me into a little shop in Handforth, where my spill occurred, and gave me a glass of lemonade with a beaten up egg in it, and I rode on, forgetting my bumps.

We had a host of friends in the club. Haylock, the captain, and almost every member of the club helped me at some time or other in mending my punctures—I was fearfully unlucky in that respect—and in pushing me up the last little bit of the steepest hills. As the youngest member of the club, I doubtless got special consideration, but everyone was kind to everyone in that genial company.

The "Clarionettes," as they called themselves, were merry people; their joyous cries of "Boots!" and "Spurs!" rang through the country lanes. Clarion slang was a fertile product, which amazed me, and which would certainly have shocked our father, who was a purist in the matter of speech, had we indulged it.

Socialists, as a rule, were very keen and strenuous in those days, and the road to socialism seemed by no means so long and difficult as it appears today, and most of the comrades, even the oldest, confidently expected to reach it in their own lifetime. The "Clarionettes" were much criticised by the ILP'ers [Independent Labour Party] and the BSP'ers [British Socialist Party] for not being sufficiently active and serious in socialist work. I have often heard the cyclists reply by telling of the good work they had done in the past in sticking little red gummed labels with appropriate mottoes on trees and fences wherever they rode. This activity was before my time, and I wished they would revert to it, being myself of strenuous mind.

Yet, though they held only very occasional meetings of any sort, and did little direct propaganda, the Clarion people carried a leaven of socialist conversation and argument into rural districts then wholly untouched by any Socialist or Labour propaganda. A copy or two of the *Clarion*, and perhaps some other literature, would generally be left behind.

Week in, week out, the Clarion clubs took hundreds of people of all ages away from the grime and ugliness of the manufacturing districts to the green loveliness of the country, giving them fresh air, exercise and good fellowship at a minimum of cost. The clubs promoted a frank, friendly comradeship among men and women, then very much less common than it is today.

When I see a pair of pink legs flash by on the back of someone else's motorcycle, I sometimes think that the owner of the pink legs is having a much less interesting journey than was ours on our humble "push bikes", noiseless, and under our own control. The miss of the pink legs cannot afford a motor-bicycle of her own in most cases, and the push bike doubtless seems to her too slow in these rapid days, but I think we had the best of it.

At our journey's end was always an enormous shilling tea, in which phenomenal quantities of bread and butter and tinned fruit rapidly disappeared, then a walk round, and frequently afterwards a brief "sing-song", sometimes joined by members of other clubs who had ridden that way. Jack Ramsden, I remember, was much admired at *Clarion* functions for his singing of the "Lowland Sea", and Harry Lowerison bubbled over with tales and songs.

One of the great events of those days was the camp at Pickmere in Cheshire, where *Clarion* people and other socialists spent a summer holiday in tents, and maintained relays of poor little children from the slums of Manchester and Salford—the Cinderella children, as Blatchford had named them.

A great factotum in the camp was "Billy de Bulwell"; his real name I have forgotten. De Bulwell was the nickname he assumed as a joke, because he had been born in Bulwell... He was ever ready with a bitter jest at the expense of the rich and aristocracy. He was kindness itself to the children and had the gift of making the naughty ones "good as gold".

"Chaise" was so called because the members of the club fancied in him a resemblance to a racing cyclist of that name. He was a great favourite, full of fun and antics and always willing to peel "spuds", wash "pots" or carry loads.

Many a puncture has he mended for me. It was pleasant when the campers sat on the grass in the evening taking turns to talk and tell tales. I remember old Mr Wadsworth telling us that as a young lad in dreary Salford he had become a socialist through studying butterflies; the loveliness of the insects had bred in him a desire for beauty also in the human world.

One of the women members who never rode, but helped with the children and the general work of the camp, was regarded, I think, by all with special affection. Tolerant, gentle and selfless, we knew that she was dying of consumption, but no word of complaining ever escaped her lips. She did not live long, but she outlived the most beautiful and popular girl in the club—one of those rare beings whose society everyone seeks. Behind her death was the common tragedy of pinching scarcity in a working class home where wages are small and life hard, as it was in those days even more than today.

The Handforth Clubhouse was an ambitious undertaking. We all looked forward to its achievement. My father took shares in it for us all. I have some of them somewhere to this day.

Before the clubhouse was established we had ceased to ride. My mother and Christabel went to Switzerland for a visit. During their absence my father was suddenly taken ill. He died before my mother could return. Christabel stayed in Switzerland for a year; for my life had become too serious and too anxious to leave time for cycling. That was the end of our membership of the Clarion Club, but afterwards, when I came to London, I wrote for some time a weekly article in the *Clarion*.

I ceased to write it only because the growing demands of our East London Federation of Suffragettes, editing its organ, *The Women's Dreadnought*, and the intermittent hunger strikes I had to endure under the "Cat and Mouse" Act at last made it impossible to fit in the *Clarion* article.

Part 5
People

Chapter 24
C L R JAMES: BEYOND CRICKET'S BOUNDARY

Christian Høgsbjerg

In a televised debate at Cambridge University Union one year on the proposition "That politics should not intrude upon sporting contacts", John Arlott replied—with characteristic erudition and humanism—that "Mr President sir, anyone who cares to support this motion will not exclude politics from sport but will in fact be attempting to exclude sport from life".[1] One who would have been to the fore in seconding Arlott in this debate was his great friend, the black Trinidadian Marxist historian C L R James (1901-89), author of among other works the seminal cultural history of West Indian cricket—and indeed cricket itself—*Beyond a Boundary* (1963).[2] As Chris Searle—a former young England cricketer and socialist activist—has eloquently noted, James "reaches three monumental purposes" in his "book of sport and book of life".

Firstly he identifies sport, one particular sport—cricket—as a vehicle of popular struggle, in his instance, of anti-imperialism, anti-racism and as an enemy of colonialism. He expresses cricket aesthetically, seeing the sport as a discourse of beauty and human culture. And finally and most importantly, he sees cricket as not simply a metaphor of life but as life itself, a way of approaching the challenges of being and living in the world. "How do men live?" he asks—or more exactly, "What do men live by?" Of course James was a man, largely speaking to other men, who played and loved a particular sport which bespoke a particular culture in a specific age. In these senses *Beyond a Boundary* may be criticised as limited, even ephemeral. Yet in its ability to connect a pursuit of leisure to the mainsprings of human life's essential progress, it is a book which has no equal.[3]

Today, as it marks its fiftieth anniversary, *Beyond a Boundary* is not only celebrated by connoisseurs of West Indian cricket but almost universally recognised as one of the finest works in cricket and sports literature.[4] Even such an unlikely figure as the former British Tory prime minister John Major has been forced to take register of how "the Marxist historian C L R James argued that, in the West Indies, cricket had a magic that was a guiding light for the dispossessed and the disenfranchised".[5] *Beyond a Boundary* was certainly a path-breaking discussion of the contradictory and complex relationship between colonialism and cricket, and how the quintessentially English game of cricket came to so profoundly shape the culture of the Caribbean.[6] Yet readers are rewarded with many rich variations on this and many other themes, including captivating biographical portraits of individual cricketers ranging from W G Grace to Garfield Sobers, thought-provoking digressions of the relationship of the birth of democracy in ancient Greece to the origins of tragic drama and the foundation of the Olympic Games, and of the parallels between these ancient Greek city states and the development of forms of mass politics and mass enthusiasm for popular sports in Victorian Britain. As a profoundly insightful and influential meditation on the aesthetics and history of cricket itself, *Beyond a Boundary* stands, as Stefan Collini once noted, as a "minor classic".

That unclassifiable work—part autobiography, part cricket history, part cultural meditation, part nationalist polemic—was remarkable for its strong sense of form, despite the apparent heterogeneity of its subject matter. A discussion of the ethical teaching of Dr Arnold, the Victorian headmaster, seemed to lead ineluctably into an argument for making Frank Worrell the first black man to captain the West Indian cricket team. It was a book by someone who was passionate about cricket, but who never lost sight of the truth that there were far more important things to be passionate about.[7]

The origins of *Beyond a Boundary* lie in James's growing awareness of the injustices of British imperial rule in Trinidad as they manifested themselves while he was busy playing, watching and reporting cricket while growing to intellectual maturity as a black colonial subject of the British Empire. "Cricket", James noted in *Beyond a Boundary* "had plunged me into politics long before I was aware of it. When I did turn to politics I did not have much to learn".[8] Given that all sections of Trinidadian society had cricket clubs that regularly played each other, from the "white and wealthy" Queen's Park to the "totally black and with no social status whatever" plebians' Stingo, it was easy to compare all the top players at close range.[9] James never failed to be shocked and outraged at continually seeing quality black players, like the Stingo player and docker Telemarque, who deserved inclusion in the West Indian national side, left out by openly ignorant and racist white selectors.[10] Moreover, the simple fact that both "white and wealthy" and "totally black" played cricket regularly against each other cast light on the totality of society. One moment both teams would be on the pitch, "playing with a straight bat", treating the other as equals and offering each other consolation ("bad luck") only to then return to all the old deference and racism in the pavilion. Given this, together with the colonial state's repression of overtly political activism—particularly after the mass dock workers strike that shook Port of Spain in late 1919—it is not surprising that some cricket matches took on immensely powerful symbolic significance, not least when the island's best "black" team, that of Shannon (with cricketers like Learie Constantine and Wilton St Hill), played Queen's Park.

James himself—as a former student turned schoolmaster at the elite Queen's Park College to which he had won a scholarship—played not for Shannon but used to open with Clifford Roach for the more middle class Maple. He later noted his decision not to join Shannon slightly delayed his intellectual and political identification with the cause of West Indian nationalism. Yet that the social antagonisms of race, class and power in this small Caribbean island implicitly played themselves out on the cricket pitch on a weekly basis meant that James always naturally felt he had the sense of seeing things whole. He later thought that a fully comprehensive and undivided vision was something that had been lost in the modern world and was last truly seen in the great English writer William Hazlitt, who wrote wonderfully about games and sports in early 19th century England, before the class conflicts of the industrial age became central to popular consciousness. James felt that early 20th century Caribbean society in some ways mirrored English society in the age of Hazlitt—the society that saw the creation of among other things the game of cricket.[11]

In 1932, ostensibly to help his friend and compatriot Learie Constantine (who had voyaged into imperial Britain in the 1920s to play professionally for Nelson in the Lancashire League) write his autobiography *Cricket and I* (1933), James himself made the move to the "mother country". Ross McKibbin notes that "sport was one of the most powerful of England's civil cultures", and James witnessed first hand cricket's popularity in the working class cotton textile town of Nelson, where thousands would turn out to watch league games.[12] James's outstandingly detailed knowledge of the game meant he soon secured a post as "the first West Indian, the first man of colour, to serve as cricket reporter for the [Manchester] Guardian", and indeed possibly the first black professional sports reporter in British history.[13] "It was a great feeling", James later recalled, "to sit beside the Times in the Number One seat allowed to the Manchester Guardian at Old Trafford," Lancashire's home cricket ground.[14] More crucially it also allowed him an opportunity to cast his gaze over a custom and practice that was not just arguably the "national game" in the imperial metropolis itself but since its "golden age" had become the game of English-speaking peoples across the empire. A dozen of some of James's finest articles for first the Manchester Guardian (1933-35) working with Neville Cardus and then the Glasgow Herald (1937-38) have been republished as part of a wider collection of his writing on his beloved game.[15]

As Andrew Smith, author of an important recent work, C L R James and the Study of Culture, notes, many of James's "central arguments" in Beyond a Boundary "are already discernible" in his early cricket writing, not least "his sense of the relationship between cricketing technique and a wider historical zeitgeist…and his passionate defence of the sport as art".[16] James's provocative and thought provoking comparison of the dramatic spectacle of cricket with "high art" was in keeping with the emerging tradition of cricket literature, and in keeping with Cardus's own philosophy. Yet as Smith notes, what always also distinguished James's analysis of cricket was "the fact that he understands it to be serious and significant because of, and not despite, its status as a popular activity".[17] Here the Marxism that James had embraced during the Great Depression as a result of his witnessing the rising threat of fascism in continental Europe first hand and his experience of reading Leon Trotsky's History of the Russian Revolution amidst the struggles of the English working class in Lancashire was arguably critical.

In 1925, in Where is Britain Going? Trotsky had suggested that any future "British Revolution" will "inevitably awaken in the English working class the most unusual passions, which have hitherto been so artificially held down and turned aside, with the aid of social training, the church, and the press, in the artificial channels of boxing, football, racing, and other sports".[18] Such an analysis of sport, stressing how the popularity of a sport like football or cricket was ultimately an expression of the intense alienation created by modern capitalist society both in and outside the workplace, an "artificial channel" into which the "unusual passions" of the British working class were "turned aside," was of course far more sophisticated than the position the official Communist movement was to take subsequently.[19] Yet for James, as we have seen, cricket in both colonial Trinidad and imperial Britain was not merely a diverting dramatic spectacle but part of the popular culture of society that Marxists could not dismiss lightly. As Smith notes, while James's "reading of cricket is irreducibly historical it operates only on the basis of a careful reading of the forms of cricket itself...he insisted that anyone seeking to understand the game in social terms had first to understand the game in its own terms".[20] Few of James's new found comrades in the tiny British Trotskyist movement seemed overly impressed by his cricket writing, so much of which was apparently obsessed with the particular styles and favourite strokes of individual players and so on, without appreciating how after attending to the specific intricacies James was then able to rise from the concrete to the general. Apparently James and Trotsky discussed cricket when they met in Coyoacán, Mexico, in 1939, and in *Beyond a Boundary* James—who would later break with orthodox Trotskyism to form his own independent Marxist current— made his disagreement with Trotsky on the "sport question" explicit: "Trotsky had said that the workers were deflected from politics by sports. With my past I simply could not accept that. I was British..."[21]

In a 1963 letter to his friend and fellow West Indian writer V S Naipaul, James confided that "I believe that, originating as we are within the British structure, but living under such different social conditions, we have a lot to say about the British civilisation itself which we see more clearly than themselves".[22] James more than justified such a statement with the publication that year of *Beyond a Boundary*, his magnum opus on "British civilisation", which came out amid the tumult of decolonisation, the decline and fall of the British Empire and the rising newly independent black nations, particularly in the Caribbean.[23] As Stuart Hall reminds us:

> James often remarked that the British said that the empire was won on the playing fields of Eton and would be lost on the playing fields of Lord's cricket ground. Just as the British had trained themselves to

create the empire on the playing fields, so on the playing fields they would symbolically lose the empire.

Moreover, because for James "it was the new drawing together of the energies of the Caribbean people that created the cricket team of the 1950s and allowed Worrell to play with grace", *Beyond a Boundary* "had a profound and imaginative anti-imperialist message".[24] If at the height of British imperial domination over a quarter of the world in 1891 the imperial poet Rudyard Kipling had famously asked, "What should they know of England who only England know?", now amidst decolonisation James stressed the wider, implicitly political, significance and symbolism of the rise of the great West Indies cricket team of "the three Ws"—Frank Worrell, Clyde Walcott and Everton Weekes—to their rightful place in the sun. As he famously declared in the preface of *Beyond a Boundary*, "This book is neither cricket reminiscences nor autobiography. It poses the question *What do they know of cricket who only cricket know?*"[25]

Overall, James certainly deserves to be remembered as "cricket's philosopher king", and it should not be forgotten that it was not only his West Indian background and experience in England but also his highly cultured Marxism that was critical for his profound understanding of sport, life and politics.[26] Indeed, Neil Lazarus has gone so far as to suggest that "in his writings about cricket, James reveals himself to be one of the truly decisive Marxist cultural theorists" of the 20th century, a figure comparable with Georg Lukács.[27] The last words might, however, go to John Arlott, who thought *Beyond a Boundary* "arguably the best book ever written about cricket", noting that "it is not only a warm and human book, but the most profound and searching discussion ever propounded on the game, if only for the reason that the writer was the most erudite, intellectual and also humanly perceptive person who ever devoted himself to its study".[28]

Chapter 25
TEST MATCH RÉSUMÉ[1]

C L R James

One of the Greatest Matches in Game's History; The Like of McCabe's Innings May Never Again be Seen; The Crowd Had An Honour All Its Own

This Trent Bridge Test has been one of the great matches in the history of the game. Australia escaped defeat, and once again Bradman saved his side—though not by a double century. At teatime on Tuesday, when he had 118 and the score was 361 for four, Australia were safe, and only then.

McCabe's innings has been lauded in prose and will doubtless be celebrated in verse. All the circumstances taken into consideration, it is the greatest piece of cricket I have ever seen or heard of, nor do I expect to see anything comparable for many years to come.

It dragged Australia from the abyss by the hair. Brown played two priceless innings, quiet and sound as a great castle. But after lunch on the last day Brown got out to Verity; McCabe followed suit. Then Hassett was caught off a ball that jumped a foot, and Badcock narrowly escaped the same fate. Despite McCabe and Brown, the match was in danger.

Duel of Duels

Only then did it become fully apparent what was happening between Verity and Bradman at the pavilion end of the wicket. Bradman was not at his best. Very rarely did he flash out a stroke. But he held his bat tight and defended with all his will and technique. Verity bowled sometimes to a rough patch whence the ball cannoned to the pads, but every now and then into a spot on the off stump or thereabouts.

And Bradman dug himself into the ground and held on for dear life. Had he gone anytime up to half an hour before tea Australia would have been in the toils. Fortune was with him, and it is probable that he will remember Tuesday between eleven-thirty and four-thirty as the most trying few hours he has ever experienced at the wicket.

Immediately after tea Wright fizzed a few balls from the breaking wicket, morally bowling Badcock twice before he shattered his stumps, and once more pulling Bradman out and leaving him there. England's moral superiority has lasted all through.

The Chosen Elevens

Both teams were badly chosen on the first day. Bradman may have been influenced by the probability of rain, but he may well have omitted Waite with his tongue in his cheek. I doubt very much if he will do it again under similar circumstances. O'Reilly, opening with the new ball, showed that Bradman does not think McCabe is really an opening bowler. McCabe did his share but a length bowler of some pace was badly needed, and Waite would just have filled the bill.

McCormick has to be very carefully nursed, but he is a good bowler, much, much better than Wall, who rendered devoted but pedestrian service in 1934. McCormick bowled Barnett with a very good ball; it had pace, lift, and something from the off. Such a ball can bowl out most batsmen at any time. We have not seen the best of McCormick, and he will take some playing on the Lord's wicket.

O'Reilly and Fleetwood-Smith we know. On that heart-breaking wicket at the start of the game they probably tried to spin the ball too much in a vain effort to get something from the unyielding turf. That and Barnett, confident but unsparing, rather broke them up. They still remain, however, the most dangerous pair of bowlers in the country. But there is one great difference. The English batsmen can face them with a new confidence. That almost visible domination that Grimmett and O'Reilly used to exercise should be beyond the reach of these two for the rest of the series. They should not be allowed to restore it.

Ward on a good wicket is a very useful bowler—no less but no more. Barnett, behind the stumps, had some strange lapses, but these were most likely incidental, and he seems a wicket keeper of the highest class. Bradman's captaincy was competent with no flashes of inspiration. When in difficulty he almost automatically tossed the ball to either O'Reilly or Fleetwood-Smith; when in great difficulty he put on both.

England in the Field

Hammond made much the same miscalculation as Bradman, and we shall probably see another fast bowler besides Farnes in the team next time unless the match begins in a downpour.

Hammond as opening bowler was simply not good enough. He bowled a good length, but the Australians played him too easily. Farnes needed better support than that at the start. Proof of this is seen in the fact that Edrich's fast bowling did valuable service. He broke the opening partnership in the second innings which gave England a chance: and later in the innings had the new ball which he used very well. Farnes bowled splendidly all through. McCabe hit him about a bit, but at a time when everybody was getting blows. Farnes never bowled short, attacked the wicket all through, and on

Monday, when the wicket gave him one or two spots clean beat Bradman two or three times in 10 minutes, besides making him play the new ball almost into short-leg's hands.

Wright bowled some of the most dangerous balls in the match. At some time or other he whipped past the bat of every batsman. Taking his bowling on the whole, he was not at all as loose as one had been led to expect, or as so many of his type who have real spin usually are.

That "Spot"

Used as Hammond used him he is a discovery. Verity returned to his best form and did a noble piece of bowling. When the ball landed in the spot it beat everything, bat, wicket-keeper, and sometimes slip. It was treated as a spot on the cheek of a beautiful woman. The batsmen patted it tenderly, Brown went behind the wicket, bent down, and had a long squint at it to see exactly where it was in relation to the stumps, while Verity searched perseveringly for it through some long and accurate spells. It held Bradman watchful as a mouse for hours. Once he jumped into Verity like a tiger, and drove fiercely with the obvious intention of distracting him from his aim. But the stroke did not come off, and Bradman retired into the cat and mouse game.

Sinfield seemed particularly easy to Brown, and he was probably helped by the tension of the situation. If the England bowling was not quite as good as it might seem when Australia was collapsing, it was much better than Australia's second innings score of over 300 for two might make it appear.

In the crucial sessions before lunch and after on Tuesday England had no luck at all. With no unusual good fortune two of three quick wickets might easily have fallen. The fielding was always good, Wright at short-leg and Hutton in the long-field doing many fine things. Hammond led the side with confidence and skill. His bowling changes were frequent, and he displayed a nice appreciation of a batsman's psychology in all his bowling changes and his placings of the field.

When McCabe was banging the bowling about there loomed a horrible prospect of some future Test on a good wicket. Bradman at one end, McCabe at the other, both using all their strokes. But sufficient unto the day... England had a long and wearisome task, and stood up well to it.

The Crowd Militant

The crowd refused to practise non-intervention, and those who study mass psychology should have been present at Trent Bridge.

On Friday and Saturday when England battered the Australians and then got them out the crowd went from delirium to delirium. It saw a catch in every bumped ball from an Australian bat and an lbw [leg before wicket] every time the ball touched an Australian pad. It heaved deep sides of regret when these baseless expectations bore no fruit. It punctuated with howls of glee the quick dismissal of the Australians on Monday, the superb stroke play and courage of McCabe giving a relish to the feast. But as McCabe manoeuvred Fleetwood-Smith from harm's way and smote his gallant way to the second century the crowd entered into the spirit of the thing and cheered each successful evasion almost, but not quite, as if England were saving the game.

It barracked when Fingleton and Brown were playing slowly, and there is no valid reason why a crowd should not barrack when it wants to. You cannot treat 30,000 people at a match as if they are children in a kindergarten. The barracking was unintelligent. But Fingleton and Brown made an appeal against the light at half-past five, reason for which was invisible to mortal eyes except theirs. When Chester approached Emmott Robinson to consult him, that sturdy Yorkshireman signified his negative when still a yard from Chester. He refused, so to speak, to discuss the matter, and the crowd was quick to see it. When it barracked as the bowler was going up to bowl it was interfering with the game, and Fingleton was quite within his rights to refuse to go on until the interruption had stopped.

Honours to the 10,000

But the crowd reasserted itself before the end of the day, and carried off all the honours. The occasion for this splendour was the dismissal of Fingleton. The greatest catch in the game, a long stretching left-handed effort at first slip sent back Fingleton, and the time was a quarter past six. Would Bradman come? He means everything to the Australian side, and I would wager that more than one of his men must have offered to go instead. "He would be a fool to come", whispered a wise and experienced critic at my side. And then in the gathering darkness came the Australian captain, striding down the pavilion steps as jauntily as ever, and never so much the "Don" as in this brave gesture.

Practically the whole ground stood up and greeted him with roars and roars of applause that lasted almost all the way. The barrackers appreciated his courage, and wanted him to let him know also that the little unpleasantness with Fingleton was merely an interlude. It was the biggest moment of a game which had many, and if only a crowd could be as unintelligent as to barrack Fingleton and Brown when they were saving the game, what else but a crowd could so spontaneously and generously lift up all hearts and justify humanity?

Chapter 26
ARTHUR WHARTON: AIRBRUSHED FROM HISTORY
Phil Turner

He was the world's first black professional footballer, who ended up a miner at the time of the 1926 General Strike. Possessed of astonishing skills in more than one area of sporting life, Arthur Wharton was not only a talented goalkeeper for the likes of Preston North End, Sheffield United and Rotherham United, but an amazing athlete and fighter against racism. He was the first 100 yards world record holder, covering the distance in ten seconds in 1886 wearing pigskin shoes on a shingle track.

But after battling against racism all his life he died in poverty in 1930 aged 65 and was buried in a pauper's grave.

Family and drink problems seem to have contributed to his retirement from sport aged 36. He then worked as a haulage worker at Yorkshire Main Colliery in Edlington near Rotherham where he was a member of the Miners' Federation of Great Britain, forerunner to the National Union of Mineworkers.

Arthur, who played in charity matches long before the PR machine proffered newspaper headlines in exchange, never shied away from a fight. Phil Vasili, his biographer,[1] said:

> At an athletics meet he was lying down in a marquee on a rolled up carpet out of view when he overheard a couple of his competitors complaining about having to run against a n....r. Arthur jumped up and said: "If you two gentlemen do not wish to race me you can always box me."

The two declined the offer.

But Arthur also faced racism at football matches. As Vasili notes:

Often at football matches he was singled out for special treatment and came in for a lot of abuse from the crowd more than others on the field and you get an impression that was due to his colour.

It is recorded that he was beaten with umbrellas when he left the field in one match. It was a rough game and there was more violence on the field than today but it does seem he came in for hard treatment...[and he] was often referred to as "Darkie" Wharton both in the press and by the crowds.

Arthur would almost certainly have been on strike in 1926. Phil Vasili went on:

What is known is that he was a member of the miners' federation and although there is nothing to establish he took part, there is no evidence that he was a scab, which would have been documented in such a strong mining area.

He was also involved in a pay dispute while at Stockport and Rotherham and he was always quite active in standing up for his rights and it can be assumed that continued in his working life outside of football.

He definitely had a sense of his own worth.

Wharton was clearly a showman, popular with team-mates and loved by fans, as this report from the Sheffield Telegraph and Independent, 12 January 1942, shows:

In a match between Rotherham and Sheffield Wednesday at Olive Grove I saw Wharton jump, take hold of the cross bar, catch the ball between his legs and cause three onrushing forwards...to fall into the net. I have never seen a similar save since and I have been watching football for over 50 years.

But for a long time his story was never told. Former Manchester United and Nottingham Forest star Viv Anderson said of him:

When I saw the exhibition on him at the National Football Museum I was totally flabbergasted. I couldn't believe he's barely heard of today after achieving so much. And you'd think I'd be one of the first to know about him. There's a connection between us that will never be broken. He was the first black professional and I was the first to win a full cap. I'm honoured to be associated with him. Arthur's story is an important part of that English football culture, and he should be more celebrated.[2]

Rotherham Town was the first club to have a fully-professional black player on their books when Arthur signed in 1889 from Preston North End. The club was a founder member of the Midland League, which it won twice in four years before being elected to the Second Division in 1893. His career lasted about 16 years and also included spells at Sheffield United and Stockport County, during which period he won the unofficial title of "the best goalkeeper in the north". Mind you, such were the wages that to supplement his club income Arthur ran two Rotherham pubs. Shaun Campbell, who set up the Arthur Wharton Foundation, said about him:

> The man was a phenomenon. The ironic thing is, back then you needed to be tough and of strong character of mind to be in goal. You could be harassed, harangued, bullied, hustled off the ball. Often the on-rushing forwards would barge into the goalkeeper so team-mates could score, and that was legal in the day.

But because no one could catch him, Arthur would run up the pitch and get two or three goals himself.

According to the foundation website, Arthur was born on 28 October 1865 in Jamestown on the Gold Coast, which is now known as Accra, Ghana, West Africa. His father was Henry Wharton, a Methodist minister who was half-Grenadian and half-Scottish, while his mother, Annie Florence Egyriba, was a Ghanaian princess. Arthur was sent to England by his father to be trained as a missionary teacher. But his talent between the posts and speed on the athletics track were first spotted when he was at college near Darlington. He also went on to play professional cricket, both codes of rugby and he cycled.

Shocking as it seems today, newspaper coverage casually referred to him as "nigger" or "darkie". Though many called for Arthur to play football for England, racism in the sport meant it would be almost a century before Viv Anderson became the first black player on the England squad in 1978.

Arthur became a working class hero in northern England. Though he had every intention of following in his father's footsteps when he arrived, aged just 19, in 1882 at Cleveland College, Durham, studying soon came second to his sporting prowess. Arthur's football skills came to the notice of Darlington Football Club. As a result he was selected to play as goalkeeper in a professional capacity.

He was also a brilliant professional cricketer, playing for teams in Yorkshire and Lancashire. In cycling he set a record time in 1887 for riding between Preston and Blackburn. He also enjoyed rugby.

Selected to play for Newcastle and District Team in 1885-86 Arthur soon became a favourite with the north east fans. He often entertained the crowds by crouching in the corner of the goal area, only saving the ball at the last minute, or doing pull-ups on the cross-bars and catching the ball between his knees.

In 1886 Arthur moved to Preston North End—then the giants of football—where he played in the FA Cup semi-final of 1887. Arthur went on to play for Rotherham Town, Sheffield United, Stalybridge Rovers and Ashton Northend. His career came to an end at Stockport County in the Second Division in 1901-2.

The racism Arthur faced in his sporting life is at the heart of explaining why he was airbrushed out of history. Quite simply he has been written out of football's history because he was black.

But Arthur was also a victim of society's hypocrisy over its moral values when a relationship while married to his first wife contributed to his fall from grace. Rotherham-born Sheila Leeson discovered that Arthur had been married to her grandmother's sister. Arthur had a relationship with Sheila's grandmother and she bore him three children, one of whom was Sheila's mother.

Sheila's grandmother was banished by her family, but Sheila has been to Ghana and discovered Arthur's huge family and visited her great grandfather's church and Arthur's school.

Sixty seven years after his death Arthur's unmarked grave in Edlington has been fully restored thanks to the Sheffield United based project Football Unites—Racism Divides and author Phil Vasili.

Several other projects have now recognised Arthur's place in history.

The Arthur Wharton Foundation aims include:

● The promotion of cultural understanding and enhanced relations between different racial groups through educational and awareness-raising programmes;

- The development of a range of events and activities, including tournaments, to foster understanding between people from diverse backgrounds;
- The ongoing raising of funds to help to ensure that young people from all backgrounds and cultures have access to the equipment and facilities which will enable them to develop their own sporting skills and talents.

The anti-racist organisation Kick It Out has created an exhibition for use by schools, youth clubs and similar organisations called Pioneers, Past Masters and Future Challenges. It features Arthur Wharton among its celebration of black and Asian football players.

In 2003 Arthur Wharton was inducted into the National Football Museum's Hall of Fame.

Chapter 27
"SPORT IS PART OF OUR RESISTANCE": MAHMOUD SARSAK, PALESTINE'S HUNGER STRIKING FOOTBALLER.

Estelle Cooch

On 16 November 2012 during the onslaught on Gaza, Israeli fighter jets chose to bombard the 10,000-seat Palestine football stadium that lies at the heart of Gaza City. I use the word "chose" because the bombing was no accident. It was a meticulously planned premeditated attack. Little remained. Photos show plastic seats strewn across cracked slabs of concrete. And in the middle of a previously patchy grass pitch there now lies a crater about 40 metres in diameter.

Considering the deaths of 162 Palestinians, a third of them children, in the eight days of Operation Pillar of Defence it could seem odd to particularly identify the destruction of a football stadium.

The crimes of the Israeli state are better known today than perhaps ever before. Global opinion polls on Israel continue to place it as one of the most negatively viewed countries in the world and have worsened considerably from 2011 to 2012.[1] As the Arab Spring deepens, borders that have been secure for decades are suddenly in flux.

At the time of writing Jordan is witnessing its largest ever strikes against the regime of King Abdullah II and protests against President Morsi in Egypt are ongoing.

Why then in an ever hostile regional context did Israel choose to open fire on a football stadium? If it was not a mistake, is it not just a trivial, almost banal, act of violence?

Far from it. For Palestinians living under occupation football is not just another pastime. Alongside basketball it is the most popular sport in the Occupied Territories. Palestine has the oldest history of organised football in the Middle East with its introduction during the British mandate and the gradual expansion of teams and leagues throughout the 1920s. The legendary Palestinian footballer Jabra Al-Zarqa refused an offer to play for Arsenal in the 1940s, instead fleeing his home in Haifa with the creation of Israel and winning the pan-Arab games in Beirut in 1957. In short, Palestinian football has a long history tied up with the struggle for justice.

The current Palestine Football Association (PFA), encompassing 259 separate clubs, was recognised by FIFA in 1998 following the creation of the Palestinian Authority (PA).

For Israel, therefore, the suppression of Palestinian sport is not a peripheral issue. It is central to the suppression of the Palestinian people.

It was in this context that the struggle of Mahmoud Sarsak, a Palestinian footballer who went on hunger strike in early 2012, became a rallying point across the globe.

In his own words:

> Resistance isn't only about armed struggle... Resistance can be through pen, brush, voice, and sport. We are all freedom fighters, but each of us has his or her own weapon. Sport is a form of non-violent resistance... Being a representative of Palestine's national football team makes me a threat to Israel.[2]

In this short piece I want to consider three things: the first is the struggle of Sarsak himself and its wider significance; the second the role of sport within Israel in reinforcing racism; and finally the role historically of the sports boycott.

Prior to 2000 the Palestinian football league attracted significant crowds to their matches. Games between Nablus, Tulkarem and Amari would easily draw over 5,000 people. The standard of the football was improving and some players managed to work their way into some of the Middle East's more prestigious leagues. All this changed with the outbreak of the Second Intifada in 2000 and the subsequent Israeli crackdown.[3]

Since that point travel restrictions have been ratcheted up and checkpoints across the West Bank have increased exponentially. According to a UN report in September 2011 there were 522 checkpoints in the West Bank and an additional 495 "ad hoc 'flying' checkpoints".[4]

Under such circumstances the very existence of the Palestinian football team seems to be a miracle.

Although most players for the team are drawn from the diaspora, in November 2007 all players based in the West Bank and Gaza were denied visas to participate in Palestine's qualifying match for the 2010 World Cup, forcing them to leave the competition.

Sports equipment donated by FIFA is routinely denied, Palestinians who play in the Israeli league are banned from transfers and the Israeli authorities regularly intervene internationally to prevent matches taking place.[5]

In addition to these obstacles, life under occupation entails the constant threat of detention or even death. Four professional footballers were among the 1,400 Palestinians killed during the Israeli assault on Gaza in 2008-9.

It was as part of this clampdown that the 22 year old Mahmoud Sarsak was arrested in July 2009 at the Gaza border. He had complete travel approval and was on the way to his new club in Balata. Sarsak was consequently held for three years without trial, without any charge and with no contact with his family.

And then on 19 March 2012 Sarsak stopped eating. By doing so he joined 1,800 other Palestinian prisoners, just under half of all those imprisoned in Israeli jails.

The impact of one of the largest coordinated hunger strikes ever reverberated around the world.

On 3 May the New York Times declared, "The newest heroes of the Palestinian cause are not burly young men hurling stones or wielding weapons. They are gaunt adults, wrists in chains, starving themselves in Israeli prisons".[6]

On 14 May 2012 Sarsak refused a deal accepted by other prisoners that would have ended his hunger strike, but seen him exiled to Norway for three months. Instead he demanded full prisoner of war status. By this time he had lost half of his original body weight.

On 8 June FIFpro, an international union of 50,000 professional football players, called for Sarsak's release and the pressure began to mount. Most significant was the myriad of sports stars coming forwards, not previously associated with the struggle for Palestinian justice. Eric Cantona, former West Ham player Frédéric Kanouté, head of UEFA Michel Platini and, incredibly, on 12 June the notoriously inept FIFA chief Sepp Blatter, all called for Sarsak's release.

Finally on 18 June, after 90 days of refusing food, Sarsak ended his hunger strike and on 10 July was released entirely and without any charge.

Hunger striking by Palestinian prisoners is not a new tactic. It was first used in Nablus in 1968 and has been repeated at least 15 times since, with three men striking to their deaths. In 2004 virtually all of the Palestinians held in Israeli prisons took part in a two-week strike, and the most ever was 11,000 prisoners in 1992.

Hunger strikes can often seem like a tactic of last resort, unless we fully understand the dynamics within Israeli jails themselves. In an interview in *Socialist Review* (July/August 2013) Mahmoud Sarsak described the contradictions within the prison system as follows:

> Supposedly, prisons are there to alter peoples behaviour and send them back out into society, but in Israel prisons are there simply to kill Palestinians. Israel uses the prison as a tool to crush people politically, ideologically, intellectually and socially. But with the resilience of the Palestinian people prison has become an academy—a university almost. It is a place where Palestinians discuss and debate different topics from what is happening on the news to the dynamics of Palestinian society to the politics of the Arab Spring. There is a strong emphasis on reading, writing and having meeting groups. So even in prison it is a continuous process of resistance. When new people come in we made an effort to encourage them to study, to develop themselves, to be teachers and to go in to academia. We have turned prison into the opposite of what Israel wants it to be.

The image we get of prison as a university helps to explain why Sarsak's campaign became such a watershed—and why personally he was able to survive it. The growing coordinated movement within Israeli jails has created an explosive situation.

Of course the novelty was not that Sarsak was imprisoned. The novelty was that he was a professional footballer who had survived 90 days without food.

To put this into perspective, the hunger strikes of Irish political prisoners in the early 1980s led to the deaths of ten prisoners between 46 and 73 days. The death of the first prisoner, Bobby Sands, after 66 days was a global scandal.

Had Sarsak died it is difficult to say what would have happened. The outrage would have provoked unpredictable protests from below and crises at the top. But why would one Palestinian be able to win such concessions from Israel?

To understand why Sarsak's death would have posed such a threat we have to look to the role that sport plays within the maintenance of the apartheid regime.

The 91st minute

Football in Israel is an ideological battleground. Despite being almost entirely Jewish the Israeli team was established during the British mandate and operated under the name Palestine—a fact worth reminding those who deny Palestine has ever existed. Its first international match saw it lose to Egypt 7-1 and it has only ever qualified for the World Cup once, in 1970. Lack of obvious success in the sporting field does not sit well with Israeli claims of superiority.

According to academic Tamir Sorek football plays a far more pernicious role than first meets the eye. What is more important than the match itself is what Sorek calls the "91st minute effect", in other words what the completion of the match represents.

The very existence of a flourishing and active Israeli league reminds Palestinians of the troubles of their own. Every match becomes part of "forging and flaunting national loyalties".[7]

As Sorek concludes, "The potential to present sports as an apolitical sphere can actually assist the rulers in using it as a political tool".[8]

Because this is the case there is a thin line between sport and violence.

In March 2012 following a defeat hundreds of Beitar Jerusalem supporters assaulted Arab cleaners in a major shopping centre in one of Jerusalem's biggest-ever ethnic clashes. A team leader for the cleaning company described it as a "mass lynching attempt".[9] No arrests were made. In this instance the "91st minute effect" had brutal consequences.

Founded in the 1940s by members of the right wing Irgun

terrorist organisation, Beitar Jerusalem is a useful model for studying the real role of sport in Israel.[10] Anti-Arab chants ring out from the stands, players extol the uniqueness of "Israeli blood" and in its 75-year history no Arab has ever been a member of the team.

The parallels with apartheid South Africa are striking. In studies of the apartheid rugby team, the Springboks, activists pointed out the use of sport "as a crucial arena of white self-esteem".[11]

The fact that qualification for the national side can only come from birth or citizenship makes the centrality of biology even more explicit. Recent attempts to reduce the numbers of Palestinians with Israeli citizenship would seem to confirm reports of a growing and virulently racist right wing within the Israeli mainstream.[12]

This racism is not complicated, nuanced, or just the result of a protracted conflict as Western media outlets would have us believe. The massacres in Gaza, the occupation and the apartheid wall are not anomalies of Israeli policy. They are at the heart of everything Israel is and has always been. As Egyptian revolutionary Gigi Ibrahim put it, "For Israel to exist Palestinians must die".[13]

It is no coincidence that Moshe Nissim, the driver who bulldozed hundreds of houses in the Jenin refugee camp in April 2002, planted a large flag of Beitar Jerusalem atop his bulldozer before beginning his "work".[14] One of his team's most popular chants is "Bulldoze the village".

Sports boycott

On 29 November 2012 a group of professional footballers released the first coordinated statement effectively calling for a sports boycott of Israel. The statement roundly condemned the Israeli assault on Gaza and denounced UEFA for "rewarding" Israel with hosting the under-21s UEFA cup in 2013. The statement was signed by five famous players of premier league team Newcastle United, former premier league players Didier Drogba and Frédéric Kanouté, and many others.[15]

While the boycott, divestment and sanctions (BDS) movement has experienced major victories since its launch in 2005, it has yet to fully make inroads into the world of sport. Its most recent campaign, Red Card Israeli Racism, looks likely to change that.[16]

Since his release Sarsak has been active in pushing for BDS. His refusal to attend "el Clasico", Barcelona versus Real Madrid, because of the presence of Israeli soldier Gilad Shalit gained much publicity.[17] Since satellite television brought La Liga into most homes the camps are awash with strips adorned with the names of Messi or Ronaldo. Considering one of the main sporting divisions in Palestine is between those whose allegiances are to either Barcelona (the majority) or Real (a sizable minority) Sarsak's refusal to attend was an important one.

The most successful anti-racist sporting initiative to date, the sports boycott of South Africa, proved that sport claiming to represent a nation, while denying rights to the majority, rests on shaky foundations

Sports matches can become constant reminders of the "enemy within". Throughout the 1970s and 1980s black South Africans packed into stadiums to cheer the opponents of the Springboks, prompting one city, Bloemfontein, to ban all black spectators.[18] Sport was, in the words of JM Coetzee, "the opium of the white masses" and as soon as they were unable to get their fix their opinions of apartheid started to shift dramatically.[19]

In a 1977 survey white South Africans ranked the lack of international sport as one of the three most damaging consequences of apartheid—needless to say black South Africans had many other grievances.[20]

In the months and years that are to come, those who struggle for justice in Palestine will confront two changing factors. The first is the increasing isolation of Israel itself which will feed into even more reckless, racist and destructive policy. The second is the ongoing Arab uprisings which offer an alternative solution to the Palestinian Authority's past record of concession. The struggle may be a long one, with detours and interruptions. But just as apartheid South Africa collapsed so will apartheid Israel.

The writer and socialist George Orwell famously wrote, "Serious sport has nothing to do with fair play. It is bound up with hatred, jealousy, boastfulness, disregard of all rules and sadistic pleasure in witnessing violence: in other words it is war minus the shooting".[21]

He is, of course, wrong. Often sport is war—and with shooting. And when that comes to be the case we should shout from the rooftops the slogan that brought the edifice of apartheid South Africa tumbling to its knees. Then, just as now, there must be "no normal sport in an abnormal society".

Chapter 28
AN ANTI-RACIST OLYMPIC REBEL: DAMIEN HOOPER[1]
Dave Zirin

Everywhere the fist-raising 1968 Olympic protester John Carlos speaks, he always remembers with respect the silver medallist on that platform, the great Australian sprinter Peter Norman.

On that fateful day Norman wore a patch in solidarity with gold medal winner Tommie Smith and Carlos, and he paid a terrible price upon returning home. Even though Norman was white, or maybe because Norman was white, he became a pariah for daring to stand up for human rights.

As Carlos says, "Never forget that there was a time that Australia was as bad as South Africa in terms of its racial policies." He's right. At the time there were laws explicitly aimed to dehumanise the indigenous Australian—often referred to as the Aboriginal—population.

Today it's still the third rail of Australian politics to claim pride and solidarity with the nation's indigenous people. Damien Hooper is finding this out the hard way. Hooper is an Olympic boxer making major waves both in and out of the ring. The light heavyweight is now a threat to win gold after dispatching highly touted US boxer Marcus Browne.[2]

He's also threatened with being sent home by the Australian Olympic Committee. Before fighting Browne the 20 year old's ring attire included a black T-shirt emblazoned with the Aboriginal flag. Hooper, who is of indigenous ancestry, knew that he was breaking the Olympics "no politics" rule, which states that you can represent only your country or approved corporate sponsors. (Worth noting that these corporate sponsors include politically neutral entities like Dow Chemicals, British Petroleum and McDonald's.)

After the bout Hooper had no regrets, saying:

> What do you reckon? I'm Aboriginal. I'm representing my culture, not only my country but all my people as well. That's what I wanted to do and I'm happy I did it. I was just thinking about my family and that's what really matters to me. Look what it just did—it just made my whole performance a lot better with that whole support behind me. I'm not saying that at all that I don't care [about a possible sanction]. I'm just saying that I'm very proud of what I did.

The next day the International Olympic Committee told the Australian Olympic Committee that they had better deal with Hooper or face the consequences. Practice for the team was halted in a very public fashion and Hooper was called in to meet with Australian Olympic chief Nick Green.

Green emerged from the meeting to inform the media that the boxer had "looked him in the eye" and was "extremely apologetic... He has learned a lesson and he will not do it again."

But what lesson is being learned? What is being taught not only to Hooper but also to Australia? The Aboriginal flag is recognised as an official Australian flag, but it's not recognised by the International Olympic Committee. The IOC is doing nothing less than asserting its sovereignty over the Australian team, and this is drawing peals of protest at home

A former world champion, the Australian/Aboriginal boxer Anthony Mundine, told the *Sydney Morning Herald* that Hooper "did the right thing".

"I take my hat off to him for that stance," Mundine said. "It takes a person with big balls to make a big stance like that. I've got his back, all day every day, because he's in the right."

Phil Cleary, an Australian politician and activist, said, "Unlike the imperial flags draped around tearful young athletes, the indigenous flag has no history of occupation of foreign territories. Sadly, it's the representation of stateless people, a people about whose history we dare not speak. Banning this flag is so pathetic it's funny."

The National Congress of Australia's First Peoples has also thrown its support behind Hooper "for being proud of who he is and where he came from".

The Congress recalled that Australian 400-metre gold-medallist Cathy Freeman held both flags following her victory at the 2000 Games in Sydney. Jody Broun, co-chair of the Congress, said, "I'm not aware of any formal action by any Olympic body when images of Cathy Freeman were beamed around the world after her 400-metre gold medal win. Those images gave an immeasurable boost to Aboriginal people and told the next generation it is possible for them to also be the best in the world."

The degradation of Damien Hooper[3] sends a very different message, one in line with what Peter Norman was forced to suffer in 1968. As Mark Twain said, "History doesn't repeat itself. But it does rhyme."

Chapter 29

"CARRIERS OF THE DREAM":[1]
TENNIS RADICALS OF THE 1960S AND 1970S

Pete Marsden and Rita Gough

Conservative, conventional and conformist would be accurate labels to ascribe to tennis in the mid-20th century. Yet even this sport, particularly so in the United States, was impacted upon by the civil rights movements and the wider political events of the 1960s and 1970s.

Progressive individuals such as Arthur Ashe, the first black male of African descent to win a grand slam title, and Billie Jean King, winner of 39 grand slam tournaments, respectively took stands against the South African apartheid regime and fought for women's rights. Both ruptured the hermetically sealed sphere of tennis, allowing into this most cosseted arena of sport the events of the outside world of apartheid, the Vietnam War, the Prague Spring, Stonewall and the Women's Liberation Movement.

Even this "lily white" sport became a radical arena because of the brave stand of some of its players and progressive dissenters, who used the world of sport as a platform to advance ideas of resistance and equality for blacks, women and lesbians.

Yet this is not the simple narrative of a "serve and volley" victory for progressive forces—the conservative elements within the tennis establishment and sport generally organised their own backlash.

Equally Arthur Ashe's stance towards the South African apartheid regime came under scrutiny from the left when in 1973 he became the first black man to play a tennis tournament in South Africa.

Arthur Ashe first brought the issue of apartheid to the forefront of America's consciousness when in 1969 he was refused a visa to play the South African Open. In an uncharacteristic comment for an avowed pacifist he said he would not mind seeing a hydrogen bomb dropped on Johannesburg, and called on South Africa to be expelled from the tennis tour and Davis Cup. He said, "South Africa was testing the credibility of Western civilisation. If you didn't come out against the most corrupt system imaginable, you couldn't look yourself in the eye".[2]

Imagine Andy Murray making a criticism in a similar vein of the Israeli government's actions against the Palestinians? The disparity is partially explained by the events in the US in the 1960s, particularly the radicalising events of the civil rights movement. In February 1960 in Greensboro, North Carolina, four black college students sat on a "whites only" Woolworth's lunch counter. Despite having lit cigarettes stubbed in their faces, being beaten and threatened, they continued their protests over many days. By 1961 50,000 people had taken part in civil rights demonstrations in 100 cities with over 3,600 participants being jailed.

The Vietnam War (or the American War as the Vietnamese more accurately called it) radicalised other sportsmen and women. Dave Zirin brilliantly describes boxer Muhammad Ali and Bill Russell, Boston Celtic basketball player, as "canaries in the coal mines signalling what was about to explode onto the sports landscape".[3]

Other players had blazed the trail in tennis including Althea Gibson, the first African-American to win a grand slam tournament in 1956 and the first black player to break the colour barrier in tennis in 1949.[4] However, racial discrimination was so rife in the 1950s, with the Ku Klux Klan operating openly and lynchings a common feature in the South, that it would have been nigh on impossible for a black tennis player to have taken an avowedly political stance.

Arthur Ashe was himself subject to discrimination within the US, having attended a segregated school. Racism was open and thriving; as a 12 year old boy he was refused permission to play in a city tournament. In 1959 he was able to play at Forest Hill, where he was seeded number 1, but was barred from playing in the South.[5] Even when he won the US Open in 1968 his prize money was only $280, yet losing finalist Tom Okker received $14,000.

So racist was American society that after Ashe contracted Aids from a blood transfusion and was asked, "Is this the hardest thing you've ever had to deal with?" he replied, "No, the hardest thing I've ever had to deal with is being a black man in this society".[6]

Ashe regarded himself as a moderate and was brought up largely by his father, a special policeman in Richmond's recreation department. Yet the impact of what was happening in wider society must have had a radicalising impact on his views, even within the stultifying conservative milieu of the world of tennis. Politics and sport had become interwoven, with black athletes having increasingly to defend their right "not to be political".

In 1973, four years after first being refused, Ashe was granted a visa and became the first black man to play in a tennis tournament in South Africa. In so doing he came under a volley of criticism from the left, although on his visit he met dissidents, including Nelson Mandela on Robben Island.

There was a major danger that his visit could be misused by the regime to interpret the visit by one of the world's most famous black sportsmen as implicit support for the apartheid regime. While his decision to visit was misguided, it should be borne in mind that similar debates had taken place among athletes about a boycott of the Mexico Olympics and about the boycott of tours by the all-white Springboks rugby team (see chapter 38). Various positions were adopted by sportsmen in this "engagement or isolation" debate.

In 1976 Ashe visited Soweto to make a documentary about sport in the area and expressed an interest in building tennis courts there. Tsiestsi Mashinini, a militant black student, challenged his visit when he said, "We don't want tennis courts. We want our land back".[7]

Afterwards Ashe continued to devote much of his life to raising awareness of the evils of apartheid. In 1985 he was arrested at the South African embassy. Just five months before his death he was again arrested, this time outside the White House in protest at the US government's treatment of Haitian refugees. He raised millions of dollars for inner-city tennis centres and the United Negro College Fund, founded the African-American Athletic Association and wrote *Hard Road to Glory*, a three-volume book on black sports history.

Despite his decision to go to South Africa he is a wonderful example of a brave and principled individual who used his position to take a stand against apartheid and was emboldened by a similar stand in the wider world. "He was an ambassador of dignity. He was an ambassador of class", said US journalist Bryant Gumbel.[8]

In an interview in the British press Ashe said he would devote himself to the civil rights movement. He even went on to express support for the radical wing of the movement when he said:

> The important thing is we are really with them, working with them. Not just as a gesture... We're not going to get what we are after quickly but we can't behave as if we are resigned to letting it come slowly. Men like Stokely [Carmichael] are absolutely right to demand and insist that it must happen now. What Stokely is doing is wonderful.[9]

Meanwhile the black revolt was also becoming a women's revolt and Billie Jean King became its standard bearer on the tennis court and beyond. The 1970s saw a push for peace in Vietnam and civil rights in the US sparking a struggle for equal rights for women, lesbians and gays. In August 1970 more than 50,000 people took part in a day of action for women's rights named the "Women's Strike for Equality" and in 1973 the women's movement achieved a significant breakthrough when the Supreme Court legalised abortion in its historic ruling "Roe v Wade".

Yet King's story of activism dates back to 1968 when she insisted that the prize money offered at Wimbledon should be offered "openly". This was a time when the official practice was for women's tournaments to be open only to amateurs and for payments to be made "under the table"—a financial handicap to working class women such as King wanting to play tennis and earn a living. Indeed even after winning her first two Wimbledons, she received nothing except the $14 daily allowance.

King became the voice for a very specific kind of feminism, one which demanded equal pay, more endorsements, better training and appropriate locker room facilities. As an activist she also participated in the broader women's movement. She fought for the women's players' union and co-founded the Women's Tennis Association. When she received $15,000 less than Ilie Natase for winning the US Open in 1972 she called for a strike if the prize money was not made equal by the following year. This aim was realised the next year at the US Open when an identical winner's purse was offered for men and women.

The most highly publicised event in her career was her tennis match with Bobby Riggs in their "Battle of the Sexes" on 20 September 1973. Riggs, a former Wimbledon champion, had challenged King after defeating women's champion Margaret Court on Mother's Day in 1973.

Riggs was quoted as saying of King:

> She's a great player for a gal. But no woman can beat a male player who knows what he's doing. I'm not only interested in glory for my sex, but I also want to set women's lib back 20 years, to get women back into the home, where they belong.[10]

King won this highly symbolic match in straight sets, 6-4, 6-3, 6-3, in front of an estimated US television audience of 50 million (90 million worldwide).

"All her life, King had been battling for equal rights for women, not only in tennis and in sports, but in society," wrote Anthony Holden. "But all her hard work and dedication were dwarfed by what she accomplished in the two hours and four minutes it took to dismantle Riggs".[11]

However, King's contribution cannot be simply reduced to a publicity stunt, no matter how significant symbolically. Her greatest contribution was the impact her career and stance had on spurring on female participation in sports and the passage of Title IX, a legal guarantee of men's and women's funding for educational opportunities. Before Title IX fewer than 32,000 women participated in college sports. By the first decade of the new millennium this had risen to over 150,000 and continues to rise. Professor of Politics at Occidental College Peter Dreier neatly sums up her career and political impact: "She broke barriers in sports and then used her celebrity to break barriers in society".[12]

King continued to make contributions to women's sport and women's liberation in general. In 1970 she signed a statement published in Ms magazine stating that she had had an abortion, putting herself on the frontline of the battle for reproductive rights. In 1981 she was "outed" by a former girlfriend and later embraced her role as the first openly lesbian sports star.

Life magazine recognised her role in the movements of the day by naming King as one of the "100 Most Important Americans of the 20th Century", the only female athlete on the list.

However, the establishment felt threatened and led a backlash. Walter Byers, executive director of the National Collegiate Athletic Association, said Title IX threatened the "impending doom" of college athletics. Sports columnist Furman Bisher of the Atlantic Journal-Constitution expressed the common sense views of the press when he commented:

> What are we after, a race of Amazons? Do you want to bring home a companion or a broad that chews tobacco? What do you want for the darling daughter, a boudoir or a locker room full of cussing and bruises?[13]

But massive social changes over the last few decades, such as the massive increase in women in the workplace, have meant that the participation of women in sport continues to rise. Basketball, volley-ball and cross country are the three most frequently offered sports for women in the US, followed by soccer (in almost 90 percent of campuses compared to just 2.8 percent in 1977), softball and then tennis.

Both Ashe and King illustrate how the social movements of the day ruptured even the conservative environment of the sport of tennis; how the social movements cross-pollinated with the world of sport. Even within tennis some players began to think beyond the tramlines imposed on them and were able to think more broadly about what was wrong with society and to participate in changing the world for the better.

The role that individuals play within movements is critical. The contributions of Ashe and King are not as widely recognised as some other sporting figures from the same era, but their stories are also important in shaping our world. Without their sacrifices perhaps the Williams sisters would not be playing, or so many tennis players willing to identify as lesbian. Indeed the stand of individuals such as Ashe and King gave others the courage to take similar political stands on the tennis courts and in wider society.

Ashe and King contributed significant challenges to the common sense of the age as millions of people witnessed their actions and speeches and began to understand how politics and sport, just as any sphere of life, are interwoven. This gave others the confidence to challenge the prejudices and hindrances to equal participation within sport.

Chapter 30
BOXING, ALI, RACISM AND RESISTANCE
Ron Senchak

Muhammad Ali is recognisable as one of the greatest sporting figures of all time. He was born into a black working class family on 17 January 1942 and was raised in Louisville, Kentucky—part of the segregated South within the US. He graduated from high school next to the bottom of the class, but he soon discovered that he possessed a great deal of talent as a sportsman in the boxing ring.

He had an outstanding amateur career culminating in a win at the Rome Olympics in 1960. Returning home he wore the gold medal around his neck constantly. He was proud to have won it for the US. He thought that his victory would bring recognition and acceptance. He thought that becoming the heavyweight boxing champ of the world would be his passport into American society. But things were to turn out rather differently.

In the United States boxing was one sport that was integrated. Throughout the first half of the 20th century it offered an avenue for black people to make it in white America. But professional boxing is brutal. Repeated bouts of sustained physical punishment mean that brain damage is common for those who play the game. So it attracts those who are literally prepared to fight their way out of the poverty and the misery that shape their lives.

Throughout most of the 20th century boxing—and the heavyweight championship in particular—carried great symbolism.

Jack Johnson was the first black heavyweight champion. When he defeated Tommie Burns for the championship in 1906 there was a backlash. Racists were desperate to find the "white hope" to defeat Johnson and restore the title to the "white race". It was the white racists who elevated the heavyweight championship into something more than a fight between two men. For them it became a "battle of the races". The search for the great white hope led to the famous "fight of the century" between Jack Johnson and Jim Jeffries. Black people saw this fight as a statement, as part of the resistance to racism; racists saw the fight as a demonstration of white superiority.

Johnson at this time was the most widely known black person in the world. The hopes of black people were on him. He was not to disappoint as he totally outclassed and destroyed Jeffries.

Undefeated in the ring, Johnson was targeted under the Mann Act (a dubious law dealing with the transporting of women for "immoral purposes", which was used very selectively) and fled the country. The "prostitute" in this case was his girlfriend and later wife. When he eventually returned he was out of shape and well past his prime and was defeated controversially by Jess Willard.

For racists in and around the ring a black heavyweight champ was a direct threat to white supremacy so all sorts of barriers were put in place to stop black fighters challenging for the crown.

Joe Louis dominated the heavyweight division and they could not keep him from the title, but there was huge pressure to ensure that if there was another black champ he would not be in the mould of Jack

Johnson. Louis had to be the champ that was acceptable to whites and would not encourage other black people to challenge the racism they faced every day. Even in order to get a shot at the title he had to pay 10 percent of his earnings to the holder James J Braddock and his manager for the next ten years.

Financial robbery was not the only price to be paid. Louis was told by his managers that he could never have his picture taken with a white woman, let alone be with one. He was never to gloat over a fallen opponent; in fact when he won he had to look like he lost. They created a media campaign featuring Joe as an all-American, clean cut, clean-living, modest fighter in a sea of scoundrels. There was a conscious attempt to create Joe as a fighter who was not a threat to white sensibilities. Nevertheless he did symbolise the hopes of black people during his years as champ. He was champion of the world. Racists hated him. Such was the impact of Joe Louis for the black community that, as black poet Langston Hughes wrote:

> Each time Joe Louis won a fight in those depression years, even before he became champion, thousands of black Americans on relief or WPA...would throng out into the streets all across the land to march and cheer and yell and cry because of Joe's one-man triumphs. No one else in the United States has ever had such an effect on Negro emotions—or on mine. I marched and cheered and yelled and cried, too.[1]

When Joe unexpectedly lost his fight to Max Schmeling (in 1936) it was more than a fighter losing a match—it was seen as a defeat for all black people:

> I walked down Seventh Avenue and saw grown men weeping like children, and women sitting in the curbs with their head in their hands. All across the country that night when the news came that Joe was knocked out, people cried.[2]

The rise of the Nazis in the 1930s posed some threats to US interests. In these circumstances the needs of the American state and the hopes of black people coincided.

Max Schmeling had become a national hero in Germany after his victory over Louis and Nazi government officials hailed him as an example of Aryan superiority. Schmeling's relationship with the Nazi regime was much more ambivalent—he refused to sack his Jewish trainer or accept a "Dagger of Honour" from Hitler.

The United States press painted Schmeling unfairly as a Nazi and Louis as a defender of American ideals. Their rematch in 1938 was one of the most famous and important in boxing history. Louis destroyed Schmeling in one round. The Nazi "white hope" was defeated. As a punishment for his "failures" Schmeling was sent to the Eastern Front by the Nazis, while Louis, the victor, joined the army and was promptly assigned to a segregated cavalry unit.

The end of the Second World War led to an unprecedented boom in the US. In the depression blacks were trapped in the segregated South; after the war there were jobs in the North and black people now had reason to move. There was a vast migration to the northern cities.

The defeat of the Nazis also created an ideological opening to push for greater equality in the US. The civil rights movement started to gather momentum from 1955 onwards. The non-violent sit-ins, voter registration drives and boycotts were met by brutal violence. And it was shown every day on American TV.

There were two more black heavyweight champs who briefly held the title until Floyd Patterson became the youngest champ in 1956.

Floyd Patterson was still part of the Joe Louis generation who knew how to do humble. He was always seen as an example of how a black person in prominent focus should act. While he supported the civil rights movement he did not have the confidence to use his position to campaign openly for black liberation. Patterson was so damaged by self-doubt that he always brought a disguise with him to his fights in case he lost. For all his moderation, when he tried to move into a white neighbourhood in the North he was driven out.

Floyd Patterson eventually lost his title to another black fighter, Sonny Liston.

Liston was the champ that nobody wanted. The leading civil rights organisation the National Association for the Advancement of Colored People (NAACP) did all they could to persuade Floyd Patterson not to give Liston a title shot. Sony was an illiterate ex-con from the bowels of the racist South. He was tied to the mob and harassed by the police wherever he went. The NAACP at this time wanted a black champ who was acceptable to white people and an example to black people. Liston was seen as neither of these.

Into these early days of great social and political struggle strode Muhammad Ali, a young black man seeking his fame and fortune.

Racism and resistance

The Jim Crow laws in the segregated South ensured black people "knew their place" with poverty and intimidation part of their daily life. But life was not much better in the desegregated North where racism, police harassment and poverty were part and parcel of everyday life for black people.

Such levels of racism bred resistance. During the 1950s the civil rights movement had been growing across the South. In 1954 desegregation legislation was passed in the Senate in the wake of the famous Brown versus Board of Education of Topeka (Kansas) Supreme Court ruling. In 1955 there was outrage at the racist killing of black teenager Emmett Till and the Montgomery bus boycott started. In 1957 Little Rock, Arkansas, became the focus of segregation protests. By 1960 the sit-ins and bus protests had started across the South.

When Ali returned from his 1960 Olympic triumph, therefore, he was returning to a world that, on the surface, seemed exactly as it had always been, but bubbling to the surface was an increasingly militant civil rights movement that was giving expression to a vibrant black resistance. And it was in this environment that he was beginning to become conscious of what it was to be a black man in the US.

1963 was a crucial year in the civil rights movement and in the transition of Muhammad Ali. That year witnessed the killing of Medgar Evers, mass arrests, violence against demonstrators, the KKK bombing of a black church in Alabama that killed four children, the march on Washington and Martin Luther King's famous "I have a dream" speech. These events had a tremendous impact on all black people in and out of the US.

That same year Ali came into contact with Malcolm X in Miami. Malcolm X was a charismatic political preacher in the Nation of Islam. At the time there were few channels for black people to express their political views, frustrations, hopes and dreams. Where black people could meet legitimately was in the churches and assembly halls of religious organisations. These arenas became significant spaces within which discontent and resistance started to be realised.

The Nation of Islam provided a sense of black pride combined with a historical view of black oppression. It was the largest black nationalist organisation in the US. Its leaders were vilified. Malcolm X was labelled the biggest racist in America by the *New York Times*.

Ali defeated Liston on 25 February 1963 to become the world champ. At the ringside were his guests and friends Malcolm X and singer Sam Cooke. Under Malcolm X's influence he came out as a member of the Nation and shortly after was given the name Muhammad Ali.

The political fallout and the politicisation of Ali now developed at a furious pace. He told a group of reporters that "I don't have to be what you want me to be".[3] It was clear that things were going to be different.

There were four key inter-linking elements to Ali's political development: his conversion to Islam and the furore over his name change; his first visit to Africa (in the period immediately after winning the championship); the unfolding civil rights struggles in the US; and the American war in Vietnam.

Names were symbolically important for many black people in the developing Black Power movement because as slaves black people had not been allowed to use their African names, but were named by the slave owners. On changing his name from Cassius Clay, Ali was attacked from every quarter. Liberals and black establishment figures denounced the Nation of Islam and refused to use his chosen name. Changing names—or adopting fight or professional names—is not at all unusual in boxing and other sports. But this was different: here was a black sportsman—and a world champ to boot—adopting a name which signalled a rejection of mainstream American society. The use of the new name became an issue that was battled out in the ring. It came to a head in his fight against Ernie Terrell. In the run up to the fight Ali poked fun at his opponent in one of his classic poems:

> I predict that Terrell will catch hell at the sound of the bell.
> He is going around saying he's a championship fighter but when he meets me he'll fall 20 pounds lighter.
> He thinks he's a champ but after I'm finished he'll just be a tramp.
> Now I'm not saying this just to be funny. But I'm fighting Ernie because he needs the money.

But when Ali met Terrell to sign the fight contract the tone changed. He asked Terrell, "What's my name?" and Terrell replied, "Cassius Clay." Ali's response was, "I'm gonna whup him until he addresses me by my proper name. I'm gonna give him a whupping and a spanking, and a humiliation." In the fight Ali destroyed Terrell,

People

calling out with nearly every punch, "What's my name? What's my name? What's my name, fool?"[4]

The second important element in his political formation was a trip he made to Africa just after becoming world champion. In the 1950s and 1960s Africa witnessed a whole series of national liberation struggles bringing a range of Pan-Arab and Pan-African leaders to power. Pan-African ideas were important within the developing Black Power movement—and in the early 1960s both Kwame Nkrumah, leader of Ghana, and Patrice Lumumba of the Congo had visited the US and spoken to large black crowds.

Ali visited Ghana (which gained its independence in 1957) where he met Nkrumah and announced that he hadn't "been home for 400 years". In Egypt, Nigeria and Ghana he noticed the respect and adulation with which he was held, in comparison to the approbation he met "at home". Across Africa he was becoming the most famous black American.

For Ali this was a qualitative break from the past. He turned his back on the trappings of fame; he was a black man first, a heavyweight champ second. When Ali visited Africa he found that he was not only champion of the US but was seen as the champion of the world. He was becoming a spokesman for the struggles of all black people the world over.

As the civil rights movement strengthened and the Black Power movement started to emerge there was also growing resistance to the war in Vietnam.

Black troops were supposedly sent to fight for democracy against the Communist North and their Southern allies. Yet in the US those same black soldiers and their families were denied all manner of basic civil rights. In Vietnam itself black troops were more likely to be sent to combat zones and died in disproportionate numbers compared to their white colleagues. Gradually the civil rights struggle from inside the US was reproduced within the US army in Vietnam as part of the soldiers' rebellion[5] and thus the civil rights movement and the movement against the war fed into each other.

In 1964 Ali sat, and failed, the entry test for the US army. But in 1966 the test was revised, Ali was forced to sit it again and this time he was classified 1A—fit for military service. But Ali refused to be conscripted. He famously proclaimed that "I ain't got no quarrel with them Viet Cong," adding, more sharply in the context of the struggle against racism in the US, "No Viet Cong ever called me nigger".[6]

His refusal to fight saw him stripped of his boxing title, and his boxing licence was suspended. He was sentenced to five years imprisonment and a $100,000 fine. He appealed the decision as a conscientious objector, but he did not fight again for nearly four years as his appeal made its way to the US Supreme Court. His conviction was eventually overturned unanimously on 28 June 1971.

He embarked on speaking tours of the college campuses where there was growing resistance to the war. Black Power and the anti-war movement were seen as part of the same struggle—and Ali was an important player in both.

He returned to the ring in 1970. Each fight took on a political and social significance. Opponents who refused to call him by his chosen name were punished in the ring, while the establishment was desperate to find someone to defeat him. On 8 March 1971 he met his match in a World Championship fight with Joe Frazier. It was the first professional fight Ali had lost in his career up to that point, and the first of a number of clashes between Frazier and Ali. Ali set up a re-match with Frazier on 28 January 1974. Frazier was by this time no longer the world champ, but Ali's victory against Frazier allowed him to take a try at George Foreman, the current world champ. That fight was to be perhaps the most famous fight ever: "The Rumble in the Jungle", held in Kinshasa on 30 October 1974.

The fight has been immortalised in the movie *When We Were Kings*. Ali used the fight and the setting to talk about his African roots and re-emphasise his anti-war and anti-imperialist stance. By defeating the American flag waving Foreman he maintained his position as a sporting icon and spokesman for the oppressed across the globe.

In boxing terms Ali's career was to hit some further peaks. In 1975 the "Thrilla in Manila" saw a brutal contest between Ali and Frazier end in victory for Ali. In 1978 Ali then lost to Leon Spinks, which led to a rematch in 1979 and Ali becoming the first man ever to win the World Championship on three separate occasions.

Ali was a boxing great. He was a man who stood up and spoke out against racism in American society and against imperialist interventions in the developing world.

Today the social and political significance of the heavyweight championship has diminished. But racism is still very much alive in the US. Future struggles to create a better world will require black and white unity to challenge the very nature of capitalist America. The great black resistance led by King, Malcolm X, the Black Panthers and encapsulated in the life of the greatest boxer, Muhammad Ali, are a shining torch that will help light the path on the next stage in the struggle.

Chapter 31
JOE LOUIS AND JACK JOHNSON[1]

J R Johnson (C L R James)

A tense political or social situation can take the simplest or most commonplace event and make it into a symbol of political struggle. The most famous of such cases is the Dreyfus case in France 50 years ago. Lenin once pointed out how this anti-Semitic attack by the military caste on a Jewish officer nearly precipitated a revolution in France.

The situation of the Negroes has in the past lifted sporting events in which Negroes took part to a level of international political interest. Observers in Europe in 1935 noted the great satisfaction with which "the left" greeted the Olympic victories of the American Negroes. These games took place in Berlin, under Hitler's very nose. His obnoxious racial theories were debunked on the presence of thousands of fanatical Nazis.

Now Joe Louis retains his title as heavyweight champion of the world. The Negroes rejoice, and the labour movement should view with sympathy and understanding their deep satisfaction.

The Negroes express by this a very simple, very human, and for that reason, social sentiment of great significance.

"Negroes are inferior? Very well then. Here is one Negro who is not inferior and beats everybody who dares to challenge him."

The British government with its long experience in colonial domination, allows no nonsense of that kind. It prohibits by law competition for boxing titles between Englishmen and coloured colonials, and we need have no doubt that if the reactionaries in the US ever got their chance they would restrict the championship to whites only. Luckily, the labour movement (whether individual workers supported Louis or Conn) would raise such a howl, that these fascistic types would have to keep their mouths shut.

Joe Louis, however, is a remarkable person, and has stamped his personality on this generation. He is a man of great personal dignity, and has borne the temptations and the publicity associated with the championship in a manner that has won the admiration of all. This has led to comments on Louis as a "representative of his race"; the announcer on the night of the big fight referred to him as such.

Jimmy Cannon of the New York Post wrote a column which ended with the phrase that Joe was a credit to his race. But he added immediately, "I mean the human race." Harlem was vastly pleased with this and the phrase has acquired wings among the Negro people.

At the opposite extreme is the New York Times.

A few days before the fight Jack Johnson, another Negro champion, died. Johnson had had a stormy and spectacular career and had served time in prison. The Times said in so many words that Johnson's conduct had cast a stain upon the Negro character which Louis's conduct was wiping away. This is a piece of ignorance and impertinence which deserves to be exposed.

Jack Johnson was champion of the old school of champions. In those days, the days of John L Sullivan, J J Corbett, etc, the champions lived fast. What made the authorities mad was that Johnson refused to act differently simply because he was a Negro. He insisted on his right to live his own way. He was persecuted but remained irrepressible to the end. Doubtless he did many wrong and stupid things. But Negro publicists who followed his career have denounced all attempts to make him into a kind of Negro black sheep.

Similarly this attempt to hold up Louis as a model Negro has strong overtones of condescension and race prejudice. It implies: "See! When a Negro knows how to conduct himself, he gets on very well and we all love him." From there the next step is: "If only all Negroes behaved like Joe, the race problem would be solved."

And yet there is a sense in which the careful public conduct of Joe Louis is a matter not only of his personal character but of his origin. Joe himself has stated in public that he would rather die than do anything which would discredit his people. In this he reflects the acute social consciousness of the generation to which he belongs.

The Negro question today is not what it was in Jack Johnson's time. Joe feels that he is not only a boxer but a social figure, someone whose actions can harm the struggle of Negroes for their full democratic rights. In that sense he feels he is a genuine "representative" of the Negro people. He feels it strongly and the Negroes, recognising this, admire him for it as well as for his boxing prowess. That is not only legitimate but is good and in its way progressive. To the Negroes, it is only another reason why they should not be deprived of their rights. The important thing is to separate this healthy sentiment from the smug and hypocritical who clasp their hands across their chests and whine: "If only Negroes conducted themselves like Joe Louis, the Negro problem would be solved."

Chapter 32
THE FLAME OF REVOLT:
AN INTERVIEW WITH JOHN CARLOS[1]

Ken Olende

The clenched-fist image of Tommie Smith and John Carlos at the 1968 Mexico Olympics is famous around the world. The two black athletes won the gold and bronze medals in the 200 metres and as the US national anthem played, they hung their heads and raised black gloved fists.

In the run up to the London Olympics John Carlos addressed 800 people at a crowded meeting. He spoke alongside Doreen Lawrence, Janet Alder and other justice campaigners at the event Resistance: The Best Olympic Spirit.

He said:

"My life has not been about winning medals; it's about being a freedom fighter... I love the Olympics, but how come the royals get the royal box and we just get a royal shove?... Racism, bias and prejudice are woven into the fabric of our society. The police try to divide us and tag us, they see us as black or white, but the reality is right versus wrong... Now I'm an old man so we have to find young recruits to take the baton."

He was cheered when he told the audience that there was one thing they can learn from him: "I am not afraid to offend my oppressor."

It was the biggest of several meetings he gave in an attempt to keep the connection between the Olympics and rebellion alive.

During the tour I spoke to him about his life and experience.

John Carlos grew up in Harlem in New York. On a sports scholarship at San Jose State University in California he met the sociologist Harry Edwards who founded the Olympic Project for Human Rights (OPHR) and his fellow protester Tommie Smith.

San Jose was only 40 miles from the city of Oakland, where the radical Black Panther Party had recently been established. Edwards was influenced by its ideas of militant action against racism and economic injustice.

John was a leading member of the OPHR, largely made up of black US athletes, which had campaigned for a boycott of the Mexico Olympics. They were angry at racism and segregation in sport and human rights issues including the participation of apartheid South Africa. Looking back on that period Edwards recently said, "Over that era you had Muhammad Ali, who was really the godfather of the revolt of the black athlete, Jim Brown, Bill Russell, Arthur Ashe, Tommie Smith, John Carlos, Curt Flood and then in some instances entire teams like the University of Wyoming football team which refused to play because of a lack of black coaches and a lack of support for black athletes on campus."

John told *Socialist Worker*:

"For two and a half years we had fought for an Olympic boycott. But many were not prepared to sacrifice their 15 minutes in the sun. We had a vote in the OPHR and it went to go to the games.

"I wasn't happy with that and at first I was going to stay home.

"Then I thought, 'If I stay home someone will go and win a medal, but they won't represent my views the way I think they need to be represented.'

"As we passed the quarter finals and semi finals I still had on my mind the thing about the boycott. Some statement needed to be made to show we had a social and humanitarian problem in society. We could no longer sweep it under the rug. We had to face up to it and deal with it.

"So I went up to Tommie and said, 'I'm disenchanted that the boycott has been called off and I want to make a statement. What's your take on it?' He said, 'Man, I want to make a statement too'."

John recalls, "We had one more step to go—we had to win the right to be on the victory stand. A lot of people seem to forget that! We went through hell and high water to be in the final and then we had to be one of the top three.

"After the race we had about 25 minutes to evaluate what we would like to do. How we were going to use the gloves, what the scarf around Mr Smith's neck meant and why I wore the black jersey over my USA uniform."

John has explained elsewhere that, "The beads were for those individuals that were lynched, or killed that no one said a prayer for, that were hung tarred. It was for those thrown off the side of the boats in the middle passage. All that was in my mind."

In an interview recorded immediately after the protest, Tommie Smith said, "The black scarf around my neck stood for black pride. The black sock with no shoes stood for black poverty in racist America. The totality of our effort was the regaining of black dignity."

The silver medallist Peter Norman, an Australian, supported them. John said, "I approached Mr Norman and asked him did he believe in human rights. He said of course he believed in human rights." Peter wore an OPHR badge as he stood on the podium.

John said, "So there you have it! We went to the victory stand and presented our message to society. We did something that had never been done before. In the greatest sporting venue. It was right up in your face.

"And this is the first time the Olympic Games had ever been televised worldwide. So the world got a chance to see it clearly and as in your face as the people sitting in the stadium."

Today the image of John and Tommie's protest is iconic.

Tommie said, in a 2008 interview with *Socialist Worker*, "As we stepped off the victory stand and walked across the green grass and across the track and back into the tunnel we received boos, catcalls. We were called animals and all sorts of names—including 'nigger'."

The US Olympic Committee sent the athletes back to the US within 48 hours of their protest.

When the pair got back to San Jose, they were treated as heroes by the other students and paraded around the campus.

The authorities took a different line. They were ostracised by the athletic world and never considered for the 1972 Olympics. This was despite Tommie holding a still unequalled 11 simultaneous track and field world records.

Olympic Committee president Avery Brundage blamed them for bringing politics into the world of sport. This still angers John. Before the Olympics OPHR had demanded his removal as a racist bigot and Nazi sympathiser. Brundage had been head of the US Olympic Committee in 1936.

John said, "Athletics and politics are intertwined. It was political when they went to the Berlin Olympics in 1936. It was political when they decided to leave Jewish athletes out of the team because they didn't want to offend Hitler.

"The fact it's done under the flags of various nations is political. If this is a sporting event why do we compete under national flags and not the Olympic rings?

"People had seen me running all over Europe with USA written on my chest. They thought that meant that everything was OK for people of colour in the United States. So I talked about the social problems we need to deal with and all of a sudden I'm a bad guy.

"We were ostracised by the sporting establishment, big business and the government.

"People I thought were friends walked away. Some felt, 'Man, I can't stand next to you. You're like a leper now. If I get too close to you I might get persecuted too.' Others said, 'Man, you've screwed up your life. You'll never get another shot. Your life is over, man'.

"As a kid god told me to stand firm to what you believe in and that's what I've done all my life."

The 1968 Olympics took place in the face of protests and state murder. John didn't know about the massacre when he made his protest. He says, "We knew there was a student movement and we had been in touch with its leaders, but we didn't know about all those young students who had lost their lives. If people today have a passion for their people like I did, they should step up against the norm and speak the truth. They have to have guts to do that."

John spoke at the radical Occupy Wall Street camp in New York during October 2011. He told the anti-capitalist protesters, "Today I am here for you. Why? Because I am you. We're here 43 years later because there's a fight still to be won. This day is not for us but for our children to come."

Chapter 33
JUSTICE FOR THE 96:
AN INTERVIEW WITH SHEILA COLEMAN

Sadie Robinson

Some 96 Liverpool football fans died as a result of the Hillsborough disaster in 1989. The disaster, and the cover-up that followed, showed the utter disdain that the entire establishment has for working class people. Survivors, relatives of the dead and others have fought for justice, in the teeth of opposition and attacks from the establishment, ever since. It took 23 years for much of the truth of the disaster, and the cover-up, to come out. And campaigners are still fighting for the whole truth and for justice for the dead.

Sheila Coleman is from the Hillsborough Justice Campaign. She described how campaigners were often dismissed in the years after the disaster:

"For too many years when people spoke about Hillsborough we would get, 'Why are you still going on about that?' Now there's this idea that fans have been vindicated so they should go away."

The publication of the independent panel report was a real breakthrough. But it was campaigners who played a key role in establishing many of the facts it contained. "The independent report was a revelation for many," said Sheila. "But to us it wasn't because we've been banging on about this for 23 years. We had unearthed a lot of the information and provided it to the authorities."

Campaigners had already shown that more people could have lived, for example, with an alternative pathologist report by Dr Ian West. But this evidence was rejected. Sheila described the inquests into those who died at Hillsborough as "corrupted". "I remember sitting in the court and every question from barristers was around drunkenness," she said. "South Yorkshire Police had a clearly defined strategy to raise again and again the idea of drunken, ticketless fans. And fans had no representation at all."

The slandering of the dead and survivors took its toll on many. "We've had survivors committing suicide," said Sheila. "We've paid for treatment for survivors who have mental health problems as a result of Hillsborough... It did enormous damage. Aside from the suicides there's been ill health and careers lost. The consequences are far-reaching."

Sheila and other campaigners faced intimidation as they fought for justice. Sheila described how many people's phones seemed to have been tapped.

"It was hardly hi-tech at that time," she said. "I would pick up the phone and listen to two Hillsborough families in different houses having a conversation. Anyone ringing me would tell me that my phone would be picked up before I heard it ring and then I would pick it up. Lots of families would say similar things about picking the phone up and hearing other people talking."

Sheila's house was broken into "several times" in the aftermath of Hillsborough. "On one occasion only my address book was stolen," she said. "I know that private investigators were paid by News International to break into people's houses and take their address books. When the inquest ended I got home and my flat had been broken into. There was nothing taken of any value on the streets. But in the park nearby was my briefcase with all my Hillsborough papers strewn all over. I saw the break-ins as warnings to back off, to frighten me. Once you stick your head above the parapet they come for you."

The extent of the cover-up and the attacks on campaigners are one of the most shocking things about Hillsborough. They expose the idea that our society is based on fairness and justice as a hollow lie. "The most frightening this is how orchestrated this cover-up was," said Sheila. "People sometimes think these things don't happen. But they do. For years we were criticised and considered extreme in our arguments. Really what we were saying was the truth."

The fact that campaigners persisted, despite such intimidation, is impressive. Sheila stressed that being militant was important in forcing some of the truth about Hillsborough to come out. "We never shied away from being political or proactive," she said. "If you wait for the state to do the right thing you're going to be waiting a long time. It's so easy to tap into the emotion of Hillsborough. The mainstream media exploit that. They don't want the facts; they want to see people crying. But we haven't got this far by crying. We've achieved what we have because we've been a thorn in the side of the establishment and we wouldn't go away. Some people say you need to maintain your dignity. I think people shouting for justice are being dignified. What is undignified is remaining silent while lies and injustice are going on."

The fight isn't over. The whole truth about Hillsborough is yet to be revealed. The police officers who lied and covered up their role in the disaster have yet to be brought to justice.

And the inquest verdicts for the dead still read, "Accidental death".

David Cameron apologised to the families of the dead when the independent report was published. But campaigners rightly want more than warm words from politicians. "It seems to be the climate for apologies," said Sheila. "It's easy to say sorry. But to me words are cheap unless they're followed by action. The report has vindicated survivors—but this isn't the end."

Part 6

Resistance

Chapter 34

ENGLAND'S TRAVELLING FANS: A TURNING WICKET

Hazel Potter

An English summer's day: outside an opulent Victorian pavilion champagne corks pop, a glorious cover drive is met with polite applause by men in blazers, while inside the faces of long-dead cricketers look down upon occupants of the Long Room who are discussing their investments. If anywhere epitomises the convergence of "the gentleman's game" with the elite of British society it is Lord's, where tradition, money and privilege are so closely bound together with cricket that you could be forgiven for thinking it must always be so.

Fast forward a few months, when winter has hit the UK and cricket is awakening in warmer climes. Somewhere on the Indian subcontinent groups of friends congregate in a dusty stadium: builders, students, retired people, teachers, decorators, accountants, plumbers, civil servants and pretty much everything in between. As the players walk onto the pitch the travelling fans launch into a rendition of "Jerusalem", before they settle down to a day of cricket, singing and socialising, that has cost about as much as a daily newspaper in the UK.

The contrast is obvious: in place of the blazers there are shorts and well-loved T-shirts; champagne is most definitely off the menu, replaced by water and (if they are lucky) beer, but, most of all, it is the demographic of supporters that is wholly different when England play abroad. It is not as cut and dried as all that, of course, and in the fancier stands, with seats and maybe even air-con, you'll find a different type of cricket tourist—one that is on a high-end package tour that ferries them from hotel to stadium and back—but over a period of almost two decades it is the independent traveller who has come to dominate England's support abroad.

For many years it was the archetypal resident of the Lord's

Pavilion who was seen to characterise the English cricket fan. It may not have been a wholly accurate representation—throughout the county grounds it is easy to find people from all walks of life—but in terms of the control of the game and at high profile matches and events it has long been a sport dominated by the elite. Perhaps this is most evident within the Marylebone Cricket Club (MCC), the members' club that owns Lord's, which has seen its governance roles ceded to a certain extent to national and global bodies, but remains the law-maker of the game. What is galling is that such an influential body within the game only finally voted to admit women in 1998, some 212 years after its foundation

Even now the governing body that runs cricket in England and Wales, the ECB, is chaired by Old Rugbeian Giles Clarke, a multi-millionaire with rather more in common with the powerbrokers in the country than the average cricket fan. No surprises then, that he has been integral in ensuring that there is now no free to air TV coverage of international matches in the UK, thus ensuring that millions have no chance at all to watch the sport (the counter-argument is that the money raised aids grassroots development, which is undoubtedly true but a short-termist view). Clarke's ECB also allocates test matches under a bidding system, something which has led to would-be host counties offering unrealistic figures to stage the most prestigious games. As a consequence several test-hosting counties have faced financial difficulties and prices for spectators have risen at an alarming rate.

Back in the early 1990s, when independent travellers planted the first seeds of any organisation, those same authorities must have shuddered a little as they heard chants reminiscent of those in football stadia ring out in grounds where England were playing cricket. Football had already seen fans begin to organise in numbers and while cricket did have an early fanzine, *Johnny Miller 96**, which dated back to the late 1980s, supporters of the domestic game had neither faced the same type of crises as their winter counterparts nor had they anywhere near the same volume in terms of numbers. At test matches though, it was a little different: here fans could congregate together and they began to develop chants along the lines of those heard at football. By 1994/95, after an Australian newspaper branded the supporters "barmy" for singing all day as their team was getting beaten, some friends printed T-shirts immortalising the "Barmy Army" chant to sell to fellow England fans at the Ashes and the name now synonymous with travelling supporters was born.

At that time the Barmy Army was a loose grouping of independent travellers who gathered to support, sing, drink and generally socialise with others of their ilk: in short, those who had little in common with the blazers from Lord's or those on organised tours. Support for the team was vociferous and a favourable exchange rate meant that travelling abroad was relatively cheap and so numbers grew.

One of the key characteristics of the fans was that, behind the songs and the drinking, there was a genuine respect for the places they visited. Whereas the tour groups would be bussed from hotel to ground to hotel, with carefully selected sightseeing in between games, the fans within the Barmy Army used whatever transport they could find, ate with locals and explored the places they visited. If the old guard toured like colonials, this new breed of fans were unpretentious travellers.

The travelling fans also developed an informal self-policing regime over the years: if there was anyone among them who wanted to sing football songs they'd be reminded that they were there to watch cricket; if someone showed disrespect to locals they would find a fellow fan having a quiet word with them. It's not a sophisticated system but it is one that works and has helped to ensure that some of the problems—notably racism—that had been seen among football fans did not develop among cricket supporters overseas.

In time the Barmy Army would become far more organised, selling not only thousands of T-shirts but also its own tours, albeit rather cheaper than the others on offer. These days fans can buy a membership of the Barmy Army—and thousands do—but what hasn't changed is the respect for people and places that was seen in the very early days. It's something that is manifested in the events and cricket matches the Barmy Army organises in the countries visited to raise funds for local charities, from the McGrath Foundation in Australia to a local children's charity in Galle. Back home "Chance to Shine", a charity promoting cricket in state schools, and the Barmy Army's Colt Teams for young players are also supported.

But while the organisation around the Barmy Army has become far more slick—indeed, a little too slick for some—the vast majority of those who make up the groups on tour remain independent travellers, many on a shoestring budget, who get together with like-minded friends. Alongside the Barmy Army merchandise, many will have a copy of *The Corridor of Uncertainty* in their hands, a fanzine produced and written by fellow fans, which encompasses the healthy disregard for the authorities and status quo that large numbers of the supporters have.

That there is little love for the governing bodies of the sport is hardly surprising, given the disdain that the ECB and others often seem to have for the average non-corporate fan and the contempt is, perhaps, something which has become more unified as a result of the growth in independent travellers. The cost of watching cricket in the UK, both on TV and live, is a particular bugbear—in 2013 the MCC is charging from £80 (for a poor view) to £120 for the first two days of the Ashes test against Australia—putting cricket out of reach for many fans. A full five days at Lord's could set you back nearly £500: more than it costs to fly to some countries, stay in a cheap hostel and watch a test match in the sun. No wonder then that among the travelling England fans many feel priced out of games at home, and with the authorities unwilling to listen to supporters while they have the corporate pound to woo it is a situation unlikely to change in the foreseeable future.

The concern for supporters is that English prices are transferred elsewhere. In the 2012 tour of Sri Lanka the local cricket board spied a chance to make some quick cash: it's a tour that is up there with the most popular among England fans and with large numbers expected on the island Cricket Sri Lanka decided to raise prices tenfold to the equivalent of £25/day for English fans, in a two-tier system that saw local fans pay the usual prices but in segregated areas. The Barmy Army met with Cricket Sri Lanka and tried to argue the case for fans but calls to the ECB were met with silence: despite repeated pleas the governing body refused to even acknowledge there was an issue.

Hundreds of England fans refused to pay the inflated prices: they either found ways to watch the games for free, inside and outside the grounds, or didn't go at all. At the end of the series Giles Clarke was booed by fans during presentations for his disregard for the plight of fans: it wasn't the first time the ECB Chair was thought to have put schmoozing above supporters and it may well not be the last.

Back at home it is true that the ECB now recognises the Barmy Army's official members, providing ticket allocations—for those that can afford them—at home games and inviting those at the top to official events, but it is this that leads to calls of a sell-out by some fans: for them the creation of trademarks, paid memberships, limited companies and, most of all, tour groups is exactly what the Barmy Army originally despised and was set up to challenge.

There is doubtless some truth in this: back in 94/95, if someone had told the friends who sold the first T-shirts that in a decade they'd be eating at formal dinners with the suits in the posh seats they'd have laughed long and hard, but regardless the importance of the Barmy Army in starting to create a culture of travelling fandom should not be underestimated. Equally true is the fact that those fans who do not align with any official group continue to travel, forming their own loose associations as they do and continuing in the same traditions as those before them. And when there is an issue that needs to be addressed, such as the Sri-Lankan ticket prices, the independent travelling supporters will by and large stand as one.

Perhaps the one thing that hasn't happened among English cricket fans is the creation of any campaigning organisation as football has with the FSF nationally and many independent supporters' groups at club level. The Barmy Army will get involved to try and help fans, but it is not an issue-based organisation that runs campaigns. There have been attempts to create a national cricket fans' group, but as yet these have been unsuccessful. However, having said that, the new breed of cricket supporters are at an earlier stage of development than their football counterparts and it may be that this will come in time.

What cannot be disputed is what has been achieved over the past 20 years to get to a stage where England's cricket fans are acknowledged at home and abroad, by players and the media, as the independent travellers that show their support vociferously win, lose or draw rather than the blazers at Lord's: if cricket in the UK can become as accessible at all levels it can only be positive for the sport.

Chapter 35
ULTRAS AND FANDOM: THE GREEN BRIGADE AT CELTIC

Michael Lavalette

There is a confusion among many people when they hear about football ultras. Many assume that "ultras" is a synonym for "hooligans"—but this is simplistic tabloid dross. Most ultras are not looking for trouble or violent clashes with fans from other teams.[1]

Similarly, the assumption—especially among many on the left—is that the term ultras is shorthand to refer to football fans with connections to the far-right. But in the world of football fandom this represents a complete misunderstanding of what the term means and the range of groups who self-define as ultras.

Ultras is a label adopted by those who want to go beyond the "normal" limits in their support of their team. It means fanatical support, a commitment to follow home and away, to bring banners, undertake tifos (collective displays with banners, placards, flags), corteos (unofficial marches to games), perhaps using pyro (pyrotechnics—flares, fireworks, etc) and singing, dancing and moving in near choreographed ways—whether winning, drawing or facing defeat.

It is certainly the case that some ultras groups (across much of Russia, the Balkans and some Italian clubs) do identify with the far-right. Ultras identify with an "imagined community" and history of their club and this can give rise to hostility to the "other". Ultras at Zenit St Petersburg, for example, released a manifesto in December 2012 that called for all "non-Europeans" and "sexual minorities" to be excluded from their club.[2] Racist abuse of black players or the anti-Semitic attacks on Tottenham Hotspur supporters in Italy in 2013 are located within a football fan culture that can foster racism and create a space for the far-right to exploit.

But there is nothing inevitable about ultras groups being right wing. There are also explicitly left wing ultras groups—notably the Commando Ultras 84 (at Olympic de Marseille), Brigate Autonome Livorno 99 (Livorno), Original 21 (AEK Athens), and those associated with Adana Demirspor in Turkey, Omonoia in Cyprus (see Ioakimidis in this volume) and Celtic's Green Brigade.

The relationship between the clubs and the ultras contains a tension.

In many respects the ultras represent a challenge to those who run football clubs. Reflecting the words of former Celtic manager Jock Stein that "football is nothing without fans", they contest the meaning and "ownership" of the clubs—often summed up in the slogan "FC not PLC". Ultras view the owners as, at best, custodians of clubs which are identified as representing a tradition, a history and a connection with fans and players from the past, resistant to the drives of commercialism and globalisation.

Yet the ultras also help create the atmosphere and the excitement that sell the game and brings more fans in. The clubs exploit the team loyalty of fans to push up prices and sell merchandise, and fans go along with aspects of this because they want their team to win— or at least to keep alive the possibility of winning.

The best known ultras group in Britain at present are the Green Brigade at Celtic. The problematic relationship they have with the club is reflective of the broader contradictions of fandom. The club has conceded the creation of a distinct Green Brigade area in the ground, "Section 111". This has effectively been handed over to the Green Brigade—and they monitor and regulate the personnel and activities within the section to some degree.

The club clearly benefits from the new songs, slogans and colourful displays the section initiates. When Celtic won the league championship in 2012, manager Neil Lennon marched the trophy over to the section and placed it on the ground in front of the fans. Generally he is effusive in his praise for the Green Brigade.

But the club is also regularly at loggerheads with the group. Throughout season 2011/12 there were announcements and leaflets from the club threatening fans who stood and made "lateral movements" during games. This was a reference to the movements of the Green Brigade as they sang. Football stadium regulations were quoted to back the club's case and the regional government issued a threat that they might close the ground because of the fans' behaviour.

Yet every time the announcement about the "lateral movements" was made it was met with resounding boos from right across the ground.

The Green Brigade gained some national prominence from their magnificent tifo at the start of the Celtic/Barcelona Champions League match in November 2012. The game coincided with the 125th anniversary of the club and the display covered every seat in the stadium (with the exception of the Barca fans).[3] It was a huge temporary public art display in green, white and red. In the days following the game Celtic quickly brought out prints of the display which sold well (though the entire cost of the tifo—running to an estimated £10,000—was carried by the fans).[4]

Yet over the course of season 2012/13 the Green Brigade was vociferous in its complaints about how its members were being treated by the club and, more importantly, by Strathclyde police.

Several members of the group were arrested at their homes. Others were picked up on the way to matches. Banners were removed. Members were served with match bans (often without prior knowledge) or travelling bans. In the ground police officers with cameras swarmed all over them in Section 111. The Green Brigade's case is that this level of police surveillance and harassment would not be possible without the cooperation of the club.

On the weekend of 16 February 2013, as many of them came into the ground, they were met by officers with lists of names of those they wanted to monitor. In response the ultras refused to take their seats. In effect this was the third boycott against harassment the group had participated in over the 2012/13 season.

Then on Saturday 16 March about 200 members and supporters of the group were kettled in Glasgow's Gallowgate area. The police claimed this was because they were trying to organise an unauthorised march to the ground—a "corteo" similar to those they had taken part in over the previous six years, which had resulted in no trouble, no arrests and had been widely reported in positive terms.[5]

At 1pm on a Saturday there are lots of Celtic fans walking the 30-minute route from the centre of Glasgow to the ground but on 16 March the police claimed they responded to "reports of a large gathering". If the police were responding to "reports" it really does represent a fantastic response rate—it took a mere nine minutes to muster several hundred officers, horses, dogs, helicopters and riot vans. They were either very efficient or else the attack on fans was pre-planned. The policing was so extreme that one leading Scottish QC suggested the events were akin to the actions of a "police state".[6] Thirteen fans were arrested. As a result many young teenage fans were facing criminal records because they wanted to march to see their team play football.

The harassment has reached such proportions that the group have put out a statement saying the existence of the Green Brigade is now being brought into question.[7]

To understand why the Green Brigade is coming under such pressure from the state we need to look at its history and activities.

Celtic ultras

The Green Brigade was formed over the summer of 2006. It was a reaction to the direction the corporate owners were taking the club.

Resistance

Like most top clubs in Britain Celtic bought into the attempt to rebrand top class football. All-seater stadiums; a more "family orientated" atmosphere (though not family-friendly in terms of pricing!); pre-match and half-time entertainment; an emphasis on "corporate hospitality": all with the intention of altering the "match day experience".

The result, at Celtic and most top clubs in Britain, was to kill the atmosphere. Stadiums were often silent. Singing was reduced to an occasional tune at matches with close rivals. It was these developments that led Roy Keane to talk about the prawn sandwich element at matches. As one of the Green Brigade's founders put it, "We are ardent Celtic fans who eat, sleep and breathe the team... As Celtic fans to the core, we are proud of the club's colourful, vocal and often humorous past, but the atmosphere at games was quite simply flat".[8]

The Green Brigade formed out of a split from an earlier fan grouping, the Jungle Bhoys. There was some disagreement over the perceived closeness of the Jungle Bhoys to the powers at the top of Celtic; the Green Brigade formed with a view to keeping a degree of distance from the club authorities. But the Green Brigade was also clear from the beginning that it was a political grouping: "a broad front of anti-fascist, anti-racist and anti-sectarian Celtic supporters".[9]

The founders were clear about their aims:

What makes the Green Brigade different is our politics. We are anti-racist, anti-sectarian, anti-fascist and left wing and proud of the fact and, similar to comrades from St Pauli, Livorno and Athletic Bilbao etc, believe that we should be allowed to show our support for political causes which have always gone hand in hand with being a Celtic supporter.[10]

And what has politics got to do with football? Well:

Politics is life. Politics has always been part of football and it's disingenuous to claim otherwise. In the 1909 Scottish Cup Final Celtic and Rangers fans rioted together against the authorities for various reasons including the widespread belief that both clubs had engineered a replay which the fans could ill afford. You cannot suspend reality when you enter a football stadium. Some of the recent decisions of Celtic plc are, in our opinion, highly contentious and could be regarded as political. For example, the shameful decision to tarnish Jimmy Johnstone's memory by having adverts for the right wing paper The S*n plastered on commemorative posters. Sponsors such as Nike, Coca-Cola and Coors are highly controversial companies criticised by watchdogs for operating sweatshops, having links to anti-union Columbian death squads and being generally anti trade union, etc. We feel these sponsorships are outwith the spirit of the Social Charter and all that Celtic stood for. Would Michael Davitt, Land Leaguer, the man who laid the centre spot, be proud of what has become of this club? To be successful does not mean sacrificing all your principles on the altar of competitiveness... We encourage Celtic's board and shareholders to take a serious look at a more ethical fair-trade sponsorship policy more in keeping with the club's socially concerned traditions.[11]

Since their inception the Green Brigade have tried to bring colour and song to home and away games through their chants, banners and tifos: "Our banners are a big part of what we do. From general banter to sending a hard hitting message, each one is carefully planned and executed to gain maximum effect".[12]

The displays also define the group's stance on a particular issue, not least the group banner itself. The Green Brigade logo has a distinctive skull with a Celtic tricolour scarf. Between 2006 and 2011 the banner was hung upside down at all matches. This was to express the group's ire at the role of the ex-MP and Blairite war apologist Dr John Reid on the Celtic board:

We know people often question or poke fun at us for hanging our banner upside down but we are resolute on this point. The custom actually comes from shipping days and was used as a sign of distress but is now common in the ultras culture. We were only a small group when we first started hanging the banner upside down so it allowed us to engage in a unique way with other fans while getting our point across.[13]

The banner remained upside down until the match after Reid's resignation. Perhaps the most notorious of their banner demonstrations came in November 2010. On the nearest Saturday to Remembrance Sunday teams in the SPL were to wear a red poppy on their shirts. Complaining about the role of British troops in the murder of civilians from Ireland to Iraq the whole section was covered with a banner proclaiming: "Your deeds would shame all the devils in Hell. Ireland, Iraq, Afghanistan. No Blood Stained Poppies on Our Hoops".

But banner protests are only one part of the group's campaigning work.

The Green Brigade has regularly protested about the treatment of fans within the new global football era, eg banners protesting at ticket prices in Britain compared to continental Europe and changes to kick-off times.

In April 2011 the group protested against cable network ESPN's demand that a mid-week Celtic-St Johnstone game in Perth kick off at 6pm. The early kick-off meant people would have to take time off work to get to the match or miss out. It had a huge impact on the crowd numbers and people's ability to watch their team. The response was the "Balls to 6pm Kick Offs" protest. As the match got under way Green Brigade supporters launched footballs onto the pitch. The players were now faced with choosing which of close to ten balls to play with! The game was stopped, the balls removed, but the point made.[14]

The Green Brigade is also part of the Alerta Network of anti-fascist fans groups.[15] As part of their anti-racist work they hold an annual anti-discrimination football tournament which involves teams made up of local asylum seekers. The slogan of the event reflects Celtic's own roots in the Irish migrant community: "Made by Immigrants, Refugees Welcome".

At the end of the 2011/2012 season the Green Brigade had a tifo in support of Palestinian hunger strikers (see Cooch, this volume). This featured a banner reading "Dignity is More Precious than Food" alongside a flurry of Palestinian flags. A spokesman for the group stated, "We did this in solidarity, to raise awareness and because it's the right thing to do. We want Palestinians to know we are thinking about them and encourage Scottish civil society to look at the injustice in Palestine".[16]

But what has undoubtedly provoked the ire of the Strathclyde police and the Scottish government is the Green Brigade's self-defined socialist republicanism. Despite newspaper reports to the contrary, the Green Brigade rarely sing pro-IRA songs. Their songs are witty renditions of a range of traditional and modern songs from "Just Can't Get Enough" (which the club have tried to cash in on with T-shirts and mugs) to "Zombie Nation" (sung about the new Rangers as a "team of the living dead"). But in their repertoire are also a small number of songs commemorating the Irish hunger strikers ("The Roll of Honour") and civilian victims of the British presence in the six counties ("The Ballad of Aidan McAnespie").[17]

These songs have been used as an excuse to target the group under the new Scottish legislation, the Offensive Behaviour at Football and Threatening Communications (Scotland) Act. This act was brought in after the so-called "shame game" in season 2010/2011. A Scottish Cup clash between Celtic and Rangers ended up with a touch-line confrontation between then Rangers assistant manager Ally McCoist and Celtic manager Neil Lennon. The match also saw three Rangers players being sent off.

In the following weeks Lennon was physically assaulted at a match against Hearts and a range of people with connections to Celtic, including Lennon and Celtic players Paddy McCourt and Niall McGinn (all of Catholic origin from the North of Ireland), were sent bullets though the post.

The problem seemed pretty obvious—sectarianism and anti-Irish racism. But the Scottish government decided to act against "offensive behaviour" at football grounds (and travelling to and from grounds). The act attempts to criminalise "offensive chanting and behaviour" at matches. But as journalist Graham Spiers notes:

> More and more people are now asking if the Scottish government is going too far in its attempt to halt "offensive behaviour" at football through incessant policing and harassing of supporters... This attempt at cleaning up Scottish society has turned into a nightmare, cutting to the very heart of civil liberty [sic]... The act seeks to do what it says on the tin: stamp out "offensive behaviour" such as bigoted or sectarian expression. There has been plenty of that around the Old Firm over the years... But what of political chanting at Ibrox or Parkhead? Indeed, how do you define political chanting? For example, should some of the Irish republican songs chanted by Celtic supporters be defined as "political" or "sectarian"?... Moreover, no matter how you define it, football club supporters the world over espouse causes or beliefs which go way beyond the game: in Spain, in Portugal, in Eastern Europe, in Latin America, as well as here in Scotland.[18]

The legislation was a panic reaction from the Scottish government and has led to the police targeting both Celtic and "new Rangers" fans. But there is no doubt that it is the Green Brigade the police have focused on.[19] They have targeted their "offensive banners" (including a banner showing someone shooting a zombie), singing songs that are "sectarian" (loosely defined to capture any songs broadly supportive of republican issues—like "The Boys of the Old Brigade", a commemoration of those who died in the Irish war for freedom,[20] the "Roll of Honour" or "Aidan McAnespie") or behaviour that is likely to cause offence—which seems to mean any involvement in the Green Brigade. Though there have been a lot of arrests, so far the police have failed to get a significant conviction.

In the aftermath of the legislation there has been a significant increase in applications for football banning orders (FBOs). FBOs were introduced in 2006 in Scotland as a result of the Police, Public Order and Criminal Justice (Scotland) Act. Between 2006 and 2010 there were low levels of FBO applications and orders issued. Since 2010 there has been a sharp increase, especially in Strathclyde (ie in the Glasgow area).

Table 1: Football Banning Orders, Scotland 2010-2012[21]

	FBOs sought		FBOs issued	
	Scotland	Strathclyde	Scotland	Strathclyde
2010	160	68	33	20
2011	348	204	86	73
2012	353	180	92	58

In response several Celtic supporters groups have come together to form Fans Against Criminalisation.[22] FAC has organised several demonstrations against the bill and the act. The Green Brigade have responded with several tifos against the Scottish government, in defence of their right to sing their songs which they strongly assert are not sectarian, and against their harassment by club and police.

To the fury of many Celtic fans there seems to be no balance and no consistency. At Hampden Park, Scotland's national stadium, in 2012 large sections of the crowd joined in songs celebrating the "Billy Boys" (a celebration of a British Union of Fascists supporter in the 1930s) being "up to his knees in Fenian blood"—yet there was little discussion of the singing in the media and no police action.[23]

The Green Brigade have been targeted by the police because they represent a politically orientated approach to football fandom. They challenge the notion that football clubs should drive their "product" upmarket and distance it from its traditional fan base. They bring colour, singing and politics to football when the state, football authorities and the PLC want to sanitise football and take politics out of the game.

The criminalisation of political football fans is part of the state's attempt to restrict our right to protest including protesting against the commodification of our social lives. As football fans and as political activists we should all support the Green Brigade—after all, if they get away with it at Celtic with the Green Brigade, who will be next?

Chapter 36
PROTEST, COMMUNITY AND FOOTBALL:
FC UNITED OF MANCHESTER AS A FAN MOVEMENT

Peter Millward and George Poulton

Notions of "community" and collective identity are important to football fans in their support of "their" football club. The story of football culture is characterised by rivalries which pit "our" team against "theirs". These values have been manifest in expressions stretching from "pub bragging rights", supporter chants/banners and sometimes even fan violence. Many football supporters believe that they have a cultural ownership of their club, even when the economic rights are owned by an investor—although it is unclear whether all investors actually receive a direct financial return on their acquisitions of football club shareholdings.

The Florida-based businessman Malcolm Glazer and his family purchased the economic ownership rights to English Premier League (EPL) club Manchester United on 12 May 2005 for £790 million. The Glazers had initially bought up a 2.9 percent stake in the club in March 2003 and by 28 June 2005 owned 98 percent of the club's shareholding. Despite the Glazers leading Tampa Bay Buccaneers—a National (grid-iron) Football League franchise in the US that they also own—to a period of sporting success, many Manchester United supporters were concerned that the buyout leveraged a £559 million acquisition debt onto the club that needed £60 million each year to repay interest on the loan. This purchase split Manchester United's fan community. For many years the club had been openly talked about as a "business" and a "commercial enterprise", which ran at odds with many supporters' understanding of the club as a community asset, and also necessarily meant extracting more money from the "consumers" of the club's "product"—the fans (many supporters were also uncomfortable at being described as "consumers"). Although the football club had become a private limited company at the time when many English football clubs professionalised, at the turn of the 20th century, it had—with other English football clubs—been protected against obvious commercial forces with the advent of the Football Association's Rule 34 (introduced in 1892) which limited shareholders' dividends to 5 percent of the share value per year. This rule was modified in 1981 to increase the return to 15 percent of the share value but the temptation to try to increase the financial return on investments meant that in many cases owners circumvented the rule by placing their "investments" in holding companies.

While leveraged buyouts are not unusual in some North American sports this move was not normal in the UK. Indeed, Manchester United was the first high-profile example of an English football club being bought with finance that would be leveraged against the club itself. Two years after the Glazers' purchase of Manchester United the economic rights to Liverpool FC were purchased in a similar way. In both instances fan protests emerged against both the perception of the strategy—a football club being bought with its own resources—and its derivatives, such as the need to generate more revenue through increasing admission ticket prices. To be sure then, a leveraged buyout is a form of corporate takeover that involves the use of borrowed money to finance the majority of the transaction and is generally conducted by private equity groups that are attempting to take over well-established firms. The financial sponsors of a leveraged buyout incur debt to buy out the target company; the private equity company incurs this debt through a mixture of debt securities and loans which may offer a high risk of default. This means that loans are set at higher interest rates with the expectation that the targeted company will pay off the debts taken to acquire it. In this case, the targeted company was Manchester United.

The Glazers' takeover split Manchester United's huge supporter community, as some fans protested by setting up FC United of Manchester in the summer of 2005. The new football club is organised as a members' Industrial Provident Society, which means that each fan who has bought a single share in the club—priced at the nominal fee of £10—can take a vote on the club's major issues. FC United runs on a semi-professional basis in the English non-leagues and is currently based at Bury FC's Gigg Lane stadium but has been developing plans to build its own ground in the Moston district of north Manchester. As with the establishment of many forms of protest action, the move to create FC United did not come from nowhere. Rather Manchester United supporters have a recent history of mobilisation. In 1995 a group of active Manchester United supporters launched the Independent Manchester United Supporters' Association (IMUSA) to oppose the club's moves to eradicate standing at matches. Then in 1998 the "Not For Sale" campaign was launched by ordinary supporters in response to the broadcaster BSkyB's proposed takeover of the club. At the time the club's board had decided to accept BSkyB's owner Rupert Murdoch's bid to purchase the club. Rallied by a confluence of IMUSA and Shareholders United Against Murdoch (SUAM, later to become MUST), fans successfully challenged the decision through the Monopolies and Mergers Commission. The Manchester United fanzines, *Red News*, *Red Issue* and *United We Stand* supported the campaign and were used as mediums to communicate with fans. Supporter accounts in these publications showed a number of concerns about the planned takeover, such as raised ticket prices, an over-mediatisation of games, the breakup of the Premier League's collective broadcasting agreement and conflict of interest within the club whereby Murdoch would deliberately not fund player transfers if Manchester United continued to be successful. In the recent protests against the Glazer family's ownership of Manchester United, the then-IMUSA chairman, Andy Walsh, worked with other important members of the group to set up FC United. By 8 July—11 days after Manchester United was delisted from the London Stock Exchange—it was claimed that over 4,000 people had pledged money to the club and FC United played its first game a little over a week later, on 16 July.

For most Manchester United/FC United fans, the delisting of the club was symbolic of the changing balance of control over the parent club. For other fans, alternative reasons to gather support for new club emerged. Thus those at FC United pushed forward an argument that the club is "a broad church" where "there's a home there for the most rabid anti-Glazer protester who out of principle will not give him a penny of their money; there's a home there for those people who can't afford to go to Old Trafford; there's a home there for people who want to watch Manchester United and just see it as an extension of the United family—first team, reserve team, supporters' team" (FC United board member Jules Spencer on *Inside Out—North West*, BBC, 26 September 2005). The club's statutes contain multiple references to the club's role in the community and its Industrial Provident Society status means that the fan communitys own the club in both its cultural *and* economic senses.

At FC United's first friendly (ie non-competitive) match, held at Leigh RMI FC, approximately 2,500 supporters of the new club travelled to the game (a huge number, given that the club are non-league and then played at the tenth level of English football). At the game the following supporter comments were made:

I'm disillusioned by what has happened at United and don't feel I can go there any more. I feel forced out of it and FC United is somewhere you can go with your mates, and stand together.
—**Dave Bergin from Warrington, who went to his first Manchester United match at two years old**

The main reason for this is opposition to Glazer, but a big part of it is the money players like Ferdinand are making. Those things are the final straw for me not going to Old Trafford any more. My season ticket would have cost me nearly £700 so I have given it up.
—**Paul Woods, 24 years old and from Sale**

I want to be part of this new team because it's what football is all about—back to the grass roots, three o'clock on a Saturday. I have played Sunday football all my life, run a Sunday team, been a referee and a secretary and have watched United for 40 years. I will still go to United, but will look at each weekend as it comes. I have applied for a ticket for the first match at Everton. I probably won't get one, so I will go to Leek, watch it on telly in the pub and then go to FC United's first league match.
—**Dave Carruthers, 48, originally from Salford**[1]

Fans of FC United do not hold uniform positions in their relationship to Manchester United. Some continue to support the mother club, and attend their matches as a priority, others continue to support Manchester United but choose attending FC United matches as their preference, while most will watch Manchester United matches on television but will never return to its home ground—Old Trafford—as they wish to avoid giving any money to the Glazers' commercial enterprises. Alternatively, a small part of FC United's support has given up its affiliation to Manchester United in its entirety.

Supporters tend to share a desire to see "their" club experience success. With that in mind, discussions about what are the aims and ambitions of FC United are common. In 2013 FC United continues as a semi-professional football club that is based in Northern Premier League—Premier Division, which is a non-league division that plays at Level 7 of the football pyramid. Fan discussions show no consensual view between those who desperately want to the club to continue to be promoted through the football pyramid and those who feared that the club's values would have to be compromised to do so. A similar compromise emerged in December 2007, when the club played Curzon Ashton in a league match that was shifted from a 3pm commencement to 12.45pm, to allow the league to screen the match through an internet live-stream. Given that one of the reasons the club was formed was to allow supporters to watch matches at their favoured time of 3pm on a Saturday afternoon—rather than having games moved to alternative days and times to suit television schedules—it presented supporters with a dilemma which many interpreted to be the first steps towards the commercialisation they had experienced as Manchester United supporters. Yet this was further complicated by supporters' contradictory relationship with the mediatisation of football generally: while most were opposed to the change of match-commencement time, the same group of supporters were excited by the possibility that the highlights of FC United's FA Cup game at Fleetwood Town on 15 September 2007 might be shown on the BBC's *Match of the Day* show, while one FC United fan on the club's unofficial internet forum argued that he wanted to see the club's scores read out on the BBC or Sky Sports News. Quite clearly, fans' rejection of the derivatives of football's commercialisation is not complete.

Fans of FC United also have differing views on the extent to which the club is bound up with wider political issues. For some supporters the club is part of a socialist or left wing fightback against dominant modes of free-market economics and the corporatisation and financialisation of everyday life. For instance an anonymous opinion piece in the FC United club programme argued:

> The nature of the anti-capitalist, all-inclusive and community friendly orientation of FC United means that we are undoubtedly a left-leaning organisation and I think we should be proud of that in a country that is in danger of vying to the dangerous, selfish right in many quarters.

However, other supporters are keen that the club does not become associated with a specific set of political principles and ideas. Rather for them their support is bound in with a set of football-specific issues and such overtures of FC United being a "left-leaning organisation" equate to "too much politics".

In the future FC United will face challenges to its "community-centred" approach to football. The club was promoted in 2005/6, 2006/7 and 2007/8 seasons due to the team's playing ability. Despite the rise through the leagues, average attendances had slipped by around 1,000 spectators per game from the club's first season to around 2,000 fans per game—a figure at which it has since stabilised. Despite Manchester United's continued success, most FC United supporters had not relaxed their views on Malcolm Glazer. However, by pushing this point forward, Crowther[2]—in his fan diary of the club's first season in existence—also admitted that some supporters "didn't get beyond Glazer" in their motivations for defecting to FC United. Given that the formation of FC United has not displaced Glazer from Manchester United it may be the case that those who have ceased to watch FC United are disillusioned at the club not meeting what they perceived to be its main aim. All of this continues to ask what type of organisation FC United is—a social movement that is opposed to, and organised by, principles that are against the supporters' "loss" of football, or a football club which happens to be concerned with the cultural politics of sport? The answers are not uniform: some supporters want the club to progress through the league pyramid, while others wanted to stabilise at the non-league level in order to resist some of the alluring commercialisation processes. Further, some fans want the club to have a greater involvement in questions of social justice across and beyond football while others believe there to be too much politics associated with the club. The future also holds promise for FC United: it continues to be a community-centred organisation that is owned by its supporters and the proposed move to its own, community-owned stadium in Moston presents even more opportunities for engagement with local residents. FC United continues as a community-led organisation and will face future challenges as an organisation that seeks to represent its supporters' *and* owners' interests.

Chapter 37
OMONOIA, NICOSIA: WHEN THE "COMMUNIST BANDITS" FORMED A FOOTBALL TEAM [1]

Vassilios Ioakimidis

On the evening of 18 May 2011 the city centre of Nicosia was taken over by thousands of jubilant Greek Cypriots, gathering from all parts of southern Cyprus. People of all ages were celebrating while waving red flags, wearing Che Guevara T-shirts and holding hammer and sickle banners. The euphoric atmosphere changed when a group of young people with covered faces started throwing missiles against the central police station in the city, housed in an imposing colonial building formerly used by British imperial forces. At the same time another group of young people smashed the makeshift kiosks of the Cypriot conservative party (DYSI) and threw petrol bombs against the stalls and pre-election billboards of the ultra-nationalist organisation ELAM. By midnight riot police had evacuated the streets after hours of street fighting. Eighteen people were arrested, five required hospitalisation, and the police station and several high street shops sustained serious damages.

Bearing in mind that the city centre of Nicosia is still divided by a ceasefire buffer zone, patrolled by the United Nations and that the recent history of Cyprus is dominated by episodes of ethnic violence, political repression, anti-communist witch hunts and nationalist hysteria, it is not surprising that several tourists thought that they were caught in the middle of yet another episode of political or ethnic violence. To their surprise however, what they had just witnessed was the OMONOIA Nicosia football club fans celebrating their team's victory in the Cyprus Cup for the thirteenth time in their history. Only four days before the parliamentary elections the line that separated football celebration from political demonstration was blurred. In reality such a line never really existed in the history of Cypriot football, which has always been bound to the volatile politics of the island. Even today the most discreet way to inquire about the political beliefs of a Greek Cypriot is to ask the question "Which team do you support?"

OMONOIA FC, one of the two most popular teams on the island, is the direct product of Cyprus's volatile political history and it still maintains constitutionally defined formal links with the Workers' Party of Cyprus (AKEL). The vast majority of OMONOIA fans are supporters of the AKEL party and the ultras are vocal members of the anti-fascist and anti-nationalist movement in Cyprus. When OMONOIA plays against its main rival, APOEL (the football team linked to the nationalist and right wing sections of the political spectrum), the matches routinely end in riots which shape party politics and fuel debates between the two major political parties for several weeks.

Even though there are several football clubs across Europe whose history is related to the struggles of labour movements and the working class, only in a handful of cases are progressive politics still seen as being inextricably linked to the formal mission of the club. OMONOIA FC is definitely one of those exceptions where politics still determine the function of the club at all levels. The largely unknown, extraordinary political history of the club was shaped by two major developments which determined the modern history of island: the formation of the Communist Party of Cyprus, and the use of nationalism as a "divide and rule" tool utilised by British colonialism. The Green Line which still divides the Greek Cypriot and Turkish Cypriot communities is a grim reminder of the impact of nationalism and colonialism in the island.

1948: The Cypriot year of discontent

In order to understand the current division in Cyprus, one has to look to the involvement of the British Empire, which in 1878 acquired the island from the declining Ottoman Empire as part of an exchange for British diplomatic support provided to the Ottomans. At the time the Greek speaking community, which constituted the vast majority of the local population, welcomed British rule, hoping for the modernisation of the island and enhancement of religious rights for the Christian community. Nevertheless, it soon became clear that the British did not intend to cultivate the local economy, let alone enhance civil or religious rights. Cyprus was primarily used by the British as a military base at the crossroads of three continents. Underdevelopment, illiteracy and severe poverty continued to overwhelm the vast majority of Cypriots irrespective of ethnic origin or religion. A small elite was educated by the British in order to run the state apparatus while most of the population lived in conditions of extreme poverty and severe exploitation. None of the social protection legislation that emerged in the UK at the end of nineteenth or the beginning of the twentieth century was transferred to the island and thus workers, many of them minors, who worked for the British-controlled industries suffered punitively harsh working conditions.

During the 1930s the widespread disappointment and disillusionment of the majority of Cypriots with British rule was channelled into two directions: the emergence of a nationalist anti-colonial movement (dominated by the Greek community and Christian church) and the development of a labour movement influenced by the ideas of socialism (supported by workers from both Greek and Turkish communities). Anderson suggests that London initially considered the latter much more dangerous that the former.[2] Nevertheless, a widespread rebellion which broke out in 1931 demanding "Enosis" (unification with Greece) met a ruthless response from the British army and launched a period of tough governance by decree, which lasted until the independence of the country in 1960. The politically regressive policy of tightening the colonial grip on the island was justified in the House of Commons on the basis of geo-strategic calculations. Tory prime minister Anthony Eden showed no reservation when he claimed "No Cyprus, no certain facilities to protect our supply of oil. No oil, unemployment and hunger in Britain. It is as simple as that".[3]

Under these circumstances the Communist Party of Cyprus (later renamed AKEL), which was the only Cypriot political party at the time, was banned. Several Greek Cypriot and Turkish Cypriot members were arrested and deported. Despite the colonial repression and the emergence of nationalism among sections of the two communities, trade unionists continued promoting working class unity and cultivating the idea of a socialist post-colonial society. Such grassroots work paved the way to the widespread popular agitation of the 1940s.

One of the most important chapters of this struggle was written in 1948 when the Cypriot working classes engaged in some of the most prolonged and combative industrial actions in the modern history of the island. The first strike of the year involved 2,100 miners working for the US mining company CMC. The industrial action lasted for 121 days and the main demands included better working conditions, a rise in wages and the development of social insurance legislation. Despite the violent attacks by the colonial authorities against the miners, the strike was victorious and workers succeeded in forcing the employers to introduce a 33 percent pay rise. The Cypriot "year of discontent" continued with the industrial actions of the asbestos workers and construction workers who fought for the creation of a social security system and the expansion of council housing. This time the British forces, who routinely used live ammunition against the strikers, were joined by the local establishment and right wing groups—led by the Orthodox Church—to form an anti-strike front. These groups were, in embryo, the prelude to the nationalist and anti-communist paramilitary groups that developed in the 1950s. Despite the orchestrated violence against the striking workers, 1948 is still considered a watershed moment in the history of the working class in Cyprus as it offered a powerful example of class unity, beyond ethnic lines, which still inspires the efforts to overcome ethnic divisions and nationalist bigotry.

"Keep the communist bandits off our football pitch..."

Not coincidentally, 1948 is also notable because it was the year that witnessed the creation of OMONOIA football club and the permanent division of Cypriot football along political lines, several years before it split into separate ethnic leagues.

Football was initially imported to Cyprus by the British colonial elite and it was "cultivated" through the English School of Nicosia—a clone of the exclusionary institution of British public schools which aimed at educating the children of the British and local elite. The first football game on the island was officially recorded in 1900 when a "British team played against a team of indigenous footballers".[4] Eventually the new sport became popular among the local population and many local "youth and cultural associations" developed football teams as part of a broader set of activities, which not infrequently revolved around nationalist principles. The first Greek Cypriot football team was founded in 1911 in Famagusta (Anorthosis) while a Turkish Cypriot team only emerged in 1932 (Chentikaya). The necessity of the establishment of ground rules and a supervisory authority led to the creation of the Cypriot Football Federation (COP) in 1934. COP was founded by seven Greek Cypriot football teams and one Turkish Cypriot one and it was largely controlled by the Greek Cypriot right wing elite.

Along with the extensive working class struggles that dominated much of the political development in 1948, Cyprus was also overshadowed by the civil war raging in Greece. Several Greek Cypriot communists had joined the war supporting Greek partisans fighting against national forces and their Anglo-American allies. In Cyprus the local establishment, supported by British authorities, had adopted the argument that this war was the outcome of the rebellion of "bloodthirsty communist gangs". Thus throughout the country there was a systematic effort to suppress expressions of solidarity to the Greek partisans. Sports were not exempted from the anti-communist witch hunt.

In May 1948 the executive board of the Nicosia-based Greek Cypriot club, APOEL, decided to send a letter of support to the Hellenic Amateur Athletics Association controlled by the right wing government of Athens. This statement breached the constitution of the Cypriot club which maintains its non-political character. The letter included a celebration of Greek nationalism concluding that our sports club "hopes for an end of the ethnocide mutiny". Such terminology was widely used by the right wing to indicate that the civil war was not the outcome of political suppression and foreign intervention but was caused by the "mutiny" of "Moscow-influenced traitor bandits".

The reaction against this letter was prompt within APOEL. Five leftist footballers refused to sign the letter and vocally denounced right wing bigotry. Unsurprisingly, they faced the backlash of right wing newspapers which stated that "we should make clear to the five or six communist footballers who refused to sign the letter: get OUT of our stadia. You can make your own stadia and play for the Russian Football Federation. In our football pitch only the Greek minded players are allowed to play football and not the ones who support bandits".[5] Under pressure from the right wing press and the broader anti-communist spirit of the time, four footballers were suspended for three months and one was permanently excluded from the activities of the club.

The reaction of the leftist athletes was widely celebrated by working class and trade unionist football fans. Many football fans saw the APOEL authoritarianism as a reflection of wider suppression of socialist ideas in Cyprus and decided to act in a way that respects the co-operative values of the Cypriot working class movement. In June 1948 a Nicosia local socialist councillor and prominent football supporter, Dr Mattheos Papapetrou, initiated a broad meeting in support of the suspended footballers. In this meeting it was decided that the footballers should not return to APOEL but instead play for a new football club. The new football club was named OMONOIA (unity), and it was decided that the colour had to be green as a gesture of respect to the colours of EPON, the Greek communist youth association that had shone as part of the Greek resistance to the Nazis during the Second World War. The emblem of the new club was the Shamrock, a symbol that clearly denoted the founders' anti-British, anti-colonial sentiment. The principles of the new club reflected some of the values of the growing co-operative movement; several notable trade unionists were included in the first executive board. The involvement of AKEL members on the board of directors has remained constant ever since.

Within weeks of the meeting, thousands of mostly working class Greek Cypriots registered as members of OMONOIA, transforming the new "association" to the most popular football club in Cyprus. This example was followed by groups of progressive Cypriots from other regions who decided to abandon the football teams formed by the local establishment and create inclusive clubs that would oppose right wing oppression. In 1949 three more football teams were created, adopting similar values. Eventually, progressive football teams founded their own league—though it was short-lived and was dismantled in 1954 in the face of oppression from nationalist paramilitary groups.

The division of Cyprus and the ultras' reprioritisation of political action

The 1950s were a decade characterised by the rise of the island's "two nationalisms". On the one hand Greek Cypriot nationalism escalated its efforts for unification with Greece (Enosis), establishing a very effective anti-colonial paramilitary movement (EOKA). This movement was supported by the right wing government in Athens which had emerged victorious from the Greek Civil War. The military wing of EOKA was led by Grivas, a veteran of the Greek civil war, notorious for his involvement in the mass murder of communists in rural Greece. Grivas was very clear that part of his struggle against British rule was the isolation and extermination of the Cypriot left. On the other hand British authorities, in an attempt to contain the growing threat of Greek Cypriot nationalism, encouraged and armed the creation of a Turkish Cypriot paramilitary group, the TMT. Turkish Cypriot nationalism developed on the basis of the idea that the two ethnic communities should be separated, thus favouring the partition of the island. A common characteristic between the two nationalist movements and their armed wings was their policy of targeting communists and trade unionists. In the peak of the ethnic conflict the Cypriot left was the only section of the political spectrum that supported the idea of a united Cyprus independent of the "motherlands" and imperialist powers. Such political objectives attracted a ferocious response from the nationalist paramilitary groups which resulted in the torture and assassination of several Cypriot communists.

In 1960 Cyprus gained its independence but the ethnic conflicts had already scarred Cypriot society in a way that seemed impossible to heal. Turkish Cypriots fortified themselves in enclaves and the rise of Greek Cypriot nationalism soon took the form of a second paramilitary campaign attempting to revive the "Enosis" (unification with Greece) agenda. In the summer of 1974 a group of right wing extremists controlled and armed by the Athens military junta attempted a coup d'état against the elected president of Cyprus. Turkey immediately intervened, invading the island and occupying the north of Cyprus. The aftermath of the short but extremely violent war of the summer of 1974 left the island divided—politically, ideologically and geographically—into two ethnic communities, which were separated by a heavily militarised ceasefire line.

The division of Cyprus radically changed the agenda of the Cypriot left, which since then has prioritised the rapprochement of the two communities as the main political objective of the movement. Since the 1970s and despite the domination of nationalist rhetoric, the Cypriot left, on both sides of the dividing line, has promoted the need for the reunification and demilitarisation of the island.

OMONOIA football club, reflecting such an agenda, has maintained its strong political character and its supporters have attempted to make use of football as a means to challenge nationalism and encourage the reunification of the two communities. As part of this campaign the OMONOIA supporters have unofficially denounced the use of the Greek Flag (still used in several government and public buildings) and have focused on symbols of class unity.

A recent report[6] indicated that today more than 80 percent of the OMONOIA football supporters politically support AKEL and the vast majority of them consider politics a "highly essential" dimension of the football team's character and mission. This is particularly evident among the OMONOIA "Gate 9" ultras who systematically participate in political mobilisations across the country. Perhaps the central aspect of such political involvement is the engagement with the growing anti-fascist movement.

Gate 9 ultras are founding members of the "Alerta" network that brings together anti-fascist football supporters across Europe. Because of their political mission, the OMONOIA supporters faced criticism from the Cypriot establishment when, in the aftermath of the reopening of checkpoints in 2003, they started using football as a platform for rapprochement with Turkish Cypriots. The relaxation at the checkpoints meant that people from both communities were able to cross the Green Line for the first time in almost 30 years. Soon after the reopening several dozen Turkish Cypriots were invited to attend a football game of OMONOIA mixing with OMONOIA ultras and holding banners displaying the word "peace". The symbolism of such action had an important impact in Cypriot society, demonstrating the willingness of the younger generation of leftist Cypriots to defy the restrictions of nationalist separation—still powerful in the island—and defend cross-community and working class unity.

The emergence of Greek neo-fascism, particularly with the rise of the fascist Golden Dawn party, which has founded a branch in Cyprus, has further crystallised OMONOIA ultras' political activism. In 2011 the ultras decided to unite with other progressive organisations and organise a summer festival which included activities, music and discussions that focused on challenging racism and fascism. During this event a space was given to Palestinian activists and the radical anti-racist organisation KISA. Moreover, OMONOIA ultras decided to distribute free tickets to immigrants and encourage their involvement in the activities of the club.

When immigrants and anti-racists were attacked by fascist groups in 2010, OMONOIA ultras did not hesitate in publicising an announcement that highlighted the need for further radicalisation of their members in order to defend social justice "in any way possible":

> A constant principle of the Gate 9 ultras is related to the struggle against racism, fascism and social divisions. The unprecedented rise of fascist attacks combined with nationalism—this incurable disease of our island!—has created a very dangerous context. At the same time, such phenomena maximise our determination for action and reaction whenever and whichever way required![7]

As Cyprus is now experiencing the reappearance of fascism and the growth of social inequality, OMONOIA supporters leave no space for misunderstanding with regard to their political commitment to the future struggles—a historical commitment which has been tested over the years and has been reaffirmed in recent times.

Chapter 38
MILITANT ACTION AGAINST SPORTS APARTHEID
Peter Hain

In 1969-70 on the back of rising direct action and strikes across Europe, sport might have appeared an unusual choice for political protest: at best peripheral, at worst eccentric.

If so, that's a fundamental misunderstanding of the white South African psyche under apartheid. Whites were sports mad, Afrikaner whites especially fanatical about rugby. Whether it was participation in the Olympics or a cricket tour, international sport gripped the white nation as nothing else—and more importantly granted them the international respectability and legitimacy they increasingly craved as the evil reality of apartheid began to be exposed abroad by horrors such as the 1960 Sharpeville massacre.

It was also more effective and easier to access, target and protest against sports links than it was to take on the might of either international capital or military alliances, both of which underpinned the white supremacist state. At that time, moreover, resistance inside the country had been suppressed: Nelson Mandela and his comrades imprisoned on Robben Island, the African National Congress (ANC) and other anti-apartheid parties outlawed, their leaders banned.

South African teams had always been all-white and the whole sports system was riddled with apartheid. Apartheid laws barred mixed clubs and mixed school sport as well as preventing teams from one racial group playing in an area designated for another. Even black-only teams playing away required special permission.

The South African Non-Racial Olympic Committee (SAN-ROC) had been forced into exile, its leaders banned and harassed to such an extent that, like the ANC, it could no longer operate legally inside the country. SAN-ROC's leader at the time, Dennis Brutus, was successively banned, put under house arrest, and finally sentenced to hard labour on Robben Island. During an attempt to escape his ban and attend an International Olympic Committee (IOC) meeting in Europe in 1963, he was arrested on the Mozambique-Swaziland border and taken back to Johannesburg police headquarters. Trying to escape again, he was shot in the stomach. An ambulance for whites arrived, found he was a "coloured" (mixed race) and drove off; he waited bleeding on the pavement for a vehicle that could take non-whites. Nevertheless SAN-ROC was successful in getting South Africa suspended from the Olympics for the first time in 1964.

That sport was an issue absolutely central to the ideology of white domination was demonstrated with devastating clarity by the mouthpiece of the government, *Die Transvaler*, on 7 September 1965. Pointing out that "the white race has hitherto maintained itself in the southern part of Africa" because "there has been no miscegenation", its editorial continued:

The absence of miscegenation was because there was no social mixing between white and non-white... In South Africa the races do not mix on the sports field. If they mix on the sports field then the road to other forms of social mixing is wide open... With an eye to upholding the white race and its civilisation, not one single compromise can be entered into—not even when it comes to a visiting rugby team.

In Britain all but the die-hard right was outraged at the South African government's refusal in September 1968 to accept Basil D'Oliveira's inclusion in the England cricket team. A coloured South African, he had qualified as a top England player after being barred from reaching those heights in his own country. The subsequent cancellation of the tour proved to be a watershed.

Yet, despite this, the English cricket authorities announced in January 1969 that they would proceed with the scheduled 1970 cricket tour by a white South African team. There was uproar. In May 1969 SAN-ROC held a public meeting in London and, among others, I raised from the floor the question of direct action to stop the tour. Dennis Brutus was in the chair and very supportive. Sports apartheid protests in Britain up to that time had been symbolic—holding up banners outside sports grounds and the like. These had been impressive and vital stages in the process of mobilising awareness. Indeed they still had an important role to play.

But the new dimension was direct action—physically disrupting the very events themselves and thereby posing both a threat and a challenge which could not be ignored by the sports elites who had been impervious to moral appeals and symbolic protest. Because it was novel and had such a potential for impact, it also had the advantage of being highly newsworthy with strong visual images in the new television age. It was the product of that unique late 1960s era of student sit-ins, Vietnam demos, the Paris 1968 revolt, the American anti-war and civil rights movements. I and others merely applied similar direct action techniques to the world of sport.

A new more militant movement gathered momentum alongside the Anti-Apartheid Movement which maintained the discreet, sometimes uneasy, distance necessary to its more conventional role. A private tour by an all-white South African club side sponsored by a wealthy businessman, Wilf Isaacs, experienced the first-ever taste of direct action against cricket in Britain. The same month a Davis Cup tennis match in Bristol between South Africa and Britain was disrupted in front of live television coverage.

The publicity for each direct action protest encouraged others. The fact that the events were taking place across the country and action could be taken locally meant the movement was characterised by considerable local autonomy and spontaneity. A network soon fell into place.

With the active encouragement of Dennis Brutus and SAN-ROC, the Stop the Seventy Tour Committee (STST) was launched at a press conference in September 1969. It had broad support from the AAM and National Union of Students, Christian groups, Young Liberals, Young Communists, to the International Socialists. Finding myself propelled into being its national chairman and spokesperson I pledged "mass demonstrations and disruptions throughout the 1970 tour". I also promised demonstrations against the Springbok rugby tour which, rather belatedly, we had realised was due to start in six weeks time and became a dummy run for stopping the following summer's cricket tour.

A mass movement was snowballing, locally based, spontaneous, independently organised, usually focused around student unions, though involving local AAM groups, trade unions, socialists, liberals, independents and the churches. It was predominantly, though by no means exclusively, a youth movement and soon took the rugby tour by storm.

The opening match against Oxford University was switched after strong opposition from both the college authorities and student activists who sprayed weedkiller on the ground and threatened to wreck the match. The tour organisers could not have played more into our hands. Switching the match to Twickenham at the last minute attracted front page lead stories on the morning of the match and set the scene for the remaining games of the 25-match tour.

Local organisers suddenly realised they were part of a mass national movement. Each of the matches saw disruptions and demonstrations of varying sizes. In Northern Ireland (already in turmoil following civil rights protests) the match was cancelled for security reasons.

The white South African establishment was apoplectic; the government-supporting newspaper, Die Beeld, stated:

> We have become accustomed to Britain becoming a haven for all sorts of undesirables from other countries. Nevertheless, it is

degrading to see how a nation can allow itself to be dictated to by this bunch of left wing, workshy, refugee, long hairs who in a society of any other country would be rejects.

In Britain the right wing was equally apoplectic. Police tactics became increasingly aggressive. Our tactics changed as well. We knew that the STST campaign had by now been infiltrated (including at a national level). My home telephone number was tapped. So an "inner group" of trusted activists was established to work on special projects, including booking a young woman into the Springbok team's Park Lane hotel. She gummed up the players' bedroom door locks with solidifying agent to delay them getting out on the morning of the pre-Christmas match at Twickenham. An STST activist also chained himself into the driver's seat of the team's coach waiting outside the hotel, while others evaded the heavy police cordon at Twickenham and chained themselves to the goalposts until they were cut free. Orange smoke pellets were thrown among the players, which, as well as interrupting play, produced dramatic television and newspaper pictures. Wherever it went, the team was under siege, resting, training or playing.

The tour finally staggered to an end, with the players bitter and unsettled. For the vice-captain, Tommy Bedford, it was cathartic. Within a year he publicly stated that the campaign should be listened to, not vilified, and praised our objectives. Although his response was a relatively isolated one in South Africa, it signalled the huge and destabilising impact of our campaign.

The reaction among the black majority in South Africa was fantastic. After their release decades later both Nelson Mandela and Govan Mbeki told me that on Robben Island news of the demonstrations had given all the political prisoners an enormous morale boost.

The rugby tour had provided the movement with a perfect springboard from which to work on preventing the cricket tour, due then to start at the beginning of May. The fact that the Springboks had gone through to the bitter end meant the protest movement had been consolidated throughout the country. But opposition, coordinated by the AAM, went much wider. The churches, led by the former England cricket captain and Bishop of Woolwich, David Sheppard, urged cancellation. The multiracial Commonwealth Games, due to take place in Edinburgh at the same time, became an important lever.

While all this was going on, a carefully timed bombshell exploded. Late in the night on 19 January 1970 demonstrators simultaneously raided 14 of the 17 county cricket club grounds. All were daubed with painted slogans. In addition a small patch in the outfield of Glamorgan's Cardiff ground was dug up and weed killer was sprayed on Warwickshire's Birmingham ground.

Pre-planned telephone reports from each small, tight group poured in throughout the night to the Press Association news agency and to my home. In the morning the coordinated protest dominated the radio bulletins and there were screaming headlines with photos in the evening papers and television programmes and the following day's national newspapers. The protests were a devastating shock to the cricket authorities and a surprise to almost everyone else. The widespread strength of the movement had been starkly revealed in an operation seemingly carried out with almost military precision. More than this, the fear at the back of the cricket authorities' mind—and probably shared by most others—had suddenly been realised: the spectre of a cricket tour collapsing amid damaged pitches and weed killer was conjured up and began to crystallise.

Speculation was rife, especially as it was not clear who was responsible. The Anti-Apartheid Movement denied all knowledge. People inevitably accused STST—as it alone had the organisational capacity necessary to mount the raids—but I said (accurately) that the STST national committee had not authorised or approved the action, thereby distancing us from it. But it was indeed a covert operation by key STST activists executed from the centre with deadly efficiency and effect.

Within weeks 300 reels of barbed wire arrived at Lord's and most county grounds introduced guard dogs and security. The pressure on the cricket authorities grew. There was speculation that African, Asian and Caribbean countries would withdraw from the Edinburgh Commonwealth Games. One by one a range of public bodies came out against the tour and there was talk of trade unions taking industrial action. Labour MPs, including the AAM's vice-chair, Peter Jackson, said they would join sit-down pitch invasions. The chair of the government-sponsored Community Relations Commission, Frank Cousins, told the home secretary that the tour would do "untold damage" to race relations.

On 12 February the governing body, the Cricket Council, met at Lord's on a snowy night, the pitch eerily surrounded by barbed wire, silhouetted against the whiteness. Lord's, the magisterial home of international cricket, looked for all the world like a concentration camp, symbolising the torment which had torn asunder this most dignified and graceful of games. It was announced that, on security grounds, the tour had been cut drastically to 12 matches from its original schedule of 28, and on just eight grounds instead of the original 22; artificial all-weather pitches would be installed as an additional security precaution.

The attorney general, Sir Peter Rawlinson, attacked the Labour home secretary, James Callaghan, for remaining "neutral" and thereby "acknowledging the licence to riot". Rawlinson also called for an injunction to be taken out against me, insisting my public statements threatening to stop the tour constituted a direct incitement to illegal action. After cabinet documents were made public 30 years later (and, ironically, when I was a serving Labour government minister), it was also revealed that ministers had discussed whether or not to prosecute me, with James Callaghan in favour.[1]

During February and March the campaign mushroomed. Committees and action groups to complement those established during the rugby tour sprang up throughout the country. The Labour prime minister, Harold Wilson, publicly opposed the tour for the first time and said that people "should feel free to demonstrate against the tour", though he specifically criticised disruptive protests. The British Council of Churches also called for peaceful demonstrations. The queen announced that neither she nor any member of the royal family would make the traditional visit to the Lord's test match, and the South Africans would not receive the traditional invitation to Buckingham Palace.

Then, with the tour just six weeks away, the Supreme Council for Sport in Africa announced that 13 African countries would definitely boycott the Commonwealth Games if the tour went ahead; Asian and Caribbean countries soon followed, raising the prospect of whites-only games running alongside a whites-only cricket tour. Sparked off by nationally-led but locally-delivered militant action, the campaign had provoked an international diplomatic and political furore.

But the Anti-Apartheid Movement, with its strong links to the labour movement, played a crucial organisational role, both as a participant in STST and in its own right. An AAM poster caught the public's imagination and was widely published in the press. Under the caption "If you could see their national sport you might be less keen to see their cricket", it showed a policeman beating defenceless blacks in Cato Manor township outside Durban. There was an ideal spectrum of protest including Bishop David Sheppard's Fair Cricket Campaign with its links to establishment opinion and SAN-ROC with its expert international contacts. Although STST's direct militant strategy powered the whole campaign, it could have been isolated without a great hinterland of broad public support.

Meanwhile our organisational preparations proceeded. Plans went ahead to blockade the team at Heathrow Airport. Thousands of tickets were being bought up by local groups (the games had been made all-ticket). The STST Special Action Group ingeniously discovered the existence of an old tube train tunnel running right underneath Lord's with an air shaft which could facilitate a dramatic entry to the ground. But, although such activity was coordinated by STST from the centre, local groups operated quite independently. There was also a considerable degree of individualistic autonomy in the campaign. People were quite literally doing their own thing.

Finally, extremely reluctantly, and under huge pressure, the Cricket Council met in emergency session and the tour was off. A campaign conceived by a few people had grown to win with mass support. STST had emerged as one of the very few British protest groups ever to have achieved its objectives completely.[2]

1970 was a cathartic year. Apart from STST's success and the Olympics expulsion, South Africa was expelled from Davis Cup tennis, international athletics, swimming, cycling, wrestling and gymnastics. This followed on from an expulsion from boxing in 1968 and judo, pentathlon and weightlifting in 1969. One by one they got the push in team sports. And the Springboks never toured Britain again until after the fall of apartheid.

Shortly after the cricket tour was stopped, the Financial Times reported:

Is it purely coincidental that the stepping up of the anti-apartheid campaign in Britain and America during the past year or so has been accompanied by a sharp falling off in the inflow of capital into the country? Those who follow these matters are convinced it is not.

For the first time in ten long bitter years since the Sharpeville massacre black South Africans and whites involved in the resistance had something to cheer about. Moses Garoeb, a leading freedom fighter in the South West African People's Organisation, told me in 1970 that STST had been an "inspiration" to SWAPO cadres in the African bush as they heard the news on their radios. I replied that it was the dedication and sacrifices of people like them which inspired us to campaign even more vigorously.

Twenty five years later the captain of the ill-fated tour, Ali Bacher, told me generously:

> There is no doubt the cancellation forced us to change. We wouldn't have done so otherwise. It was the turning point. There was no way back for us. You were right—we were wrong.

Chapter 39
THE WORKERS' SPORTS MOVEMENT[1]
Simon Basketter

Most people watch sport and there was a time when the left debated and organised participation in sport on a mass scale. Between the First and Second World Wars, hundreds of thousands of workers took part in left wing sports movements. These movements, mostly ignored by today's history, were set up in conscious opposition to the growing sports industry—and were highly political.

German Communist leader Ernst Grube declared, "Worker sport has nothing in common with the petty bourgeoisie's craving for freedom; it is Marxist class war on all fronts of sport and physical exercise." That sounded a bit less bombastic in those days—because this was a global movement.

A Socialist Gymnastics Union had existed in the US as early as 1850. But it was in response to sport organised by the bosses in the 1880s and 1890s that workers' sporting events started to take off. Workers' gymnastics and cycling societies were formed across Germany in 1893. In 1895 a British workers' cycling club was organised around the Clarion newspaper. Hiking groups grew up around Europe. Germany was the centre of the movement. There were over 350,000 worker sportsmen and women organised there before the First World War.

Workers' sports were consciously different from "bourgeois" sports, in that they were open to all. A good example was the setting up of a "Workers' Wimbledon" tennis championship. The idea was that workers' sports would remove class barriers from participation in sport, but also substitute socialist values for capitalist ones. That's why, prior to 1914, there was an emphasis on activities that could be less competitive, such as gymnastics, cycling, hiking and swimming. The German newspaper *Volksstimme* (*The People's Voice*) deplored "our youth's interest in sport which is solely concerned with contest and victory".

However, after the First World War competitive sport became ever more dominant. So left wing sports groups embraced more competitive activities—partially to keep members.

Political divisions also shaped the form of labour sports' organisation. The International Union of Red Sports and Gymnastics Associations, better known as the Red Sport International (RSI), was founded in Moscow on 23 June 1921. It hoped to run sports with the values of the Russian Revolution. It wanted "revolutionary proletarian sports and gymnastics organisations in all countries of the world" as "support centres for the proletariat in its class struggle".

The RSI aimed to act as a counter-balance to the Lucerne Sport International (LSI). Established in 1920 by representatives of European worker sports federations, the LSI was allied to the Socialist (meaning Labour-type social democratic) parties. The president of the All-Union Council of Physical Culture, V Mikhailov, said:

> The reformist Lucerne Sports International helps the bourgeoisie with its policy of using sport to divert the workers from the revolutionary-class tasks of the proletariat Everyone remembers how the English trade unionists, in the midst of the [1926] general strike sought to divert the workers with their "portentous" resolution: "To call on workers to organise soccer games with the police on the days of the strike." The Red Sport International must use all means to strengthen its work in the struggle against using sport to divert the broad masses from the revolutionary tasks of the working class.

This reflected the key division in the labour movement after the First World War. The Communists believed that capitalism could only be beaten by revolution, while the Socialists looked to reforms from above. This battle reflected one going on in Russia between revolution and counter-revolution. One consequence of the Civil War after the revolution was that sport essentially moved from a factory domain—bosses setting up soccer teams, etc—to the military; fit people make better soldiers.

But nonetheless there was an ideological debate on the nature of sport. One post-revolutionary faction called the "Hygienists" rejected all competitive sports, contrasting sports with healthy exercise and physical culture. Such games as soccer, boxing and weightlifting were deemed injurious to mental and physical health. The Hygienists instead favoured participation over watching sports, calling for an end to grandstands and spectators.

The Proletarian Culture Movement, or Proletkult, which rejected all prior culture as bourgeois, sought to advocate a specifically class approach to all areas of culture, including sports. The practices of the pre-revolutionary period had to be abandoned, and an entirely new culture, practised by and for the working class, was to take its place. This concern led them to criticise any form of competitive sport derived from bourgeois society. They preferred instead what they called "production gymnastics, excursions, and pageants". At times they invented specifically proletarian games, two of which were "Rescue from the Imperialists" and "Smuggling Revolutionary Literature across the Frontier". These and other Proletkult pastimes were participatory activities. No Proletkult member dreamed of creating a "National League of Literature Smuggling" for spectators. For both the Proletkult and the Hygienists spectator sport was anathema.

These experimental and utopian approaches survived well into the early 1930s before their eventual eradication under Stalin. But through the 1920s there were moves to a competitive approach that could inspire proper values. Anatoli Lunacharsky, the first head of the Commissariat of Enlightenment, argued that workers must train for "the coming struggle with the bourgeoisie".

With the full domination of Stalinism it became straightforward. Russia was in competition with the West and sport was one of the ways of doing it. This required the creation of a highly trained sports elite. In 1935 Alexander Kosarev, head of Komsomol, the party's youth organisation, would announce, "Soviet athletes must not only improve All-Union records but beat world records as well. In the Soviet physical movement 1935 must be the year of the world record."

Outside of Russia membership of the Communist RSI groups in most countries was significantly smaller than the LSI ones. But the

RSI was still substantial. So in Germany the mainstream workers' sports organisation ATUS had some 1.2 million members in 1929. But there were also 250,000 workers in Communist sport groups. They were expelled from the ATUS in 1928 for insisting that sport groups should commit themselves to revolution.

This reflected Communist policy at the time—and it didn't always fail. In both France and Germany the majority of workers' football clubs joined the Communist group after the split.

But the Socialist groups were on a different scale. In 1926 ATUS opened the most modern sports facility in Germany, the Bundesschule in Leipzig. One affiliate, the Workers' Cycling Association, was the largest cycling organisation in the world with 320,000 members. It even ran its own bicycle factory. In Austria and Czechoslovakia the movement was also impressive. The Czech groups, for instance, taught over 10,000 people a year how to swim.

A further measure of the flourishing movement was the labour sports press. The German groups published 60 newspapers with a combined circulation of 800,000—and that's excluding local editions. On top of this the Communist sports groups were printing 11 regional and four national sports papers of their own by 1932.

The most imposing part of the labour sports movement was the Workers' Olympiads. These were organised as a counter to the national chauvinism of the recently revived mainstream Olympics. The first was held in Prague in 1921. At the time the losers of the First World War were banned from competing in the Olympics. In sharp contrast, the Prague games featured competition between worker athletes from "enemy" nations. This theme was also prevalent at the first official Labour Olympiad in 1925. Held in Germany under the motto "No more war", more than 150,000 people attended.

The 1931 Second Olympiad in the Austrian capital, Vienna, was in many ways the high point of the workers' sports movement. The social democrats who governed "Red Vienna" built a brand new stadium and even offered their guests reduced fares on public transport. Tens of thousands of athletes stayed in workers' houses in the city. On the last day of the Olympiad some 250,000 people came to watch the "festive march" through Vienna of an estimated 100,000 people from 26 nations. They toppled a symbolic figure that represented capitalism.

But sports groups associated with the Communist RSI were excluded. Besides the Russians, these included some 250,000 Germans and 100,000 Czechs plus smaller contingents from Europe and the US. The RSI organised its own competitions, the international "spartakiada" (named after the rebel slave gladiator Spartacus). They were held in Moscow in 1928 and in Berlin in 1931. This division wasn't fully bridged until the third and final workers' Olympiad, held in 1937 in Antwerp, Belgium.

In response to the rise of fascism, the Communists—under the influence of Stalin—declared the popular front. Political differences were to be ignored in the name of unity. So Antwerp offered a huge display of labour solidarity. Some 50,000 filled the stadium on the final day, and 200,000 marched.

But the movement suffered heavily as fascism swept through Europe. A workers' Olympiad scheduled for Barcelona in 1936 had to be aborted after Franco's attempted military coup led to civil war. The German ATUS had been one of the Nazis' first targets in 1933. And Hitler's armies suppressed others as they marched across the continent. Within two years a similar fate befell the labour sports movement in Czechoslovakia as Hitler's armies occupied.

But it wasn't just repression that hurt the labour sports organisations. More and more the labour press gave pride of place to the spectacle aspect of organised sport. In 1931 a front page headline in the Viennese socialist daily during the workers' Olympics proclaimed "Austria's Victories at the Olympiad". The "spartakiada" eventually became internal Russian events for displays of pomp.

The growth of corporate sport, combined with the Cold War, meant that the workers' sport movement never recovered. But nonetheless their attempts to organise workers' sport are worth remembering.

Chapter 40
WORKING ON THE CHAIN GANG AT
THE TOUR DE FRANCE

Michael Lavalette

In July 2014 the annual highlight of the world's cycling road-race calendar, the Tour de France, will return to the roads of Britain. For two days the peloton* will race across Yorkshire, while a third day will be spent in Cambridge and London.

The race offers people the chance to follow the team tactics of road racing, while marvelling at the riders' athleticism and will power. Twenty two teams of nine riders will race over 2,000 miles on the road, and in the process traverse some of the highest mountains in France. They will race through wind, rain, extreme heat and, occasionally, snow.

Road racing is very tactical. Each race, or each day of a "Grand Tour",[†] can be between 100 and 200 miles in length and the point is to get one of your team over the line first—or on a Grand Tour to get your leader to the finish ahead of, or alongside, his main rivals. But this means trying to second guess what other teams are trying to do. It means trying to control the race over the day, but doing so while looking after your leader. It means trying to ensure that your leader is protected from the wind and the elements so that in the last few miles he has the energy to win or to stay at the front and get home safely ("drafting", riding close behind another rider, means saving up to 25 percent of your energy output compared to the rider you are following).

Cycling is an unusual team sport. Teams dedicate themselves to the demands of their leader, but at the end of the race each rider gets an individual classification within the race. In any race it is perfectly possible that a strong "rouleur"[‡] could head the peloton on his leader's behalf for much of the race. But towards the end, exhausted, he will drop off and finish last (sometimes struggling over the finish line 15 or 20 minutes behind the winner). But if his team leader or team sprinter has done well then that will, in no small part, be because of his role controlling the race from the front at the start.

In Tour teams each of the nine riders has their own task to perform. Some will be expected to gain stage victories; others will lead out the (specialist) sprinter; mountain specialists will protect their

---

* French terms dominate road cycling. The peloton refers to a large group of racing cyclists, riding in close formation. Sometimes races break up and here you have several pelotons within the race. The word means a "ball of wool or string" but was used figuratively to refer to a group of soldiers—and is the origin of the English word "platoon".

† There are three "Grand Tours": the Tour de France, the Giro d'Italia and the Vuelta a España.

‡ A rouler is a cyclist who is capable of riding at the front of the peloton for a long period of time.

leader in the mountains or set off at high speed up one of the slopes to try and grab a victory. Others will be the domestiques* who fetch and carry water, food, rain jackets and clothing for the others.

But no matter their job in the team, each will also work to protect their nominated team leader who will be going for a good position on the GC (the overall standings on the "general classification" at the end of the three-week race). They are all expected to drive themselves into the ground to protect and shelter him. Be on hand to bring him back to the peloton if he needs to stop for a comfort break, or has a mechanical problem. They will be expected to get him out of all and any difficulties—and this can include giving him their bike, or one of their wheels, if he needs it.

Today the Tour pulls in phenomenal sums of money: it is worth more than the total income of all the other European races put together.

Yet only a tiny proportion of this will go to the 400 or so professional cyclists on the European circuit. One might expect the typical professional cyclist to be earning a huge wage—like Premier League footballers. The accountants Ernst Young produce an annual report for the UCI (the professional cycling governing body) and the most recent report suggests that the average annual salary of a rider with a UCI Pro Team has risen from €190,000 in 2009 to €264,000 in 2012.[1]

But these figures mask the vast inequality within the peloton. A Pro Tour rider for example, riding for one of the top teams in the sport, will be on a basic annual salary of £30,000. At the end of 2010 the Cyclingtips website found that:

> The minimum salary for a Pro Tour rider is €35,000 (€24,000 for a new professional). A good domestique will make between €40k-€100k per year. A very good domestique (perhaps a lead-out man) will make between €100k-€200k.[2]

It is only the top team leaders who can command contracts worth hundreds of thousands of pounds.

For pro-cyclists seasons are relatively long (about six months of hard racing) but careers are short and injury is common. On average there are five injuries a week during the season, which means each rider has a one in four chance of injury. In fact, the injury rate is so

---

* A domestique is a rider whose task is to work in order to further his team leader's prospects of victory.

high that most firms will not provide health cover for tour cyclists.[3] As Daniel Coyle notes:

> They crash in sprints and on downhills, on greasy roundabouts and on sun-melted tar. They lose eyes. They go into comas. They break their backs with such regularity that they have a nifty-sounding term for it: "percussion fracture".[4]

As Coyle suggests, the injuries are usually serious. Riders travel at high speed, with little protection. When they crash, their bodies hurtle into metal machines and onto road surfaces. Flesh is ripped and burned, and bones are broken—yet riders are under intense pressure to get back on the bike and carry on.

Famously (or perhaps infamously, given his later disqualifications for doping), American cyclist Tyler Hamilton finished second in the 2002 Giro D'Italia despite fracturing his shoulder earlier in the race. In the 2003 Tour he crashed in the first stage of the race and broke his collar bone. But he got back on the bike, winning stage 16 and finishing fourth overall. By the end of the 2003 Tour race he had ground his teeth so hard to deal with the pain that he required emergency dental treatment.[5]

The racers will be driven to the very limits of human endurance by their managers and the organisers. Both are keen to create the kind of spectacle that will encourage interest from TV and investment from sponsors.

And the sponsors are key. In 2012 there were 61 principal sponsors for the 40 elite professional teams. These sponsors provided 73 percent of team revenues. When we add other sponsors into the mix the figure increases to 95 percent of all team revenue being sponsor-dependent. In fact teams adopt the names of the main sponsors and so, as sponsors change, so does the name (thus Lance Amstrong's US Postal Team became Team Discovery Channel, though the management, medical and racing team remained more or less intact).

The scale of this funding is significant. In 2009 the total budget for the 39 professional men's teams was 235 million euros. In 2012 there were 40 professional teams with a total budget of 321 million euros (an increase of 36.5 percent over the three-year period).[6]

Ensuring sponsors are happy means getting television coverage. So riders will be pushed to win races or, if that's not possible, to ensure riders are in a breakaway, or in a leading group racing up a mountain or that a rider will head off on a "suicidal" solo break—with no chance of winning but gaining plenty of air-time.

All of this means putting pressure on the riders to stretch themselves up to, and beyond, their limit.

The average speed of the Tour is on an upward curve. The riders will cover the Tour at an average speed of 39 to 40 kilometres per hour. The table below gives a flavour of how the Tour is speeding up.

Each year the organisers include more mountains for the riders to climb and more mountain top finishes, because this immense hardship is what makes "good" television, which in turn attracts the sponsors.

This conflict between "sporting endeavour" and commercial interests has been central to the Tour since its inception.

The Tour de France was born out of a circulation war between two French cycling magazines at the start of the 20th century L'Auto (which was printed on yellow paper, and hence gave birth to the leader's "yellow jersey") and Le Velo. The first "Grande Boucle" took place in 1903 with participants expected to ride 2,428 kilometres between 1 and 19 July. The first stage was from Paris to Lyon (467 kilometres) and was won in 17 hours 45 minutes. The distances covered immediately generated huge interest in the event. Cyclists were greeted by large crowds along the way and the circulation of L'Auto rocketed.

But the event also led to criticism that the sponsors were exploiting working class athletes for their own gain. Analogies were drawn between the dehumanising, overly regulated life of the tour cyclist and that of the industrial factory worker.

The following year's event was marred by all sorts of "cheating". Riders were sponsored by other papers, magazines, cafes and bike manufacturers. Riders took lifts in cars, drinks were spiked and all sorts of activities were undertaken to try and put opponents out of the race.[8] From the beginning, therefore, the Tour tested riders' physical endurance while being steeped in all sorts of shady activities.

The Tour organisers have always attempted to control the race with a series of rules and regulations that have nothing to do with cycling and everything to do with an attempt to codify and regulate the race as a national spectacle.

Riders were banned from getting any help, were prohibited from "drafting", had to carry their own food, could not accept water from anyone but had, instead, to stop and fill their bottles at wells and

Table 1[7]

Year	Stages	Riders	Dropped out (%)	Distance (km)	Average speed	Winner
1903	6	60	65	2,428	25.68	M Garin
1906	13	82	83	4,637	24.46	R Pottier
1920	15	113	81	5,503	24.07	P Thys
1924	15	157	62	5,425	24.25	O Bottecchia
1928	22	162	75	5,476	28.40	N Frantz
1938	21	96	43	4,694	31.56	G Bartali
1948	21	120	63	4,922	33.44	G Bartali
1952	23	122	36	4,898	32.23	F Coppi
1990	21	198	21	3,504	38.62	Le Mond
1992	21	198	34	3,983	39.50	M Indurain
1996	21	198	35	3,765	39.23	B Riis
1998	21	189	49	3,875	39.98	M Pantani
1999	20	180	22	3,870	40.28	L Armstrong
2000	21	177	28	3,662	39.57	L Armstrong
2001	20	189	24	3,458	40.07	L Armstrong
2002	20	189	19	3,278	39.92	L Armstrong
2003	20	198	26	3,427	40.94	L Armstrong
2004	20	188	22	3,391	40.55	L Armstrong
2005	21	189	18	3,593	41.65	L Armstrong
2006	21	176	21	3,657	40.78	O Pereiro
2007	21	189	25	3,570	39.23	A Contador
2008	21	180	19	3,559	40.49	C Sastre
2009	21	180	13	3,460	40.32	A Contador
2010	20	198	14	3,642	39.59	A Schleck
2011	21	198	16	3,630	39.79	C Evans
2012	20	198	23	3,497	39.83	B Wiggins

could not even discard any of their clothing. If the stage started in the cold, but later the day heated up, riders had to carry all their original clothing with them or face a fine.

But from the beginning the cyclists started to subvert the rules in an ongoing conflict over interpretation. The stages were so incredibly long that soon riders started to work together unofficially. Sometimes this would involve drafting; at other times it would involve collective agreement to take it easy at points in the race. So they would ride slowly all day and then race for the last hour, for example (a practice they still engage in today on some stages).[9]

In response Tour organiser (and editor of *L'Auto*) Henri Desgrange created even more rules to control the "laggards" who wouldn't race hard enough. He demanded the "ouvriers de la pedale'" increased their "productivity". A time limit was introduced. Now all riders had to complete the stage within a set period (calculated as the winner's time, plus an additional 10 percent of his time). Failure to complete within this limit resulted in disqualification. In response, in 1933, the entire peloton cycled in together, outside the time. The rule was broken. No one was disqualified.

For the future the rule was adapted so that if 15 percent of the peloton were outside the time there would be no disqualifications. This led to the creation of the gruppetto[†] or the "autobus" where, during difficult or mountainous days, riders from all teams work together, not to win but to finish collectively within the day's time limit.

But the battle was not over. Now the race organisers tried to enforce a rule that required that any day's winner had to average at least 30 kilometres per hour, or else winnings would not be paid. The battle over "speed ups" and the cyclists' "productivity" continued.

The Tour also quickly became enveloped in all sorts of discussions about "Frenchness" and this was heavily promoted by *L'Auto*. The paper did not simply cover race results. It included long descriptions of local scenery, regions, departments and famous or significant historic sites that the racers were travelling through (a practice which continues today as French television coverage includes shots of churches, castles, rivers, dams and other landmarks). These descriptions were particularly prominent during the inter-war years. The Tour organisers sold the race as a great "national healer". Cyclists were promoted as "giants" of the road and as "ouvriers de la pedale". They were portrayed as heroic and hard-working—the kind of individuals that were needed to rebuild France and French prestige in the inter-war era.

But this imagery was also turned against the Tour and the Tour organisers by the French left—and, at significant points, by the riders themselves. In 1924 the defending champion, Henri Pelissier, quit the tour in protest at the distance of the race and the petty rules riders were meant to adhere to. Campaigning journalist Albert

---

*   Pedal or bike workers.

†   The gruppetto is a large group of cyclists far behind the leaders who calculate the time they need to achieve to allow them to start the following day—and ride collectively to achieve that goal.

Londres took up the case, recounting the effects the race had on the cyclists, the illnesses they endured, the weight loss they suffered and the drugs they used to put up with the pain.

Londres described the race as a "tour of suffering" and the cyclists as the "forçat de la route" (the convicts, or chain gang labourers, of the road). Pelissier wrote to the Communist Party paper L'Humanité saying that he accepted the "excessive fatigue, suffering, pain" of his profession but he and his fellow racers wanted to be "treated as men, not dogs".

L'Humanité kept up the pressure during the inter-war years, denouncing the criminal exploitation of the "pedal workers" by the "sports profiteers". They linked their attack to a general critique of overwork, speed-ups and exploitation by French capitalism on all workers.

In the immediate aftermath of the Second World War the Tour was again promoted as an exercise of national healing. The Tour visited some of the most devastated cities and towns and seemed to promise a further "national renewal".

But again the rules and regulations of the Tour and the conflict between commercialism, profit and the "pedal workers' rights" began to emerge. There were three notable episodes.

In the 1950 Tour the cyclists found themselves racing along the Mediterranean on a particularly hot day. As temperatures reached 41 degrees celsius the riders stopped and ran into the sea to cool down. The press reported the event as a comedic break—the organisers, however, saw it as a breach of the racing code and fined all the racers. In the 1952 Tour, during a similarly hot day, on a 200 kilometre stage between Perpignan and Toulouse the cyclists decided that, rather than stop and swim, they would race slowly for the first half of the race. The organisers called the slowdown a "115 kilometre strike" and cancelled the day's winnings.

More spectacularly in 1978 the cyclists collectively walked across the finish line at Valence-D'Agen in protest at the length of the day's stage and the poor conditions they were facing as organisers put profit and commercial considerations ahead of rider safety and recovery. The grievances were varied. The riders complained that transfers were too long. When they finished racing they had to get on a bus and travel to the location of the next day's race start. But this ate into recovery time. They complained at the excessive length of the day's race. On the day in question they were expected to cover two stages of 254 kilometres between Tarbes and Valence-D'Agen and Valence-D'Agen and Toulouse. For the organisers, two stages meant twice as much income from two finishing stage hosts but for the riders it meant an excessive amount of racing. Long stages also meant early starts. The start at Tarbes was scheduled for 7.30am to enable the two stages to be completed. But this meant riders had to rise at 5am—after a long transfer the night before.

So in the face of these attacks on their working conditions the riders effectively went on strike. They cycled together and, as they approached the finishing line, all stepped off their bikes and walked across the line.

In 1998, during the height of police operations against drug taking on the Tour, the riders went on strike again. On stage 17 they stopped mid-race, sat in the road and a furious argument took place between those who wanted to go on, those who wanted to quit the Tour and those who wanted to end racing for the day. Eventually the riders got back on their bikes and rode together—refusing to race.

Cycling and the Tour are full of contradictions. And in this sense they are no different to other sports under capitalism—or indeed to other areas of cultural life under capitalism.

Road racing combines the drama, excitement and unpredictability of the race, the complex tactics, great athleticism and the spectacle of individual sacrifice for the team cause. The excitement as riders race up one of the great mountain stages of the Tour is truly awe inspiring. Yet, like all sports, the Tour also embodies conflict and exploitation. There is conflict between athletes and organisers and between the sportsmen and the global advertisers and media outlets who try to force greater, more "spectacular" efforts from riders to feed their commercial interests.

The pain, suffering and demands placed on participants have one other notable outcome. Professional cycling is, and always has been, racked by drug use. The teams demand quick recoveries and improved performances. Failure means contracts will not be renewed.

In this atmosphere the teams encourage riders to do "what is necessary"[10] and this means using all types of performance enhancers. When individuals are caught they are abandoned as "cheats". Yet there is no doubt they are the victims of a callous system of exploiting the modern day "forçat de la route".

Part 7

Alternative futures?

"PHYSICAL CULTURE", SPORT AND REVOLUTION: THE DEBATE IN POST-REVOLUTIONARY RUSSIA

Gareth Edwards

> People will divide into "parties" over the question of a new gigantic canal, or the distribution of oases in the Sahara (such a question will exist too), over the regulation of the weather and the climate, over a new theatre, over chemical hypotheses, over two competing tendencies in music, and over a best system of sports.
> —Leon Trotsky[1]

At the start of the 20th century sport had not flourished in Russia to the same extent as in countries such as Britain. The majority of the Russian population were peasants, spending hours each day on backbreaking agricultural labour. Leisure time was difficult to come by and even then people were often exhausted from their work. Of course people did still play, taking part in such traditional games as lapta (similar to baseball) and gorodki (a bowling game). A smattering of sports clubs existed in the larger cities but they remained the preserve of the richer members of society. Ice hockey was beginning to grow in popularity, and the upper echelons of society were fond of fencing and rowing, using expensive equipment most people would never have been able to afford.

In 1917 the Russian Revolution turned the world upside down, inspiring millions of people with its vision of a society built on solidarity and the fulfilment of human need. In the process it unleashed an explosion of creativity in art, music, poetry and literature. It touched every area of people's lives, including the games they played. Sport, however, was far from being a priority. The Bolsheviks, who had led the revolution, were confronted with civil war, invading armies, widespread famine and a typhus epidemic. Survival, not leisure, was the order of the day. However, during the early part of the 1920s, before the dreams of the revolution were crushed by Stalin, the debate over a "best system of sports" that Trotsky had predicted did indeed take place. Two of the groups to tackle the question of "physical culture" were the Hygienists and the Proletkultists.

Hygienists

As the name implies, the Hygienists were a collection of doctors and healthcare professionals whose attitudes were informed by their medical knowledge. Generally speaking they were critical of sport, concerned that its emphasis on competition placed participants at risk of injury. They were equally disdainful of the West's preoccupation with running faster, throwing further or jumping higher than ever before. "It is completely unnecessary and unimportant", said A A Zikmund, head of the Physical Culture Institute in Moscow, "that anyone set a new world or Russian record".[2] Instead the Hygienists advocated non-competitive physical pursuits—like gymnastics and swimming—as ways for people to stay healthy and relax.

For a period of time the Hygienists influenced Soviet policy on questions of physical culture. It was on their advice that certain sports were prohibited, and football, boxing and weightlifting were all omitted from the programme of events at the First Trade Union Games in 1925. However, the Hygienists were far from unanimous in their condemnation of sport. V V Gorinevsky, for example, was an advocate of playing tennis, which he saw as being an ideal physical exercise. Nikolai Semashko, a doctor and the People's Commissar for Health, went much further, arguing that sport was "the open gate to physical culture" which "develops the sort of will-power, strength and skill that should distinguish Soviet people".[3]

Proletkult

In contrast to the Hygienists the Proletkult (proletarian culture) movement was unequivocal in its rejection of "bourgeois" sport. Indeed it denounced anything that smacked of the old society, be it in art, literature or music. It saw the ideology of capitalism woven into the fabric of sport. Its competitiveness set workers against each other, dividing people by tribal and national identities, while the physicality of the games put unnatural strains on the bodies of the players.

In place of sport Proletkultists argued for new, proletarian forms of

Alternative futures?

play, founded on the principles of mass participation and cooperation. Often these new games were huge theatrical displays looking more like carnivals or parades than the sports we see today. Contests were shunned on the basis that they were ideologically incompatible with the new socialist society. Participation replaced spectating, and each event contained a distinct political message, as is apparent from some of their names: Rescue from the Imperialists; Smuggling Revolutionary Literature Across the Frontier; and Helping the Proletarians.

Bolsheviks

It would be easy to characterise the Bolsheviks as being anti-sports. Leading members of the party were friends and comrades of those who were most critical of sport during the debates on physical culture. Some of the leading Hygienists were close to Leon Trotsky, while Anatoly Lunacharsky, the Commissar for the Enlightenment, shared many views with Proletkult. In addition, the party's attitude to the Olympics is normally given as evidence to support this anti-sport claim. The Bolsheviks boycotted the games, arguing that they "deflect workers from the class struggle and train them for imperialist wars".[4] Yet in reality the Bolsheviks' attitudes towards sport were somewhat more complicated.

It is clear that that they regarded participation in the new physical culture as being highly important; a life-affirming activity allowing people to experience the freedom and movement of their own bodies. Lenin was convinced that recreation and exercise were integral parts of a well-rounded life. "Young people especially need to have a zest for life and be in good spirits. Healthy sport—gymnastics, swimming, hiking, all manner of physical exercise—should be combined as much as possible with a variety of intellectual interests, study, analysis and investigation... Healthy bodies, healthy minds!"[5]

Unsurprisingly, in the aftermath of the revolution, sport would play a political role for the Bolsheviks. Facing internal and external threats which would decimate the working class, they saw sport as a means by which the health and fitness of the population could be improved. As early as 1918 they issued a decree, "On Compulsory Instruction in the Military Art", introducing physical training to the education system.

This tension between the ideals of a future physical culture and the pressing concerns of the day were evident in a resolution passed by the Third All-Russia Congress of the Russian Young Communist League in October 1920:

> The physical culture of the younger generation is an essential element in the overall system of communist upbringing of young people, aimed at creating harmoniously developed human beings, creative citizens of communist society. Today physical culture also has direct practical aims: (1) preparing young people for work; and (2) preparing them for military defence of Soviet power.[6]

Sport would also play a role in other areas of political work. Prior to the revolution the liberal educationalist Peter Lesgaft noted that "social servitude has left its degrading imprint on women. Our task is to free the female body of its fetters".[7] Now the Bolsheviks attempted to put his ideas into practice. The position of women in society had already been greatly improved through the legalisation of abortion and divorce, but sport could also play a role by increasingly bringing women into public life. "It is our urgent task to draw women into sport," said Lenin. "If we can achieve that and get them to make full use of the sun, water and fresh air for fortifying themselves, we shall bring an entire revolution in the Russian way of life".[8]

And sport became another way of conveying the ideals of the revolution to the working classes of Europe. The worker sport movement stretched across the continent and millions of workers were members of sports clubs run mainly by reformist organisations. The Red Sports International (RSI) was formed in 1921 with the express intention of connecting with these workers. Through the following decade the RSI (and the reformist Socialist Worker Sports International) held a number of Spartakiads and Worker Olympics in opposition to the official Olympic Games. Worker-athletes from across the globe would come together to participate in a whole range of events including processions, poetry, art and competitive sport. There was none of the discrimination that marred the "proper" Olympics. Men and women of all colours were eligible to take part irrespective of ability. The results were very much of secondary importance.

So were the Bolsheviks anti-sport? They certainly did not seem to go as far as Proletkult's fervent ideological opposition and, as we have seen, were prepared to utilise sport in the pursuit of wider political goals. No doubt there were many individual Bolsheviks who despised sports. Equally many will have greatly enjoyed them. Indeed, as the

Alternative futures?

British secret agent Robert Bruce Lockhart observed, Lenin himself was a keen sportsman: "From boyhood he had been fond of shooting and skating. Always a great walker, he became a keen mountaineer, a lively cyclist, and an impatient fisherman".[9] Lunacharsky, despite his association with Proletkult, extolled the virtues of both rugby union and boxing, hardly the most benign of modern sports.

This is not to say that the party was uncritical of "bourgeois" sport. It is clear that it tackled the worst excesses of sport under capitalism. The emphasis on competition was removed, contest that risked serious injury to the participants was banned, the flag-waving nationalist trappings endemic to modern sport disappeared, and the games people played were no longer treated as commodities. But the Bolsheviks were never overly prescriptive in their analysis of what physical culture should look like.

The position of the Bolsheviks in those early days is perhaps best summarised by Trotsky in the quote that opens this chapter. It was not for the party to decide what constituted the "best system of sports" or produce the correct line for the working class to follow. Rather it was for the mass of people to discuss and debate, experiment and innovate, and in that process create their own sports and games. Nobody could foresee exactly what the play of a future socialist society would be like, but equally no one could doubt that the need to play would assert itself. As Trotsky said, "The longing for amusement, distraction, sightseeing and laughter is the most legitimate of human nature".[10]

Stalinism

The hopes of the revolution died, alongside thousands of old Bolsheviks, with the rise of Josef Stalin. The collectivist ideals of 1917 were buried, replaced by exploitation and brutal repression. Internationalism was jettisoned in favour of "socialism in one country". As the values and imperatives of the society changed so too did the character of the country's physical culture. By 1925 the Bolsheviks had already turned towards a more elitist model of sport. Around this time Stalin is reported to have said, "We compete with the bourgeoisie economically, politically, and not without success. We compete everywhere possible. Why not compete in sport?"[11] Team sports reappeared, complete with capitalist style league and cup structures. Successful sports people were held up as heroes in the Soviet Union and the quest for records resumed. Many of the

Hygienists and Proletkultists who had dared to dream of new forms of physical culture perished in the purges.

Eventually sport became a proxy for the Cold War. In 1952 the Soviet Union was re-integrated into the Olympic movement, ensuring that the medal table at each games became a measure of the relative strength of East and West. As the country was inexorably compelled into economic, political and military competition on the international stage, so it also found itself drawn into sporting competition with the West.

Just as it would be a mistake to judge the ideals of the Russian Revolution by the horrors of Stalinism, so we should not allow the latter days of Soviet sport to obscure those remarkable early experiments in physical culture. Sport in Russia may have ended as a steroid-enhanced caricature, but how far removed that was from the vision of Lenin when he said, "Young men and women of the Soviet land should live life beautifully and to the full in public and private life. Wrestling, work, study, sport, making merry, singing, dreaming—these are things young people should make the most of".[12]

Chapter 42
PHYSICAL EDUCATION: A CLASS ISSUE?[1]
Sue Caldwell

I want to use the example of competitive sport at the Olympics to lead a revival of competitive sport in primary schools. We need to end the "all must have prizes" culture and get children playing and enjoying competitive sports from a young age.[2]

Thus prime minister David Cameron sought to blame teachers for the perceived under-representation of state school medallists at the London 2012 Olympics. Ironically, one day earlier he had been defending his proposal to scrap two hours of weekly compulsory physical education from the school curriculum, claiming that schools were spending it "doing things like Indian dance or whatever, that you and I probably wouldn't think of as sport".[3]

Of course it should not be surprising that public schools are vastly over-represented in sports such as rowing, sailing and horse-riding, where Team GB won the majority of their medals. No comprehensive

Alternative futures?

school can begin to match the resources that elite public schools are able to provide, and their parents are unlikely to own the horses and yachts that children of the very privileged grow up with. On the athletics track and in the boxing ring it was a very different story, with gold medallists such as Nicola Adams, Jessica Ennis, Mo Farah and Greg Rutherford thanking their state school teachers for the opportunities they had been given. Such realities did not stop Rupert Murdoch from tweeting, "No wonder China leading in medals while US and UK mainly teach competitive sport a bad thing."

The remarks from Eton-educated Cameron and his chum from a fee-paying grammar school in Australia reveal a lot about the way that the ruling class view state schools in general and physical education in particular. Education has always been tied up closely with class, from the length of time a child is likely to spend in education to the quality of resources they are likely to have access to and the expectations that underpin their school curricula. Public, fee-paying schools have always been the preserve of the rich, designed to foster the self-confidence and self-esteem appropriate for those born to rule. This includes access to decent leisure activities—essential for intellectual development—and to competitive sports intended to build leadership skills and "toughness" in preparation for their entry into the boardrooms of multinational companies and the corridors of state power, and for a century and a half to run the empire.

Education for the working class has always been given grudgingly, and then only to the extent that it prepares them for jobs much lower down in the pecking order. At a basic level this initially meant a diet of literacy, numeracy and some simple skills. The fact that middle class children have often been educated alongside those of the working class, together with attempts by progressive teachers to raise the expectations and self-esteem of their pupils, has meant that a wider range of subjects is on offer, often taught in imaginative and inspiring ways. Nevertheless, it is the needs of the employing class that overwhelmingly dictate what happens in education. Employers are routinely asked to comment on and influence education policy, and with the creeping privatisation of schools through the Academies programme their influence is set to increase.

When physical education was first brought into schools it was in the form of military-inspired physical training, with the aim of distilling discipline and obedience. In the late 19th century this was replaced by a Swedish form of "medical" gymnastics. For a while this was a closely fought battle, with the Swedish version eventually winning out partly because it was cheap, requiring little in the way of equipment, and partly on the basis of an argument about a perceived decline in the "health of the nation"—an argument with echoes into 21st century debates about obesity among schoolchildren. (It is worth noting that the person with responsibility for school physical education in the early 20th century was the national Chief Medical Officer.)

There was nothing altruistic in the authorities' concern for working class health and physical education. The turning point was concern among generals, politicians and *Times* leader writers at the poor physical state of rank and file soldiers sent to fight the Second Boer War of 1899-1902. The British state wanted an average level of fitness so that young men could be sent to fight for its interests—which they were in vast numbers just a decade later. So the principle of systematic exercises performed on command persisted, in line with the general desire to ensure that the children of the working classes be kept under control and know their place.

The 1902 Education (Balfour) Act brought in nationwide compulsory state secondary education. Over the next few decades the numbers of working class teenagers in state education rose dramatically, and at the same time a shift took place in educational psychology. Gradually the Swedish system fell out of favour to be replaced with an "English" system aimed at developing the individual through a broad based curriculum. Following the Second World War responsibility for physical education (as it now became called, replacing the old "physical training") moved from the Chief Medical Officer to the Ministry of Education. Their 1950s document "Moving and Growing" introduced a "child-centred" approach, especially in primary schools and especially with regard to gymnastics.

As a result of the 1944 Education Act schools began to be resourced with gymnasiums and playing fields, and in secondary schools sport and games came to be seen as a way to educate pupils in physical skills, first for boys and later for girls as well.

Throughout this time there were left wing and right wing positions around the role of physical education. A more libertarian focus on health and well-being for all ultimately lost out to a more militaristic vision based around notions of the survival of the fittest, something that found an extreme embodiment in fascist Germany.

In Britain the left failed to challenge the drift towards competition, partly because the influence of eugenics on organisations such as the Fabians led them to concede ground to the right. So although by the 1950s teachers had more flexibility over the syllabus, the reality was that a combination of drill exercises and public-school influenced competitive sport still very much prevailed.

It was not until the advent of comprehensive schools and the progressive movements in education of the 1970s that a significant group of teachers began to experiment with more radical forms of PE based on ideas of equality and participation. It is this development that Cameron and Secretary of State for Education Michael Gove are attacking when they accuse state schools of being hostile to competitive sport.

These attacks by the right wing are not new, and they are also without foundation. In 1987 the Thatcher government commissioned an inquiry into sport in schools which found "no evidence of any philosophy that is against competition".[4] Two years later the *Times* discovered only one of 60 Labour-controlled education authorities—Sheffield—opposed competitive games and even this was ambiguous. The authority's PE adviser said that although many primary children were too young for full-side team sports, "it was not their policy to discourage competition in schools" and certainly not team games in secondary schools.[5]

If anything, secondary schools nowadays offer a much broader range of physical activities, including sports, than the narrow football/cricket/rugby/hockey options of the 1950s inherited from public schools, with the addition of basketball, dance, tennis (Andy Murray is also state educated) and athletics, for example. The total number of British pupils taking part in competitive sport at their school was 78 percent for the years 2009-10, up from 58 percent in 2006-7, and the average secondary school now offers participation in around 25 sporting disciplines. Four years ago a typical piece in the *Daily Mail* bemoaned the fact that 438 state schools no longer had annual sports days—not mentioning that they represented just 2 percent of the total.[6]

It is, however, true and to be applauded that progressive teachers did try to challenge the emphasis that had emerged on competitive sport by the 1970s, an emphasis that grew as successive governments started to equate success on the world sporting stage with success on the political stage. This was a reflection of the wider Cold War conception of sport as war minus the shooting that ran through every international sporting event from the Olympics to chess.

Physical education had come a long way from its roots in "medical gymnastics" for all, and physical educators were becoming coaches for the sporting elites of the future. The effect of a "winner takes all" philosophy was to turn off generations of young people from any kind of physical activity and leave them with embarrassing memories of being the last person picked for the team. It was quite right to try to counter this, in what the right wing parody as a move towards "all must have prizes",[7] but was in fact an attempt to make all children feel included and valued. For example a movement around "teaching games for understanding" (TGfU) emerged at Loughborough University in the early 1970s that emphasised breaking games down into smaller units to encourage thinking and understanding rather than drill practice. Primary school sports days included sack races and other fun activities.

The 1995 National Curriculum marked an end to any form of experimentation, which in any case had not spread very deeply into schools. The sports-based focus was re-emphasised, with the then prime minister, John Major, making the following telling contribution to the White Paper "Sport—Raising the Game":

> Competitive sport teaches valuable lessons which last for life...[sport] is one of the best means of learning how to live alongside others and make a contribution as part of a team...it is at the same time one of the defining characteristics of nationhood and pride.[8]

The same document revealed that the government believed that "pair play, self-discipline, respect for others, learning to live by laws and understanding one's obligations to others in a team are all matters which can be learnt from team games properly taught".[9]

Putting aside for the moment the fact that characteristics such as "nationhood and pride" and "learning to live by laws" clearly reveal the class nature of those who wish to impose this curriculum on working class children, socialists should challenge the notion that competitive team sports do indeed foster positive values in young people. Competitive sport is about obeying arbitrary rules, being better than everyone else and doing whatever it takes to win—hardly values likely to encourage respect for others or moral development.

This policy shift marked a backward step for physical education. The emphasis was not on mass participation and increasing involvement of specific groups such as people with disabilities, but on school sport and elite performance.

The debate around the Olympic legacy has once again brought the demand for competitive sport in school to the fore, this time with an emphasis on primary schools. It should be seen in the context of an attempt by the coalition government to turn the education clock back to the Victorian era with a narrow emphasis on grammar, phonics, drilling in long division techniques and so on. There is a crying need for young people to engage in greater amounts of physical activity, as evidenced by rising levels of child obesity. Sadly, the government's emphasis on competitive sport falls wide of the mark.

A report from the Young Foundation launched by Tory mayor of London Boris Johnson after the Olympics rather embarrassingly concluded that the government's emphasis is misguided, saying:

> The emphasis on traditional, competitive team-based sports is out of line with the way many young people want to participate. The over-riding emphasis on competitive sports is at odds with the motivations and drivers of many of the young people who are currently inactive.[10]

Instead the report recommends street-running, parkour, frisbee and Zumba-type activities that are much more informal and less competitive forms of activity.

The sheer hypocrisy of the government is revealed in its selling off of school playing fields, with the coalition selling off over 20 in two years. (A staggering 10,000 playing fields were sold off between 1979 and 1997.) The government has also scrapped the £160 million School Sports Partnership that allowed schools to share resources and have access to expert tuition. Such actions betray the real priorities of Gove and Cameron—to use school sport to instil the values that they deem appropriate in working class children, while continuing to use lottery money to fund the occasional youngster who shows prodigious talent.

The rich of course will suffer no such constraints. Rugby public school, for example, boasts eight squash courts, 12 grass tennis courts, nine hard tennis courts, a gymnasium, swimming pool and playing fields covering 86 acres. Radley College near Oxford can add to that a permanent county standard athletics track and a golf course. There will never be such a thing as a level playing field as long as we have an education system divided along class lines.

What then should be the demands of socialists with regard to sport in education? In the first instance we should fight for working class children to have access to the same resources as the rich. Many young people do enjoy competitive sport and they have every right to the same opportunities as those who attend Eton, Harrow and Rugby. We should vigorously oppose any cuts in school sport provision.

At the same time we need to appreciate that many more young people are completely alienated from school sport and drop out at the earliest opportunity. Sport is not the same as physical education and we should support and encourage educators who want to develop a more inclusive approach. Among other things this could include various outdoor activities such as rock climbing and orienteering which working class children really enjoy but again have limited access to relative to their rich counterparts. As one socialist PE teacher puts it:

> In my experience [young people] want PE that gives them pleasure, enjoyment, respect and self-worth. They want to be challenged, to be creative, to think, to understand and to learn. What they certainly don't want is to be embarrassed, stereotyped and left out, to feel incompetent or be seen to be a failure. Most of the time kids want to work together, co-operate and have fun.[11]

Among the strategies that he suggests are students coming up with their own methods for getting over a vault rather than following a predetermined sequence, or the scorer of a goal in a football match swapping sides. Far from bashing progressive teachers for undermining school sport they should be encouraged to develop such ideas.

Ultimately, this means challenging the nature of competitive sport itself. Physical education should be about the enjoyment of one's body, human company and the environment. As long as we are stuck with a capitalist system that glorifies success for a sporting elite there will be young people who want to be a part of that, and they have every right to do so. But we should understand that the price of success for the few is failure for the many. We need to have a better vision of ways for people to enjoy the physicality of their bodies than bending them to an arbitrary set of rules designed to foster allegiance to the system. It will be up to young people growing up in a socialist society to decide how they do that, but I strongly doubt that competitive sport will have anything to do with it.

Conclusion

THE CONTRADICTIONS OF CAPITALIST SPORT

Michael Lavalette

As many of the chapters gathered together in this volume attest, sport gives pleasure to countless millions. For the sports worker it can be a way out of poverty and an opportunity to excel in a sphere of life where the poor, despite the barriers of class, race, gender and disability, seem to have a chance of "making it". As the boxer Muhammad Ali famously said, "I hated every minute of training, but I said, 'Don't quit. Suffer now and live the rest of your life as a champion'."[1]

For the spectator and the fan, sport is a major source of pleasure, enjoyment and escapism. It offers relief from the daily humdrum of life and can bring a sense of belonging. As footballer Thierry Henri said, "I eat football. I sleep football. I breathe football. I'm not mad. I'm just passionate".[2]

For the countless millions of amateur players, athletes, cyclists, gymnasts, joggers and swimmers taking part in sport, playing is fun. The benefits are obvious—escape from the routine of daily life, relaxation and the chance to improve one's health and level of fitness. Further, such play seems to exist in a social space where the normal restrictions of society don't apply—or don't apply so rigorously. Here playing sport and games seems to offer a glimpse of a freer, less alienated existence.

But of course, this is only part of the story. There is another, darker, side to sport.

Far from liberating our bodies and minds sport is used to exploit the sports worker, the amateur player and spectator while making huge profits for multinational companies and sporting organisations. And the sums made by these organisations can be vast. Manchester United, for example, was the first ever sports team to be worth £3 billion pounds. The second most valuable sports team in the world is the NFL Dallas Cowboys, worth $2.1 billion.[3] The World Wrestling Federation was floated on the US stock exchange for $1.5 billion in 1999.[4]

Then there are the profits made by the sports industry more broadly. Both Nike and Adidas, for example, posted "significant" increases in profits for the first quarter of 2013. Adidas saw its net profits rise 6.5 percent to €308 million (£260 million),[5] while Nike, the world's largest athletic shoe and clothing company, posted third-quarter net income of $662 million, against $569 million for the same three-month period last year. As a result Nike's revenue increased 9 percent to $6.2 billion (£4 billion).[6] These are the same sports manufacturers who have been mired in all sorts of reprehensible employment practices. Nike have found themselves at the forefront of campaigns against their use of child labour. Adidas made the uniforms for the British Olympic team in 2012 at their factory in Indonesia, where workers were paid 54 cents a day for a 65-hour working week.[7]

Then there are the huge sums generated by global sporting spectacles like the Olympics or World Cups. The IOC's own "Olympic marketing file" 2012 tells us that:

> The Olympic Movement generates revenue through several programmes. The IOC manages broadcast partnerships, the TOP worldwide sponsorship programme and the IOC official supplier and licensing programme, the OCOGs manage domestic sponsorship, ticketing and licensing programmes within the host country, under the direction of the IOC. In addition, NOCs generate revenue through their own domestic commercial programmes.

The results of this are shown in the table below.

Olympic Marketing Revenue [8]

	1993-96	1997-2000	2001-04	2005-08	2009-12
Source					
Broadcast	1,251	1,845	2,232	2,570	3,914
TOP Programme	279	579	663	866	957
OCOG Domestic sponsorship	534	655	796	1,555	Not yet available
Ticketing	451	625	411	274	NYA
Licensing	115	66	87	185	NYA
Total	2,630	3,770	4,189	5,450	NYA

All figures in US$ millions

And finally there is the huge turnover generated by sport for broadcasters, media outlets and advertisers. Multinational broadcasters pay vast sums to show sports events, but in return they charge huge amounts to advertisers. Multinational corporations are prepared to pay huge amounts for sponsorship of major sporting events. Take for example the London Olympics in 2012. In the run up to the games the *Guardian* published a breakdown of the amount companies were paying in sponsorship:

> Firstly, there's the worldwide sponsors—these are the 11 big companies such as Coca Cola, who sponsor the games to the tune of around $100m through the International Olympic Committee. They include Dow's controversial sponsorship of the wrap that will surround the stadium. Also, some of the IOC worldwide numbers include more than one game. Then there are the London 2012 "tier one" partners, such as Adidas, BT and BMW, who each pay around £40m—there are seven of these. That's followed by another seven "supporters" who pay £20m and then 28 "suppliers" who pay around £10 million.[9]

It is hard to imagine a major international sporting event, the Olympics, the cycling Grand Tours, or the cricket, rugby or football World Cups, without the participation of big business, corporate sponsors, and flag waving patriots.

And, of course, when investing such sums in sport, big business expects sport to bend to its will. In 2013, for example, the FA Cup Final between Wigan and Manchester City started at 5.15pm instead of the usual 3pm kick-off, in order for ESPN to maximise its advertising revenue. However, for the fans it meant that if the game had gone into extra time, both sets of supporters would have been stranded in London having missed the last train home.

So, on the one hand, sport seems to offer a sphere where we are less controlled than in work or other areas of social life, that generates excitement and passion, and that offers participants, at all levels, a space to play, albeit in often rule-bound ways. On the other hand, the hopes and dreams of sport are confined and restricted by the very nature of the modern sporting industry. Sport is tied into the commercial drives of big business and restricts, regulates and limits our sporting lives in myriad ways.

In the gap between the promise of sport playing and activity and the structural reality of the world of capitalist sport, conflict and contest over the meaning of sport and its location in the world can develop.

We have explored this aspect of sport by looking at the ways that sports men and women, fans and spectators have challenged the sporting institutions and regulatory bodies to try and assert control over their games and activities (chapters 8, 35, 36, 40). We have considered the ways that the range of social divisions in society—around class, "race", gender, disability—are reproduced within sport (see chapters 15 to 22). We have looked at the conflict between sporting institutions and sports workers (chapters 19 and 40), between fans and clubs (chapters 34 to 37) and alternative forms of sporting organisations set up in opposition to traditional ones (chapters 36 and 39). And we have also looked at a range of sporting rebels who have used the sporting spectacle to challenge the iniquities of sport or of society more generally: from Ali to John Carlos; from Damien Hooper to Mahmoud Sarsak.

Sport is played and watched by millions of people every day across the globe. It is an important and central cultural activity engaged in by working people. For those of us on the political left it is vital that we can relate to those who love to watch and play sport, and that we always seek to infuse sport with politics. Above all this means being aware of the vast iniquities and huge profits that the sports capitalists make at our expense, to celebrate the sporting rebels and varying forms of resistance that exist within and around sport, and to demand a future where we will all be free to take part in social production in the morning, philosophise in the evening and play whenever we want.

Notes

Introduction: Capitalism and sport: politics, protest, people and play

1 R Lipsky, *How We Play the Game: Why Sports Dominate American Life* (Beacon Press, 1981), p34

2 www.sportengland.org/about_us/recognition_of_sports_and_ngbs.aspx

3 oxforddictionaries.com/definition/english/sport

4 Tobby Miller, Geoffrey Lawrence, Jim McKay and David Rowe, *Globalization and Sport* (Sage, 2001), p13.

5 See S Waiton, *Snobs' Law: Criminalising Football Fans in an Age of Intolerance* (Take A Liberty Press, 2012) for a review of the Offensive Behaviour at Football and Threatening Communication (Scotland) Act.

6 The Tifo was from the Celtic/Barcelona game and can be viewed on-line here: www.thecelticnetwork.com/2013/03/07/fantastic-voyage/

7 See J Hargreaves, *Sport, Power and Culture: A Social and Historical Analysis of Popular Sports in Britain* (Polity Press, 1987).

8 "First Among Equals: The Laurie Cunningham Story", sport-onthebox.com/2013/03/04/football-first-among-equals-the-laurie-cunningham-story-new-documentary-on-itv/

9 As above.

10 "Greek footballer given lifetime national ban after apparent Nazi salute", *Guardian*, 17 March 2013, www.guardian.co.uk/football/2013/mar/17/greek-football-lifetime-ban-nazi-salute

11 On this see Dave Zirin's piece, "The Verdict: Steubenville Shows the Bond Between Jock Culture and Rape Culture", *The Nation*, 18 March 2013, www.thenation.com/blog/173387/verdict-steubenville-shows-bond-between-jock-culture-and-rape-culture

12 Durham Miners Association, "Durham Miners Demand Banner Back from the Statement of Light", durhamminers.org/News/Stadium%20of%20light.html

13 S Moore, "How Can Football Be A Beautiful Game and Justify Paolo Di Canio's Nazi Salute?", *Guardian*, 3 April 2013, www.guardian.co.uk/commentisfree/2013/apr/03/football-beautiful-game-paolo-di-canio-nazi-salute?INTCMP=SRCH

14 S Morris, "Sheffield United Striker Ched Evans Found Guilty of Rape", *Guardian*, 20 April 2012, www.guardian.co.uk/football/2012/apr/20/ched-evans-found-guilty-rape

15 "Rio Ferdinand Shocked At Claims England Fans Sang Racist Songs", BBC News, www.bbc.co.uk/sport/0/football/21973672

16 D McRae, "Robbie Rogers: Why Coming Out As Gay Meant I Had To Leave Football", *Guardian*, 29 March 2013, www.guardian.co.uk/football/2013/mar/29/robbie-rogers-coming-out-gay

17 S Moore, as above.

18 R Moore, *The Dirtiest Race in History: Ben Johnson, Carl Lewis and the 1988 Olympic 100 Metres Final* (Wisden, 2012).

19 *Competitive Advantage*, "Coaching ABUSE: The dirty, not-so-little secret in sports" (no date), https://www.competitivedge.com/%E2%80%9C coaching-abuse-dirty-not-so-little-secret-sports%E2%80%9D

20 M Cookson, "Juan Antonio Samaranch: A Fascist Who Moulded the Olympic Games", *Socialist Worker*, 27 April 2010, www.socialistworker.co.uk/art.php?id=21026

21 E Palmer, "Cristiano Ronaldo Versus Israel: Eric Cantona, Eden Hazard and the Football Stars Backing Palestine", *I B Times*, 26 March 2013, www.ibtimes.co.uk/articles/450487/20130326/christian-ronaldo-pro-palestine-footballers-israel.htm

22 www.labournet.net/docks2/9703/fowler.htm

23 L Edwards, "AC Milan's Kevin-Prince Boateng Leads Team Off Pitch In Protest At Racist Chanting In Friendly Match With Pro Patria", *Telegraph*, 3 January 2013, www.telegraph.co.uk/sport/sportvideo/9778415/AC-Milans-Kevin-Prince-Boateng-leads-team-off-pitch-in-protest-at-racist-chanting-in-friendly-match-with-Pro-Patria.html

24 B Peck, "St Pauli Fans Choreograph Demonstration Against Homophobia During Match", 2 April 2013, sports.yahoo.com/blogs/soccer-dirty-tackle/st-pauli-fans-choreograph-demonstration-against-homophobia-during-072841259--sow.html

25 See G Edwards, "Marx, Lenin, Chess", 29 November 2012, Inside-left.blogspot.co.uk/2012/11/Marx-Lenin-Chess.html

26 D Zirin, *A People's History of Sport in America* (The New Press, 2009).

27 T Collins, *Sport in Capitalist Society* (Routledge, 2013), p1.

28 E P Thompson, *Customs in Common* (Penguin, 1991).

29 On football see G Myerson, *Fighting for*

Football: From Woolwich Arsenal to the Western Front: The Lost Story of Football's First Rebel (Aurum Press, 2009).

30 Collins, as above, pviii.

31 J-M Brohm, Sport: A Prison of Measured Time (Pluto Press, 1987).

32 D Conn, "In sickness and in wealth", Guardian, 19 April 2013.

33 Manchester United have carefully cultivated their relationship with companies such as Toshiba, Singha beer and Hong Kong's PCCW among their list of sponsors: www.football.co.uk/manchester_united/ferguson_brought_football_to_asia__say_fans_rss4132020.shtml

34 news.sky.com/story/1062882/david-beckham-tops-richest-footballers-list

35 D Conn, "Premier League players just keep getting richer...and directors cashing in too", Guardian, 19 April 2013.

36 £5 billion is the amount EPL clubs receive from global television rights. This is made up of £3.01 billion for domestic live rights from Sky and BT for three seasons from 2013-14; £178 million from the BBC for Match of the Day highlights and it is well on course to improve on the £1.4 billion it currently receives from overseas broadcasters. If the total revenue breaks through the £5 billion barrier as expected, the amount that the title-winning club receives from 2013-14 is likely to top £100 million for the first time—Guardian, 12 November 2012, www.guardian.co.uk/football/2012/nov/12/premier-league-tv-rights-5-bn

37 "Olympic athletes see limited sponsorships", ESPN, espn.go.com/blog/playbook/dollars/post/_/id/811/olympic-athletes-see-limited-sponsorships (accessed 9/12/20-12)

38 J Cobin, When Friday Comes: Football, War and Revolution in the Middle East (De Coubertin Books, 2013).

Part 1: Sport in a capitalist society

Chapter 1: Capitalism and the birth of modern sport

1 M Huggins, Flat Racing and British Society 1790-1914 (Frank Cass, 2000), p153.

2 M Marqusee, Anyone But England: Cricket and the National Malaise (Verso, 1994), pp35-36.

3 A Harvey, The Beginnings of a Commercial Sporting Culture in Britain, 1793-1850 (Ashgate, 2004), p119.

4 R Holt, Sport and the British (Clarendon

Press, 1989), p26.

5 Harvey, as above, p127.

6 Marqusee, as above, p44.

7 T Collins, and W Vamplew, Mud, Sweat and Beers (Berg, 2002), p5.

8 A Guttmann, From Ritual to Record: The Nature of Modern Sports (Columbia University Press, 1978), p37.

9 Quoted in D Pickering (ed), Cassell's Sports Quotations (Cassell & Co, 2000), p381.

10 R Carew, Survey of Cornwall (1602) quoted in H Hornby, Uppies and Downies: The Extraordinary Football Games of Britain (English Heritage, 2008), p139.

11 B Russell, "In Praise of Idleness", in In Praise of Idleness and Other Essays (George Allen & Unwin, 1935), p17.

12 E Dunning and K Sheard, Barbarians, Gentlemen and Players: A Sociological Study of the Development of Rugby Football (Routledge, 2005), p20.

13 Quoted in Pickering, as above, p32.

14 R W Malcomsen, Life and Labour in England: 1700-1780 (Hutchinson, 1981), p47.

15 J Rule, The Labouring Classes in Early Industrial England: 1750-1850 (Longman, 1986), p216.

16 E P Thompson, "Time, Work-Discipline, and Industrial Capitalism", Past and Present 38 (1967), p56.

17 W Vamplew, Pay Up and Play the Game: Professional Sport in Britain, 1875-1914 (Cambridge University Press, 1988), p39.

18 Thompson, as above, p90.

Chapter 2: In defence of sport

1 L Trotsky, Trotsky's Writings on Britain, volume 2 (New Park, 1975), chapter 8: Prospects.

2 On "sportification" see A Ingham, "The Sportification Process: A Biographical Analysis Framed by the Work of Marx, Weber, Durkheim and Freud", in R Giulianotti, Sport and Modern Social Theorists (Palgrave Macmillan, 2004).

3 J Huizinga, Homo Ludens: A Study of the Play-element in Culture (Beacon Press, 1955); R Caillois, Man, Play and Games (University of Illinois Press, 1961).

4 J Riordan, Sport, Politics and Communism (Manchester University Press, 1991).

5 See H U Gumbrecht, In Praise of Athletic Beauty (Harvard University Press, 2006).

6 P Stack, "Over the Bottom Line", Socialist Review (September 2002).

Chapter 3: Sport and capitalism

1 The ideas presented here were first explored in A Budd, "Capitalism, Sport

and Resistance: Reflections", *Culture, Sport, Society*, volume 4, number 1 (2001), and A Budd, "Sport and capitalism", in Roger Levermore and Adrian Budd (eds), *Sport and International Relations: An Emerging Relationship* (Routledge, 2004), and initially stimulated by Chris Bambery, "Marxism and Sport", *International Socialism* 73 (1996). Those works remain useful, but are marred by a one-sidedness in their approach. The approach of this chapter owes a debt to Ian McDonald, "One-dimensional Sport: Revolutionary Marxism and the Critique of Sport", in Ben Carrington and Ian McDonald (eds), *Marxism, Cultural Studies and Sport* (Routledge, 2008). See also Richard Gruneau, *Class, Sports, and Social Development* (University of Massachusetts Press, 1983).

2   J Maguire, *Global Sport: Identities, Societies, Civilizations* (Polity, 1999), p79.

3   J Ryan, *Little Girls in Pretty Boxes: The Making and Breaking of Elite Gymnasts and Figure Skaters* (Women's Press, 1996), explores how girls' bodies are damaged in the search for gymnastic perfection, referring to "legal, even celebrated child abuse" (pp3-4).

4   For a recent re-statement of the state's continuing importance for capitalism see A Budd, "Characterising the Period or Caricaturing Capitalism? A Reply to Nigel Harris", *International Socialism* 138 (2013).

5   E Cashmore, *Making Sense of Sport* (Routledge, 1990), p62.

6   C Mercer, "A Poverty of Desire: Pleasure and Popular Politics", in Fredric Jameson et al, *Formations of Pleasure* (Routledge & Kegan Paul, 1983), p89.

7   One of capitalism's smaller ironies is that, in the more economically liberal US, the regulation of the major sports is designed to give all clubs a (sporting) chance of winning while in the traditionally more regulated Europe the larger clubs have successfully demanded a larger slice of the cake, thereby perpetuating their dominance.

8   R W Lewis, "'Touched Pitch and Been Shockingly Defiled': Football, Class, Social Darwinism and Decadence in England, 1880-1914", in J A Mangan (ed), *Sport in Europe: Politics, Class, Gender* (Frank Cass, 1999), p118.

9   Cashmore, as above, p171. R Beamish, "Marxism, Alienation and Coubertin's Olympic Project", in Carrington and McDonald, as above, is more positive, but concludes that the Olympics' inspirational and transformative potential is fundamentally limited by the fact that high-performance sport is a specific form of alienated labour.

10 When the American Communist Party led an attempted boycott of the Berlin Olympics, Avery Brundage, president of the US Olympic Committee and later of the International Olympic Committee, argued that "certain Jews must now understand that they cannot use these Games as a weapon in their boycott against the Nazis" (quoted in P Hain, "The Politics of Sport Apartheid", in J Hargreaves (ed), *Sport, Culture and Ideology* (Routledge & Kegan Paul, 1982), p233).

11 Hargreaves, as above, p41.

12 W J Morgan, *Why Sports Morally Matter* (Routledge, 2006), p6.

13 D Robins, "Sport and Youth Culture", in Hargreaves, as above, p145.

14 A Gramsci, *Selections from Prison Notebooks* (edited and translated by Quintin Hoare and Geoffrey Nowell Smith) (Lawrence and Wishart, 1971), p175.

15 Cashmore, as above, p42. J Hoberman, "Sport and Ideology in the Post-Communist Age", in L Allison (ed), *The Changing Politics of Sport* (Manchester University Press, 1993), p17, argues similarly that "the competitive impulse is a basic human drive".

16 K Marx, "A Contribution to the Critique of Hegel's Philosophy of Right: Introduction", in Karl Marx, *Early Writings* (Penguin, 1975), p244.

17 N Geras, *Marx and Human Nature: Refutation of a Legend* (Verso, 1983), p96.

18 I McDonald, "One-dimensional Sport" (2007), www.idrottsforum.org/articles/mcdonald/mcdonald071212.html, p5.

19 Quoted in A Tomlinson and G Whannel (eds), *Five Ring Circus: Money, Power and Politics at the Olympic Games* (Pluto, 1984), p28. On the persistence of racism in sport see *Ethnic and Racial Studies*, special issue "Sport Matters: Politics, Identity and Culture", volume 35, issue 6 (2012).

20 Resistance to oppressive social structures can be indirect and take surprisingly mediated forms. For examples from Brazilian and Argentinian football under military regimes in the 1960s and 1970s see Budd, 2001 and 2004, as above, and S Kuper, *Football Against the Enemy* (Phoenix, 1996), pp170-204. Here leftist managers saw entertaining and creative football as an expression of freedom

and the feelings of ordinary people.
Argentina's 1978 World Cup winning
manager Cesar Luis Menotti even
referred to left wing and right wing
football (see J Wilson, "Get-well
Wishes to Argentina's El Flaco Whose
Football Moved the World" (2011),
www.guardian.co.uk/football/
blog/2011/mar/16/cesar-luis-menotti-
argentina? commentpage=2).
21 Geras, as above, p108.
22 McDonald, as above, p6.

Part 2: Global sport

Chapter 4: Think local, act global: Football and globalisation

1 On 26 December 2012. Sources: www.
football-lineups.com and en.wikipedia.
org (don't knock it).
2 www.sportingintelligence.com/2011/
10/28/a-football-competition-and-a-
headline-about-a-global-audience-of-
billions-and-yet-its-actually-true-what-
on-earth-is-going-on281002/
3 Just pandering to my City supporting
friends there. Source: www.dailymail.
co.uk/sport/football/article-2151762/
Manchester-United-claim-10-cent-
world-support-them.html Source:
www.dailymail.co.uk/sport/football/
article-2151762/Manchester-United-
claim-10-cent-world-support-them.html
4 Particularly in Sheffield apparently. See
A Harvey, Football: The First Hundred Years
(Routledge, 2005).
5 S Dobson and J Goddard, The Economics of
Football (Cambridge, 2001).
6 www.independent.co.uk/sport/
football/premier-league/ios-
investigation-footballs-tax-
shame-8373895.html
7 news.bbc.co.uk/1/hi/sport/football/
293678.stm
8 www.fifa.com/aboutfifa/social
responsibility/news/newsid=920094/
index.html
9 See Chris Harman, "Globalisation:
Critique of a New Orthodoxy",
International Socialism 73 (winter 1996), for
a fuller discussion. Available at www.
marxists.de/imperial/harman/global-e.
htm
10 M Lewis, Moneyball: The Art of Winning an
Unfair Game (WW Norton, 2004).

Chapter 5: Cycling: History and globalisation

1 In Italian: "Il tunnel era di modeste
dimensioni, appena cinquanta metri,

ma il 19 marzo 1946 assunse
proporzioni eccezionali agli occhi del
mondo. Quel giorno era lungo sei anni
e perso nella tetraggine della guerra [...].
Si udì un rombo dalle profondità di quei
sei anni e all'improvviso comparve alla
luce del giorno un'auto verde oliva che
sollevò una nube di polvere. "Arriva
Coppi" annunciò il messaggero, una
rivelazione che solo gli iniziati avevano
previsto"
2 In Italian: "Ha segnato la mia vita, nella
gioia e nel rimpianto"

Chapter 6: Cricket and globalisation: From ICC to IPL

1 Thanks to Neil Robinson and the MCC
library staff for their assistance in
researching this chapter.
2 The Duckworth Lewis Method, "The
Age of Revolution" (1969 Records
Limited, 2009).
3 A Pritchard, "The IPL: The Balance of
Power Shifts to Asia" (2009), www.
playthegame.org/uploads/media/
Adrian_Pritchard_-_Cricket_IPL.pdf,
p3.
4 G Haigh, Sphere of Influence: Writings on
Cricket and its Discontents (Simon &
Schuster, 2011), p30.
5 Haigh, as above, p50.
6 M Herborn, "Indian Premier League
Signals New Era in World Cricket", 4
May 2008, www.playthegame.org/
news/detailed/indian-premier-league-
signals-new-era-in-world-cricket-1293.
html
7 E W Swanton, "The Presidency of
Cricket", Playfair Cricket Monthly (June
1962).
8 Quoted in D Birley, A Social History of
English Cricket (aurum, 2003), p219.
9 www.icc-cricket.com/the-icc/icc_
members/overview.php
10 Haigh, as above, p110.
11 Quoted in Haigh, as above, p103.
12 www.icc-cricket.com/the-icc/about_
the_organisation/history.php. They
were later joined by Pakistan, Sri Lanka,
Zimbabwe and Bangladesh.
13 www.icc-cricket.com/the-icc/about_
the_organisation/history.php.
14 Quoted in M Marqusee, Anyone But
England: An Outsider Looks at English Cricket
(Aurum, 2005), p128.
15 BBC News, 2 April 2012, "Murdoch's
Star Wins India Cricket TV Rights",
www.bbc.co.uk/news/world-asia-
india-17581216
16 J Buttler, "The Champions League

Twenty20: Cricket's Divided Republic", *All Out Cricket* (December 2012), p67.

17 Mike Marqusee in R Steen (ed), *The New Ball*, volume 2: Universal Stories (Mainstream, 1999), p203.

18 M Bose, "Mihir Bose's blog", 31 May 2007, www.bbc.co.uk/blogs/the reporters/mihirbose/2007/05/politics_ surrounds_sonns_succe_1.html

19 Haigh, as above, p3.

20 Haigh, as above, p12.

21 See Ugra in R Steen (ed), *The New Ball*, volume 6: Co-stars (Mainstream, 2001), pp33-49.

22 Though a court in India has recently overturned this, and the BCCI is studying the judgement at the time of writing. See BBC News India, 8 November 2012, "Ban on India Cricketer Azharuddin Overturned", www.bbc.co.uk/news/world-asia-india-20248113

23 Haigh in Steen, 2001, as above, p29. For example, Australia's Mark Waugh and Shane Warne were penalised for a lesser charge of providing information to a bookmaker.

24 Quoted by Haigh in Steen, 2001, as above, p15.

25 Birley, as above, p318.

26 M Adams, "What Sports Stars Really Earn", MSN Money, 10 February 2011, money.uk.msn.com/news/money-in-sport/articles. aspx?cp-documentid=154629146

27 Cricinfo, 2012, www.espncricinfo.com/ england/content/player/210777.html

28 *Times of India*, 19 April 2010, quoted in Haigh, as above, p56.

29 Quoted in Haigh, as above, p47.

30 Quoted in M Atherton, *Glorious Summers & Discontents* (Simon & Schuster, 2012), p72.

31 BBC News, 14 June 2012, "Allen Stanford Jailed for 110 Years for $7bn Ponzi", www.bbc.co.uk/news/world-us-canada-18450893

Chapter 7: The Meaning of Murdoch: Sport in the New World Order

1 *Independent*, 16 October 1996.

2 For soccer see D Conn, *The Football Business*, 2nd edition (Edinburgh, 2002). For the NFL see M Oriard, *Brand NFL* (North Carolina, 2010). For rugby see T Collins, *A Social History of English Rugby Union* (Abingdon, 2009).

3 G Whannel, "Television and the Transformation of Sport", *Annals of the American Academy of Political and Social Science*, vol 625, no 1 (2009), pp205-218.

4 For the origins and use of Lombardi's saying, see S J Overman, "'Winning Isn't Everything. It's the Only Thing': The Origin, Attributions and Influence of a Famous Football Quote", *Football Studies*, vol 2, no 2 (1999), pp77-99.

5 *Guardian*, 22 November 2011.

6 Y Pallade, C Villinger and D Berger, *Antisemitism and Racism in European Soccer* (Berlin, 2007).

7 Quoted in the *Guardian*, 12 July 2011.

8 WADA, *Q&A: Whereabouts Requirements*, undated pdf at www.wada-ama.org/ rtecontent/document/qa_whereabouts_ requirements_en.pdf

9 "Cleaners to act as doping spies at London Olympics", *Guardian*, 4 October 2011.

10 J Tuckman, "It's a Man's Game", *Guardian*, 5 January 2005.

11 *Guardian*, 17 September 2009.

12 *IAAF, Competition Rules 2010-11* (Monaco, 2009), p112. IOC Press Release, "IOC approves consensus with regard to athletes who have changed sex", 18 May 2004, www.olympic.org/ media?articleid=56234. IOC Press Release, "IOC Addresses Eligibility of Female Athletes with Hyperandrogenism", 5 April 2011, www.olympic.org/medical-commission?articleid=124006.

13 For an exhaustive discussion of the issue, see G N Callahan, *Between XX and XY: Intersexuality and the Myth of Two Sexes* (Chicago Review Press, 2009).

14 Jeré Longman, "In African Women's Soccer, Homophobia Remains an Obstacle", *New York Times*, 21 June 2011.

15 R Gruneau and R Neubauer, "A Gold Medal for the Market: The 1984 Los Angeles Olympics, the Reagan Era, and the Politics of Neoliberalism", in S Wagg and H Lenskyi (eds), *The Palgrave Handbook of Olympic Studies* (London, 2012).

16 H Lenskyi, *Inside the Olympic Industry: Power, Politics, and Activism* (New York, 2000), pp108-112.

17 *The Province* (British Columbia), 8 October 2008.

18 D Lyon, *Surveillance Society: Monitoring Everyday Life* (Milton Keynes, 2001), pp51-58.

19 G Kuhn, *Soccer versus the State* (Oakland, 2011), pp68-69.

20 *Guardian*, 26 April 2011.

21 K Marx and F Engels, "The Communist Manifesto", *Collected Works*, vol 6 (London, 1976), p487.

Chapter 8: The jogging boom

1   M Perryman, "The Running Boom", Marxism Today, October 1984.
2   New York Times, 1975.
3   www.playfair2012.org.uk
4   C McDougall, Born to Run: A Hidden Tribe, Super Athletes, and the Greatest Race the World Has Never Seen (Knopf, 1984), p129.
5   B Whalley, Run Wild (Simon & Schuster, 2012), p80.
6   O Gibson, "Grassroots Clubs Say Government is Endangering London 2012 Legacy", Guardian, 19 October 2012.

Part 3: The sporting gods that failed

Chapter 10: Cycling and drugs: It's not about the bike

1   In 2001 Lance Armstrong's autobiography It's Not About the Bike became a best seller. It was a remarkable story that covered his recovery from life-threatening cancer, his return to elite professional cycling and first victory in the Tour De France (now removed from the record books). The title is, however, suggestive of a reality that is more accurate than many realised at the time—L Armstrong (with S Jenkins), It's Not About the Bike (Yellow Jersey Press, 2001).
2   Lance Armstrong, victory and farewell speech from the podium on the Champs-Elysee after his seventh and last Tour De France "victory" in 2005. Available at en.wikiquote.org/wiki/Lance_Armstrong
3   See W Voet, Breaking the Chain: Drugs and Cycling: The True Story (Yellow Jersey Press, 1999).
4   L Armstrong, It's Not About the Bike, as above.
5   L Armstrong (with S Jenkins), Every Second Counts (Yellow Jersey Press, 2003).
6   Journalist David Walsh has been chasing the Armstrong story from 1993. His book L A Confidentiel: Les secrets de Lance Armstrong (Points, 2006) with Pierre Ballester earned him Armstrong's condemnation and exclusion from the media tent. At the end of 2012 and beginning of 2013 he published a number of books that brought together his story and articles tracing Armstrong's downfall—see: Seven Deadly Sins: My pursuit of Lance Armstrong (Simon & Shuster, 2012); From Lance to Landis: Inside the American Doping Controversy at the Tour de France (Ballantine Books, 2013) and (with Paul Kimmage and John Follain),

Lanced: The Shaming of Lance Armstrong (Sunday Times, 2012). Walsh's case includes significant evidence that suggests the UCI were prepared to cover up Armstrong's doping.
7   USADA Report on Allegations Against Lance Armstrong, online.wsj.com/article/SB10008723963904447999045780486731578 64186.html p7
8   USADA Report on Allegations Against Lance Armstrong, online.wsj.com/article/SB10008723963904447999045780486731578 64186.html p8
9   M Zeigler, "Cycling: Lance Armstrong failed four drugs tests in 1999, UCI admits", Independent, 17 April 2013.
10 See J Whittle, Bad Blood: The secret life of the Tour de France (Yellow Jersey Press, 2009), pp135-136.
11 See J Whittle, as above, p133.
12 D Walsh, P Kimmage and J Follain, Lanced: The Shaming of Lance Armstrong (Sunday Times, 2012).
13 "Lance Armstrong and Oprah Winfrey: Cyclist Sorry for Doping", BBC Sport, www.bbc.co.uk/sport/0/cycling/21066354
14 Australian Crime Commission (2013), Organised Crime and Drugs in Sport, www.crimecommission.gov.au/publications/other/organised-crime-drugs-sport
15 Australian Crime Commission, as above.
16 As of March 2013 Fuentes was on trial in Spain charged with "endangering the health of athletes whilst treating them with banned drugs and banned procedures". The trial was due to end in early April 2012.
17 A Dymock, "Doping Comments Labelled 'Degrading' by Players' Union for French Rugby", Independent, 10 April 2013, www.independent.co.uk/sport/rugby/rugby-union/news-comment/doping-comments-labelled-degrading-by-players-union-for-french-rugby-8567515.html
18 C S Thompson, The Tour De France (University of California Press, 2012).
19 Cited in an article in L'Equipe, 23 July 1994.
20 See J Newsinger, The Blood Never Dried (Bookmarks, 2006).
21 Taylor Hamilton reports that many cyclists have eating disorders as they struggle to keep their weight down to anorexic proportions—T Hamilton and D Coyle, The Secret Race: Inside the World of the Tour de France: Doping, Cover-ups and Winning at all Costs (Bantam Press, 2012).
22 Older, retired footballers are well

known to suffer a range of joint problems in later life, the result of playing through an injury, or playing with the help of a cortisone injection.

23 See D Millar, *Racing Through the Dark: The Fall and Rise of David Millar* (Orion Books, 2011).

Chapter 11: Hillsborough:
The disaster and the cover-up

1 Hillsborough Independent Panel, *Hillsborough: The Report of the Hillsborough Independent Panel* (The Stationery Office, September 2012). The report is available for free download at hillsborough. independent.gov.uk/repository/report/ HIP_report.pdf

2 Hillsborough Independent Panel, as above.

3 Quoted in R Taylor, A Ward and T Newborn (eds), *The Day of the Hillsborough Disaster* (Liverpool University press, 1995).

4 See M Thatcher, "Speech to the Conservative Party Conference", 14 October 1988, www.margaretthatcher. org/document/107352; the quotation is taken from "The Blame Lies With Them", *Socialist Worker*, 22 April 1989.

5 "The Blame Lies With Them", as above.

Chapter 12: Mexico 1968:
Massacre at the Olympic games

1 Originally published in *Socialist Worker*, 22 May 2012.

Chapter 13: Anyone but England:
Not flying the flag in the World Cup

1 Originally published in *Socialist Worker*, 15 June 2010.

Part 4: Sporting divisions

Chapter 15: Sexism in sport

1 R Guinness, "'We're in the 21st Century': Women Step Up Campaign for Minimum Pay", www.smh.com.au/ sport/cycling/were-in-the-21st-century-women-step-up-campaign-for-minimum-pay-20110925-1krq7. html#ixzz21FdcymRq

2 O Gibson, "Women's Sport Attracts 0.5% of All Sponsorship", *Guardian*, 5 November 2011, www.guardian.co. uk/tv-and-radio/2011/nov/05/women-sport-point-five-sponsorship

3 A Topping, "Women's Sport is Underfunded and Ignored, Charity Claims", *Guardian*, 24 October 2012, www.guardian.co.uk/lifeandstyle/ 2012/oct/24/womens-sport-underfunded-ignored-charity-claims and "Even Elite sportswomen face challenges", www.wsff.org.uk/the-challenge-elite-sportswomen

4 N Subbaraman, "Olympic Athletes Win Big On Social Media", 13 August 2012, www.fastcompany.com/3000373/ olympic-athletes-win-big-social-media

5 E McDonagh and L Pappano, *Playing with the Boys: Why Separate is not Equal in Sports* (Oxford University Press, 2009), p164.

6 C S Thompson, *The Tour De France: A Cultural History* (University of California Press, 2006).

7 "Sports: Breaking Records, Breaking Barriers: Gertrude Ederle", Smithsonian National Museum, amhistory.si.edu/ sports/exhibit/firsts/ederle/index.cfm

8 E Cashmore, *Making Sense of Sports* (Routledge, 1996), p129.

9 Cashmore, as above, p131.

10 www.sports-reference.com/olympics/ athletes/mu/margaret-murdock-1.html

11 McDonagh and Pappano, as above, p13.

Chapter 16: Wrestling with the prophet:
The politics of Muslims and sport

1 "British Mentors Beat Afghan Soldiers 3-0", British Forces News, www.bfbs. com/news/afghanistan/british-mentors-beat-afghan-soldiers-3-54736. html

2 "Female Football Gaining Ground in Afghanistan", British Forces News, www.bfbs.com/news/afghanistan/ female-football-gaining-ground-afghanistan-47947.html

3 M Mamdani, *Good Muslim, Bad Muslim: A Political Perspective on Culture and Terrorism* (American Anthropological Association, 2002).

4 "Mo Farah Reveals He Was Detained in 'Terror Bungle' at US Airport", *Independent*, 30 December 2012, www. independent.co.uk/news/uk/home-news/ mo-farah-reveals-he-was-detained-in-terror-bungle-at-us-airport-8433440. html

5 "Newcastle 'Planning Prayer Room' for Papiss Cisse, Demba Ba and Hatem Ben Arfa", *Metro*, 6 May 2012, metro.co. uk/2012/05/06/newcastle-planning-prayer-room-for-papiss-cisse-demba-ba-and-hatem-ben-arfa-415438/

6 "The Whitechapel Wanderer", *Emel Magazine*, www.emel.com/article? id=9&a_id=1844

7 See T Fletcher, "'All Yorkshiremen are From Yorkshire, But Some are More

'Yorkshire' than Others': British Asians and the Myths of Yorkshire cricket", www.academia.edu/435458/_All_Yorkshiremen_are_from_Yorkshire_but_some_are_more_Yorkshire_than_Others_British_Asians_and_the_myths_of_Yorkshire_cricket

8 D Zirin, "Let Them Play: Behind FIFA's Decision to Ban Iran's National Women's Team", The Nation, 8 June 2011, www.thenation.com/blog/161228/let-them-play-behind-fifas-decision-ban-irans-national-womens-team#

9 "FIFA President: Gay Fans 'Should Refrain From Any Sexual Activities' During 2022 World Cup In Qatar", www.huffingtonpost.com/2010/12/13/fifa-president-gay-fans_n_796068.html

10 J Dorsey, "World Cup Qualifier: A battle for Iranian Women's Rights", mideastsoccer.blogspot.co.uk/2012/10/world-cup-qualifier-battle-for-iranian.html

11 Human Rights Watch country report, www.hrw.org/middle-eastn-africa/jordan

12 www.oonaking.com/issues/diversity/item/184-what-we-need-is-a-muslim-rooney.html

Chapter 17: Cricket: Gentlemen and Players

1 David Kynaston, WG's Birthday (Bloomsbury, 2010), p26.

2 John Major, More Than A Game: The Story of Cricket's Early Years (Harper Perennial, 2008).

3 Ric Sissons, The Players: A Social History of the Professional Cricketer (Pluto, 1988).

4 Major, p267.

5 Sissons, p52.

6 Major, p374.

7 Major, p268.

8 Sissons, p290.

9 Kynaston, p5.

Chapter 18: Cricket, racism and the Yorkshire Leagues: Prospects for a more inclusive cricket in Yorkshire

1 C L R James, Beyond a Boundary (Stanley Paul, 1963).

2 Duncan Hamilton (ed), Wisden on Yorkshire: An Anthology (J Wisden, 2011), p1.

3 Quoted in Rob Steen, "What Happened to the Black Cricketer?", Wisden Cricket Monthly (August 2004).

4 Mike Marqusee, Anyone but England: Cricket and the National Malaise (Verso, 1994).

5 Marqusee, p144.

Chapter 19: Rugby League: Sport, class and politics

1 Wray Vampley, Pay Up and Play the Game (Cambridge University Press, 1988), p33.

2 Richard Holt, Sport and the British (Oxford University Press, 1989), p138.

3 Eric Hobsbawm, The Age of Empire (Weidenfeld & Nicholson, 1987), p76.

4 C L R James, Beyond a Boundary (Sportsmans Book Club, 1963), p88; see James Mangan, Athleticism in the Victorian and Edwardian Public School (Cass, 2000).

5 Tony Collins, A Social History of English Rugby Union (Routledge, 2009), pp42-46; Tony Collins, 1895 and All That... (Scratching Shed, 2009), p35.

6 Tony Collins, Rugby's Great Split (Routledge, 1998), p112.

7 James Walvin, The People's Game (Mainstream Publishing, 1992), p77.

8 Arthur Budd, "Past Developments in Rugby Football, and the Future of the Game", in Frank Marshall (ed), Football: The Rugby Game (Cassell & Co, 1892), p132. The anti working class prejudice of middle class footballers was at times visceral. One Corinthian (amateur ex public schoolboy and university player) wrote that if he fell on the pitch at Millwall "the smell wouldn't come off for weeks". See John Lowerson, Sport and the English Middle Classes: 1870-1914 (Manchester University Press, 1995), p183.

9 Tony Collins, Rugby League in Twentieth Century Britain (Routledge, 2006), chapter 10.

10 Sport was big business. In 1895 it has been estimated that British annual expenditure on sport amounted to £47 million or approximately 3 percent of GDP (Lowerson, as above, p225).

11 Collins, Rugby League in Twentieth Century Britain, as above, p8.

12 Edward Thompson, "The Long Revolution I", New Left Review 9 (1961), p33.

13 Geoffrey Moorhouse, At the George (Sceptre, 1989), p10.

14 Marc Perelman, Barbaric Sport (Verso, 2012), p39.

Chapter 20: What's different about the Paralympics?

1 Arthur Williams, "Paralympics cannot be something that is just every four years", Guardian, 9 September 2012, www.guardian.co.uk/sport/blog/2012/sep/09/paralympics-2012-funding-

athletes
2 Peter Walker and Zoe Holman, "Paralympics Boom Echoes Around British Sport", *Guardian*, 2 October 2012, www.guardian.co.uk/sport/2012/oct/02/paralympics-boom-echoes-around-british-sport?INTCMP=SRCH
3 www.sportspromedia.com/notes_and_insights/paralympics_confirms_huge_london_2012_global_audience_eyes_four_billion_in/
4 Peter Walker, "Paralympics Tries to Shake off Image as Games for Rich Countries", *Guardian*, 30 August 2012, www.guardian.co.uk/sport/2012/aug/30/paralympics-games-for-rich-countries
5 BBC News, 11 September 2012, www.bbc.co.uk/news/magazine-19503755
6 Anne W Strike, "There's More to Paralympic Injustice than Just Blade Length", *Guardian*, 6 September 2012, www.guardian.co.uk/commentisfree/2012/sep/06/paralympic-injustice-oscar-pistorius?INTCMP=SRCH
7 Matthew Syed, "Inspiration to all but not a Magic Wand for the Future", *Times*, 5 September 2012, www.thetimes.co.uk/tto/sport/paralympics/article3528542.ece
8 *ITV News*, 7 September 2012, www.itv.com/news/story/2012-09-07/paralympics-not-changing-attitudes-as-hoped/

Chapter 21: From the factory to the field: the story of Dick, Kerr Ladies FC (1917-1965)
1 Dedicated to the memory of Emma Gough... "So much promise and so little time".
2 Spartacus Educational, "Women and Football", www.spartacus.schoolnet.co.uk/Fwomen.htm
3 Barbara Drake, *Women in Trade Unions* (Virago Press, 1984), pp111-118, 181.
4 Gail J Newsham, *In a League of their Own* (Pride of Place Publishing, 1994), Introduction.
5 Chris Hunt, "Belles of the Ball: Dick Kerr's Ladies", www.chrishunt.biz/features14.html
6 Newsham, p55.
7 Hunt, as above.
8 Spartacus Educational, as above.
9 Newsham, p84.
10 Spartacus Educational, as above.
11 Spartacus Educational, as above.
12 Newsham, p64.
13 Spartacus Educational, as above.

14 Spartacus Educational, "Dick,Kerr Ladies", www.spartacus.schoolnet.co.uk/Fwomen.htm
15 Shelley Alexander, "Trail-blazers who pioneered women's football", BBC Sport Football, htmp://news.bbc.co.uk/sport1/hi/football/women/4603149/stm
16 Newsham, p112.
17 Newsham, p138.
18 Spartacus Educational, "Dick, Kerr Ladies".
19 Spartacus Educational, "Dick, Kerr Ladies".
20 Newsham, p140.
21 Hunt, as above.

Chapter 23: Pedalling Days
1 This article first appeared in the *Clarion*, March 1931.

Part 5: People

Chapter 24: C L R James: Beyond cricket's boundary
1 Chris Searle, *Pitch of Life: Writings on Cricket* (The Parrs Wood Press, 2001), p110.
2 For my brief introduction to James, see Christian Høgsbjerg, "C L R James: The Revolutionary as Artist", *International Socialism* 112 (autumn 2006).
3 Searle, as above, p152.
4 Some important critical appraisals of the work can be found in Hilary McD Beckles and Brian Stoddart (eds), *Liberation Cricket: West Indies Cricket Culture* (Manchester University Press, 1995).
5 John Major, *More Than a Game: The Story of Cricket's Early Years* (Harper Collins, 2007), p390.
6 On these themes, see also Brian Stoddart and Keith A P Sandiford (eds), *The Imperial Game: Cricket, Culture and Society* (Manchester University Press, 1998).
7 Stefan Collini, "Radical on the Boundary", *Times Literary Supplement*, 25 September 1987.
8 C L R James, *Beyond a Boundary* (Hutchinson, 1969), p71.
9 James, as above, p56.
10 James, as above, p77.
11 James, as above, p158.
12 Ross McKibbin, *Classes and Cultures: England 1918-1951* (Oxford University Press, 1998), p332.
13 Paul Buhle, *C L R James: The Artist as Revolutionary* (Verso, 1993), p42.
14 Alex Hamilton, "Profile: An Interview with C L R James", *Guardian*, 25 June 1980.

15 See C L R James, *A Majestic Innings: Writings on Cricket* (Aurum, 2006). This collection was first published in 1986 by Allison and Busby and entitled simply *Cricket*.

16 Smith, Andrew, "'Beyond a Boundary' (of a 'Field of Cultural Production'): Reading C L R James with Bourdieu", *Theory, Culture & Society*, 23/4 (2006), p95. See also Andrew Smith, *C L R James and the Study of Culture* (Palgrave Macmillan, 2010).

17 Andrew Smith, "'A Conception of the Beautiful': C L R James' *Glasgow Herald* Cricket Articles, 1937-1938", *The International Journal of the History of Sport*, 23/1 (2006), pp49, 64.

18 Leon Trotsky, *On Britain* (Monad Press, 1973), p148. See also Chris Bambery, "Marxism and Sport", *International Socialism* 73 (winter 1996), p50.

19 The official Communist position went from a crude denunciation of sport as "bourgeois" during the "class against class" Third Period "line" during the late 1920s and early 1930s, and then embracing sport in an uncritical manner during the Popular Front period and thereafter. While this needs more investigation, it seems the Communist Party of Great Britain paper the *Daily Worker* accordingly went from saying very little about sport to devoting pages to sports coverage. For some discussion of the complicated relationship between the CPGB and sport during the 1930s, see Stephen G Jones, *Sport, Politics and the Working Class: Organised Labour and Sport in Inter-War Britain* (Manchester University Press, 1998), pp73-103.

20 Smith, "'A Conception of the Beautiful'", as above, p52.

21 James, *Beyond a Boundary*, as above, pp151, 205-206.

22 James, *A Majestic Innings*, as above, p117.

23 For more on how *Beyond a Boundary* was shaped by James's critical American sojourn from 1938-53, see Bill Schwarz, "C L R James's American Civilization", in Christopher Gair (ed), *Beyond Boundaries: C L R James and Postnational Studies* (Pluto, 2006), and by decolonisation after his return to Britain in 1953, see Christian Høgsbjerg, "Facing Post-Colonial Reality? C L R James, the Black Atlantic and 1956", in Keith Flett (ed), *1956 and All That* (Cambridge Scholars Press, 2007).

24 Stuart Hall, "C L R James: A Portrait", in Paget Henry and Paul Buhle (eds), *C L R James's Caribbean* (Duke University Press, 1992), pp13-15.

25 James, *Beyond a Boundary*, as above, p11.

26 Dave Renton, *C L R James: Cricket's Philosopher King* (Haus, 2007).

27 Neil Lazarus, "Cricket and National Culture in the Writings of C L R James", in Paget Henry and Paul Buhle (eds), as above, p93.

28 John Arlott, "C L R James: Behind the Marxist Crease", *Guardian*, 1 June 1989.

Chapter 25: Test match résumé

1 This article originally appeared in *The Glasgow Herald* on 16 June 1938. It is published here with the permission of the C L R James Estate. Thanks are due to Andrew Smith for help locating the article and to Christian Høgsbjerg for transcription.

Chapter 26: Arthur Wharton: Airbrushed from history

1 Phil Vasili, *The First Black Footballer: Arthur Wharton 1865-1930: An Absence of Memory* (Routledge, 1998). Read more at suite101.com/a/arthur-wharton-worlds-first-black-professional-football-player#ixzz2ItgWhdWJ

2 Chris Webber, "Black Football Pioneers from Arthur Wharton to Viv Anderson and Beyond", *Observer*, 30 August 2009, www.guardian.co.uk/football/ 2009/ aug/30/arthur-wharton-pioneer-black-footballer

Chapter 27: "Sport is part of our resistance": Mahmoud Sarsak, Palestine's hunger striking footballer

1 "Poll: Israel viewed negatively around the world", *Jerusalem Post*, 2 December 2012, www.jpost.com/NationalNews/ Article.aspx?id=270291

2 Shahd Abusalama, "Meeting Mahmoud Sarsak: 'It's not my Victory, it's Yours'", Electronic Intifada, 16 July 2012, electronicintifada.net/blogs/shahd-abusalama/ meeting-mahmoud-sarsak-its-not-my-victory-its-yours

3 Chris Jones and Michael Lavalette, *Voices from the West Bank* (Bookmarks, 2011).

4 Movement and Access in the West Bank, United Nations Office for the Coordination of Humanitarian Affairs occupied Palestinian territory, unispal. un.org/UNISPAL.NSF/0/8F5CBCD2F464 B6B18525791800541DA6

5 Documents sent to the author by the Palestinian Football Association including, "Israeli FA Transfer & Reg of Players According FIFA Regulations", "Report on Cancelled Matches to Sepp Blatter" and "Obstacles that Confront us Because of Occupation Practices Report".

6 Jodi Rudoren, "Palestinians go hungry to make their voices heard", *New York Times*, 2 December 2012, www.nytimes. com/2012/05/04/world/middleeast/ palestinian-resistance-shifts-to-hunger-strikes.html?pagewanted=all

7 Rob Nixon, "Apartheid on the Run: The South African Sports Boycott", *Transition* no 58 (Indiana University Press, 1992), p70.

8 Tamir Sorek, *Arab Soccer in a Jewish State: The Integrative Enclave* (Cambridge University Press, 2007), p34.

9 Oz Rosenburg, "Hundreds of Beitar Jerusalem fans beat up Arab workers in mall; no arrests", *Ha'aretz*, 2 December 2012, www.haaretz.com/print-edition/ news/hundreds-of-beitar-jerusalem-fans-beat-up-arab-workers-in-mall-no-arrests-1.420270

10 Tamir Sorek, "Soccer Fandom and Citizenship in Israel", Middle East Research and Information Project, 2 December 2012, www.merip.org/ mer/mer245/soccer-fandom-citizenship-israel

11 Rob Nixon, as above, p72.

12 "Citizenship law decision a stain on Israeli law", *Jerusalem Post*, 2 December 2012, www.jpost.com/DiplomacyAnd Politics/Article.aspx?id=253281

13 Gigi Ibrahim, "One Night in Gaza", 2 December 2012, theangryegyptian. wordpress.com/2012/11/22/free-gaza-end-israel/

14 Tamir Sorek, "Soccer Fandom and Citizenship in Israel", as above.

15 Chris McGreal, "Footballers condemn plans to hold U21 European championship in Israel", *Guardian*, 2 December 2012, www.guardian.co.uk/ world/2012/nov/30/footballers-u21-european-championship-israel

16 Red Card Israeli Racism, redcardapartheid.weebly.com/

17 Sal Emergui, "El ex preso palestino Al Sarsak rechaza ir el clasico", *El Mundo*, 2 December 2012, www.elmundo.es/ elmundodeporte/2012/10/01/ futbol/1349080783.html

18 Rob Nixon, as above, p72.

19 Christopher Merrett, "'We don't Want Crumbs, We Want Bread': Non-Racial Sport, the International Boycott and South African Liberals, 1956–1990", *English Academy Review: Southern African Journal of English Studies*, volume 27, issue 2 (2010), p82.

20 Rob Nixon, as above, p75.

21 George Orwell, "The Sporting Spirit", 2 December 1945, orwell.ru/library/ articles/spirit/english/e_spirit

Chapter 28: An anti-racist Olympic rebel: Damien Hooper

1 This article first appeared on 3 August 2012 at www.edgeofsports.com/2012-08-03-764/index.html

2 Light heavyweight Hooper was beaten 19-11 by Russian fourth seed Egor Mekhontcev.

3 By way of a postscript, after he was beaten by Mekhontcev, Hooper was quoted in the Australian press: "I was proud that I did it. I don't regret doing it... It was disappointing [to be banned from wearing the T-shirt for the Mekhontcev fight], I think there should be awareness of that. We are two cultures living in one nation"—*Herald Sun*, "Aussie Boxer Damien Hooper Thumped by Russian, but Wants to Turn Pro Immediately", 5 August 2012, www.heraldsun.com.au/sport/london-olympics/russian-boxer-egor-mekhontcev-too-experienced-for-aussie-hope-damien-hooper/ story-fn9dheyx-1226443084917

Chapter 29: "Carriers of the dream": Tennis radicals of the 1960s and 1970s

1 Dave Zirin, *A People's History of Sports in the United States* (The New Press, 2008), pxii.

2 Zirin, as above, p199.

3 Zirin, as above, p156.

4 iml.jou.ufl.edu/projects/Spring02/ hessing/agibson.htm

5 Syndiata Djata, *Blacks at the Net* (Syracuse University Press, 2006)

6 Bob Carter, "Ashe's Impact Reached far Beyond the Court", espn.go.com/ classic/biography/s/Ashe_Arthur.html

7 Zirin, as above, p201.

8 Carter, as above.

9 Djata, as above, p201.

10 Zirin, as above, p202.

11 Zirin, as above, p203.

12 Peter Dreier, "Billie Jean King and Remarkable Success of Title IX", www. huffingtonpost.com/peter-dreier/billie-jean-king-and-rema_b_1621359.html

13 Zirin, as above, p202.

Chapter 30: Boxing, Ali, racism and resistance

1   Langston Hughes, *Autobiography: The Collected Works of Langston Hughes*, vol 14 (University of Missouri Press, 2002), p307.
2   Langston Hughes, as above, p307.
3   Mike Marqusee, *Redemption Song: Muhammad Ali and the Spirit of the Sixties* (Verso, 1999), p81.
4   Dave Zirin, "John Harbaugh Summons the Poetry of Muhammad Ali", *Edge of Sports*, www.edgeofsports.com/2013-02-10-813/index.html
5   Jonathan Neale, *The American War* (Bookmarks, 2001).
6   See the Ian Wooldridge interview with Ali, www.youtube.com/watch?v=dLam_GiQ2Ww

Chapter 31: Joe Louis and Jack Johnson

1   Originally published in *Labor Action*, 1 July 1946. Available on-line at the Marxist Internet Archive www.marxists.org/archive/james-clr/works/1946/07/louis-johnson.html. Published here with the permission of the C L R James Estate.

Chapter 32: The flame of revolt: an interview with John Carlos

1   This is an extended version of the interview first published in *Socialist Worker* Issue 2304, 22 May 2012.

Part 6: Resistance

Chapter 35: Ultras and fandom: The Green Brigade at Celtic

1   Some ultras do engage in violence or are involved with fighting with fans from other clubs. Passion for the club can spill over into clashes between rivals—it would be naive to assert otherwise!
2   Howard Amos, "Liverpool head to Zenit St Petersburg fearing racism may rear its head", *Guardian*, 13 February 2013. www.guardian.co.uk/football/2013/feb/13/liverpool-zenit-st-petersburg-racism
3   You can get a glimpse of the display (and the atmosphere that night!) here: www.youtube.com/watch?v=phKo0Qo6PXQ. Or look at some of the still images here: greenbrigade.proboards.com/index.cgi?board=picsandvids&action=display&thread=57730
4   forum.celtictalk.org/topic/25093-125th-anniversary-tifo-v-barcelona/
5   Angela Haggerty, "'Disproportionate' Police Presence and Batons Used on Marchers at Glasgow's Green Brigade Football Fan March", 16 March 2013, angelahaggerty.com/disproportionate-police-presence-and-batons-used-on-marchers-at-glasgows-green-brigade-football-fan-march/
6   Gerry Braiden, "Top QC Says Response to Green Brigade March Like a 'Police State'", *Herald*, 18 March 2013, www.heraldscotland.com/news/home-news/top-qc-says-response-to-march-like-a-police-state.20524316
7   ultras-celtic.com/blog/
8   TNT interview with the Green Brigade (2011), Part I, www.twistsnturns.net/content.php?160-The-Green-Brigade-Part-I
9   Roddy Forsyth, "Demented Atmosphere in Scottish Football Led to SPL Referees Calling for Strike Action", 25 November 2010, www.telegraph.co.uk/sport/football/competitions/scottish-premier/8160406/Roddy-Forsyth-demented-atmosphere-in-Scottish-football-led-to-SPL-referees-calling-for-strike-action.html
10 Green Brigade Ultras, forum.celtictalk.org/topic/16391-green-brigade-ultras/
11 Green Brigade Ultras, forum.celtictalk.org/topic/16391-green-brigade-ultras/
12 TNT interview with the Green Brigade (2011), Part II, twistsnturns.net/content.php?206-The-Green-Brigade-Part-II. You can see a range of their tifos at the group's own YouTube summation of season 2011/2012 here: www.youtube.com/watch?feature=player_embedded&v=dyTh4VWhdME. This includes (at 11 mins 40 secs) the unfurling of the fantastic banner of the four men of the apocalypse created to celebrate the demise of rivals Rangers.
13 TNT interview with the Green Brigade Part II, as above.
14 You can see a clip of the protest here: www.youtube.com/watch?v=P9nOe8soWO0
15 Details of the Alerta Network are here: https://www.facebook.com/pages/Alerta-Network-Antifascist-movement-celtic-fc/266427420060121?sk=wall&filter=12
16 Andrew McFadyen, "A Celtic Message to Palestine", *Al-Jazeera*, 13 June 2012, www.aljazeera.com/indepth/features/2012/06/2012612204354413741.html
17 Henry MacDonald, "British Government admits regret over McAnespie Killing", *Guardian*, 27 July 2009, www.guardian.co.uk/uk/2009/jul/27/british-

government-regret-mcanespie-killing

18   Graham Spiers, "How the SNP have made policing fans a minefield", *Herald*, 19 March 2013 www.heraldscotland.com/sport/opinion/spiers-on-sport-how-the-snp-have-made-policing-fans-a-minefield.1363789179

19   Spiers, as above.

20   In the summer of 2011 the Queen laid a wreath at the commemoration head stone in Dublin to those who died for Irish freedom between 1796 and 1921. So the Queen can lay a wreath in Dublin, but you can't sing about them in Glasgow! www.bbc.co.uk/news/world-europe-13425722

21   The result of an FOI request: www.strathclyde.police.uk/assets/pdf/22915/Response_for_website.pdf00242013

22   ultras-celtic.com/blog/?page_id=686

23   You can see the crowd singing this rather bilious dirge here: www.youtube.com/watch?v=6ZYGYXAdITM

Chapter 36: Protest, community and football: FC United of Manchester as a fan movement

1   Stuart Brennan, "Amir's Land of Hope", *Manchester Evening News*, 18 July 2005.

2   P Crowther, *Our Club Our Rules: FC United of Manchester* (Lulu Books, 2006), p152.

Chapter 37: OMONOIA, Nicosia: When the "communist bandits" formed a football team

1   I am indebted to my good friend and comrade Nicos Trimikliniotis who kindly provided me with archival information and constructive insights on the topic.

2   Perry Anderson, The divisions of Cyprus, *London Review of Books*, vol 30, no 8 (24 April 2008), pp6-7.

3   Anderson, as above, p7.

4   "Adventures of Ideas", *Politis* newspaper, 29 April 2007, edited by Nicos Trimikliniotis.

5   "Adventures of Ideas", as above.

6   N Peristianis, "Football Violence", Research Report, Intercollege Nicosia (1999).

7   Ultras announcement 7 December 2010, www.gate9.com.cy/site/index.php?option=com_k2&view=item&id=57:ανακοίνωση-07/12/10&Itemid=120

Chapter 38: Militant action against sports apartheid

1   I was subsequently put on trial for conspiracy in 1972: see Derek Humphry

(ed), *The Cricket Conspiracy* (National Council for Civil Liberties, 1973).

2   For an account see Peter Hain, *Don't Play with Apartheid* (Allen & Unwin, 1971).

Chapter 39: The workers' sports movement

1   Adapted from "A League of Our Own: the Story of the Workers' Sports Movement", *Socialist Worker*, 14 July 2012.

Chapter 40: Working on the chain gang at the Tour de France

1   "UCI Report Reveals Men's Professional Cycling's Healthy Position", 24 February 2012, www.uci.ch/Modules/ENews/ENewsDetails2011.asp?id=Nzg5Ng&MenuId=MTYzMDQ&LangId=1&BackLink=%2FTemplates%2FUCI%2FUCI8%2Flayout.asp%3FMenuID%3DMTYzMDQ

2   Cycling Tips, "How Much Money do Pro Cyclists Make?", 23 November 2010, www.cyclingtips.com.au/2010/11/how-much-do-pro-cyclists-make/

3   Daniel Coyle, *Lance Armstrong: Tour de Force* (Harper Collins, 2006).

4   Coyle, as above, p14.

5   Taylor Hamilton and Daniel Coyle, *The Secret Race: Inside the Hidden World of the Tour de France: Doping, Cover-ups, and Winning at All Costs* (Bantam Press, 2012).

6   "UCI Report Reveals Men's Professional Cycling's Healthy Position", as above.

7   "Every Tour de France Winner Listed from Garin to Wiggins", *Guardian*, 23 July 2012, www.guardian.co.uk/news/datablog/2012/jul/23/tour-de-france-winner-list-garin-wiggins

8   Christopher S Thompson, *The Tour de France: A Cultural History* (University of California Press, 2006).

9   Thompson, as above.

10   There has been a rash of books looking at the misuse of drugs in cycling. Perhaps the two most poignant are Tyler Hamilton's biography, as above, and David Millar's *Racing Through the Dark* (Orion Books, 2011).

Part 7: Alternative futures?

Chapter 41: "Physical culture", sport and revolution: the debate in post-revolutionary Russia

1   Leon Trotsky, *Literature and Revolution* (Bookmarks, 1991), p200.

2   Quoted in Barbara Keys, *Globalizing Sport: National Rivalry and International Community in the 1930s* (Harvard University Press, 2006), p161.

3   Quoted in Jim Riordan, "Worker Sport Within a Worker State: The Soviet Union", in Arnd Krüger and Jim Riordan (eds), The Story of Worker Sport (Human Kinetic, 1996), p56.

4   Quoted in Jim Riordan, "The Rise and Fall of Olympic Champions" in OLYMPIKA: The International Journal of Olympic Studies, volume II (1993), pp25-44.

5   Jim Riordan, "Worker Sport Within a Worker State: The Soviet Union", as above, p57.

6   Jim Riordan, "Worker Sport Within a Worker State: The Soviet Union", as above, p49.

7   Quoted in Jim Riordan, "The Rise, Fall and Rebirth of Sporting Women in Russia and the USSR", in Journal of Sport History, vol 18, no 1 (Spring, 1991), pp183-199.

8   Quoted in Jim Riordan, "The Rise, Fall and Rebirth of Sporting Women in Russia and the USSR", as above, pp183-199.

9   Jim Riordan, "Marx, Lenin and Physical Culture", in Journal of Sports History, vol 3 (2) (1976), p156.

10   John M Hoberman, Sport and Political Ideology (University of Texas, 1984), p181.

11   Quoted in Barbara Keys, Globalizing Sport: National Rivalry and International Community in the 1930s (Harvard University Press, 2006), p163.

12   Quoted in Jim Riordan, "Marx, Lenin and Physical Culture", as above, p156.

Chapter 42: Physical education: a class issue?

1   The author would like to thank Chris Blakey, Shaun Doherty and Kevin Ovenden for their helpful comments.

2   David Cameron, Daybreak, ITV1, 10 August 2012.

3   Quoted in Times Educational Supplement, 9 December 2009.

4   "Raising the Game" (Department for National Heritage, 1995), p2.

5   Quoted in Times Educational Supplement, 9 December 2009.

6   John Harris, Guardian, 5 August 2012.

7   This phrase comes from the title of a much-maligned 1996 book by Melanie Philips that was roundly dismissed by academics at the time, with John Sutherland in the London Review of Books calling it "second-hand tittle-tattle". It is now being revived by the Tory right.

8   "Raising the Game", as above, p2.

9   "Raising the Game", as above, p7.

10   "Move It: Increasing Young People's Participation in Sport" (Young Foundation, 2012), p14.

11   Chris Blakey, "Can there be a Radical Pedagogy for PE?", Education for Liberation Magazine.

Conclusion: The contradictions of capitalist sport

1   addicted2success.com/motivation/video-muhammad-ali-shares-his-most-powerful-quotes/

2   expertfootball.com/quotes/?p=Thierry_henry

3   www.forbes.com/sites/mikeozanian/2013/01/27/manchester-united-becomes-first-team-valued-at-3-billion/

4   Mike Marqusee, "This Sporting Lie", Index on Censorship, no 4 (2000), p45.

5   "Adidas Profits Rise Sends Share Price Higher", BBC, 3 May 2013, www.bbc.co.uk/news/business-22394723

6   "Nike shares jump as earnings beat forecasts", BBC, 21 March 2013, www.bbc.co.uk/news/business-21889880

7   Pratap Chatterjee, "Exploiting Indonesia: Adidas for London Olympics 2012", Corpwatch, 16 April 2013, www.corpwatch.org/article.php?id=15705

8   Olympic Marketing Fact File (IOC, 2012), www.olympic.org/Documents/IOC_Marketing/OLYMPIC-MARKETING-FACT-FILE-2012.pdf

9   Guardian DataBlog, www.guardian.co.uk/sport/datablog/2012/jul/19/london-2012-olympic-sponsors-list